HORACE'S COMPROMISE
The Dilemma of the American
High School

Theodore R. Sizer

HORACE'S COMPROMISE
The Dilemma of the American High School

*The First Report from A Study of High Schools,
Co-sponsored by the National Association of
Secondary School Principals and the Commission
on Educational Issues of the National Association
of Independent Schools*

HOUGHTON MIFFLIN COMPANY
Boston • New York • London

For our children,
Tod, Judy, Hal, and Lyde,
whose adolescence brought us joy,
and for Becky, who shares our
hopes for schoolchildren

For information about permission to reproduce selections from
this book, write to Permissions, Houghton Mifflin Company,
2 Park Street, Boston, Massachusetts 02108.

Library of Congress Cataloging in Publication Data
Sizer, Theodore R.
Horace's compromise—the dilemma of the American
high school.
Includes bibliographical references.
1. High schools—United States. I. Title.
LA 222.S54   1984   373.73   83-18500
ISBN 0-395-34423-9
ISBN 0-395-61158-X (pbk.)

Printed in the United States of America

FFG 10 9 8 7 6 5 4 3 2 1

Contents

Preface to the 1992 Edition   vii
Introduction   1
Prologue: Horace's Compromise   9

I THE STUDENTS   23

1 Five Adolescents   25
2 Diversity   35
3 Commonality   40
4 Docility   53
5 Incentives   59

II THE PROGRAM   69

1 What High School Is   71
2 Purpose: Mind and Character   84
3 Skills: The Importance of Coaching   99
4 Knowledge: Less Is More   109
5 Understanding: The Importance of Questions   116
6 Character: Decency 120
7 Principals' Questions   131

III THE TEACHERS 141

1 Three Teachers 143
2 Agreement 154
3 Motivation 161
4 Conditions 172
5 Teachers 180
6 Trust 195

IV THE STRUCTURE 203

1 Hierarchical Bureaucracy 205
2 Better Schools 214
3 A Paralysis of Imagination 218

Afterword: An Experiment for Horace 222

Acknowledgments 241

Notes 248

Preface to the 1992 Edition
Better Compromises for Horace?

"I AM Horace, a high school teacher. Let me tell you how it hurts."

Since the 1984 publication of *Horace's Compromise,* I have received scores of letters from school people that open with some form of this agonized statement. The Horace of the book is a composite character, both fictional and real, a fine person and teacher who knows that his school's traditional routines force him into activity that virtually guarantees inadequate work from the students. However, no one seems to care much about the surely unintentional mindlessness of Horace's Franklin High, its often generous but profoundly flawed practices and attitudes. Everyone goes along—in effect, compromising.

Things have always been this way, many assume. Most people are happy; Franklin pride is everywhere. Franklin is just like most other schools, and they don't see any need to redesign themselves. So why bother? Anyway, changing anything is a stressful business. Teaching is already difficult work; kids are messy, demanding, and distracted; and the community really doesn't care very much. The folks out there *like* Franklin High, just as it is. So let's all go along, even if in our heart of hearts we know better.

This rankles Horace. It appears that some of his colleagues in the real world are similarly disturbed. It's not that their schools are all that bad or ungenerous or aren't trying to serve their students. It is just that with a dose of honest self-scrutiny and a willingness to make and stick to some hard decisions, these schools could be so much better.

Horace's Compromise was one of three volumes (all published by Houghton Mifflin) to emerge from A Study of High Schools, an inquiry into the state of American secondary education conducted from 1979 to 1984. Arthur G. Powell, Eleanor Farrar, and David K. Cohen published *The Shopping Mall High School: Winners and Losers in the Educational Marketplace* in 1985, drawing on their own and their colleagues' careful observation of fifteen secondary schools over the 1981–1982 academic year. They too exposed compromises, the "treaties" made by schools and in schools for all involved to "get along." The final chapter, written by David Cohen, is a meditation on why Americans have the schools they do and why they tolerate an institution that clearly fails to challenge the intellects of a majority of its students. Perhaps, Cohen suggests, Americans have purposes for high schools other than traditional academic education, and these—sorting the students out in a genial, ritual-filled setting—may be well served by current practices. Horace may feel compromised, but his goals might be different from those of a larger public.

In 1986, Robert Hampel published the third volume, *The Last Little Citadel,* a series of essays on the history of American high schools since 1940. He chronicled the periodic efforts to change the schools and the usual failures of those attempts. Only the actions of the late 1960s, he found, left much of a trace on the system. Once again, the basic satisfaction of Americans with their schools, whatever their leaders may have told them, was clear. Yes, citizens might assert, there may be an Educational Crisis, but it's at somebody else's school, not mine. I'm satisfied with our Franklin High. Don't change it. Don't put my offspring at any risk of not graduating with their classes. Don't make my child a guinea pig. Don't upset the fragile compromises that I have already made.

In the years since our books were published, all of us on the staff of A Study of High Schools have pondered our work, wondering if there were themes or areas that we missed, ones that might have shed further light on the schools. Hampel, for instance, feels that we all underestimated the important role of the principal. By looking so much at teachers, we may have underplayed the nature of the force, for whatever end, of those in the central office. Indeed, Horace Smith's principal at Franklin High School remains a shadowy figure, removed, it seems, from compromises.

In addition, Hampel thinks now that we underestimated the importance of faculty politics, or at the least the ebb and flow of groups of faculty in the shaping of a school's important cultures. There are the Horaces, he argues, those who are ready and eager to try to improve their situation. But there are also the "yes, but . . ." staff members, the ones who, intentionally or unintentionally, jeopardize any divergent effort by persistently raising concerns that snarl reform. Further, there are the indifferent ones, people who show up at staff meetings but rarely talk; their passivity, of course, speaks volumes. Indifference effectually creates profound drag. Finally, there are the actively hostile forces, usually small in number, bitter and carping, whose primary political tactic is the use of corrosive gossip.

The interactions of these groups explain much in schools, Hampel says, and their functioning sheds light on why there has been so little apparent constructive movement even in places that appeared to have a core of committed reformers such as Horace. A core group alone means little, it seems. It is for this reason, for example, that pilot projects, ostensibly the forerunners of change, are in effect pedagogical Siberias, places where the troublemakers, the questioners of the status quo, can be safely sequestered, out of the way. These encapsulated units include not just the Horaces but also the children of aggressive parents. They siphon off dissent of all sorts. The core of reformers is thereby neutralized.

Hampel also feels that we underestimated the influence on the schools we studied of district and state authorities and of the character of their particular communities. No school is an island, and although our books did address issues of politics and of class and setting, our research approach unintentionally seemed to assume that each was indeed operating in a vacuum.

Arthur Powell wonders if we stressed enough the weakness of the incentives for serious learning that the culture as a whole lends—the signals that hard work and high standards are expected of everyone. Kids need strong incentives to engage at school, and to leave responsibility for providing them to teachers alone is to guarantee failure. A community that starves its schools financially, that tolerates administrative and contractual arrangements which undermine the schools' sensible functioning, and that signals by its own activities a superficial interest in, if not scorn of, learning is one in which a school cannot succeed, even if it is staffed with a score of Horace Smiths. Further, children who come to school hungry, frightened, neglected, and abused are unlikely to settle down readily to Coleridge and calculus, and the America of the early 1990s has a growing number of such adolescents. Poverty in this country today is found primarily among children and youth and their mothers. School reform must often be the daughter of social reform.

Written today, *Horace's Compromise* would have benefited from these new awarenesses. Its original message, however, continues to be important. Whatever the nature of the larger community or the internal politics of a school might be, the familiar and often ineffective practices of teaching persist: the rushed procession of fifty-two-minute classes; the jumble of "subjects," none either thoroughly defined or related well to any other, leaving even the ablest and most devoted students in a swamp of intellectual confusion; the predominance of teacher-talk and student-listen, with its attendant docility; the reduction of the goals for a school to the collection of credits (meaning "seat time"); and the procession of mindless, brief tests that relate little, if at all, to the curriculum the students have supposedly traversed. The waste of most people's time, students and teachers alike, and the costs to the society are prodigious. The many Horaces out there know this, and it does truly hurt.

Since 1984, I have joined a growing group of school and university colleagues who are struggling to address this hurt, to identify and to put into practice better compromises for Horace.

x

We call ourselves the Coalition of Essential Schools, and the basis of our effort is laid out in the afterword to this volume, written in 1985. While based at Brown University and teaching here, I have had opportunities to visit schools, to listen and to watch my friends there, to reflect on what is meant by and for these schools, and also to study the process under way in those places where the Horaces and others are directly attempting reform. A first report on my take on all this appears as *Horace's School: Redesigning the American High School,* published by Houghton Mifflin in 1992.

When one is not in high school classrooms, it is all too easy to forget both the intense dailiness of schools—the urgency of the immediacies found in any swirl of adolescents—and the senselessness of the regimens that most students follow. One has to shadow kids for a day or two to be forceably reminded of what it is like to change subjects abruptly every hour, to be talked at incessantly, to be asked to sit still for long periods, to be endlessly tested and measured against others, to be moved around in cohorts by people who really do not know who you are, to be denied any civility like a coffee break and asked to eat lunch in twenty-three minutes, to be rarely trusted, and to repeat the same regimen with virtually no variation for week after week, year after year.

Students are remarkably good-natured about all of this; they often cavil with my hostile description of their school lives, and many are content with the low intensity and expectations at school. They make do, make their treaties, make their compromises. They assume that this is what they are supposed to do: this is Going to School in America. They exude genial acceptance. And as a result, there is all too often no edge to their thinking, no deep habits of intellectual interest, little curiosity beyond the immediate. Even in elite schools they have been cheated, and they don't know it. The exceptions among them, the academic or athletic tyros who are regularly heralded by their communities, prove the rule. The unspecial majority cheerfully mark time.

How to crack through these barriers to sensible reform? Is the task so difficult that the reform will have to come from the outside, leveraged by centrally controlled examinations of students and certification of teachers? Is it necessary to circumvent the existing educational establishment by means of some sort of competitive market system? Are the conventional habits of schooling so deeply inbred—reinforced by a system of teacher education that largely affirms them—that wholly new sorts of schools, or other kinds of educating systems, must be created, again and deliberately circumventing Horace and his Franklin High colleagues? Many today think so; and here the change since 1984, when *Horace's Compromise* was first published, is most telling. The political and business leaders of this country may not wait for Franklin to change itself; they may have utterly lost patience with the existing system.

In 1984 the critique embodied in the three books of the Study of High Schools was called radical. Today, in 1991, it is assumed in many influential quarters not to be radical enough. The argument behind *Horace's Compromise* draws on the belief that the best schooling will come only when the Horace Smiths harness themselves to the task. Horace is to be trusted—trusted to know what is best for kids, what kids need to flourish in the world beyond school—and Franklin High's immediate community is to be trusted to know what standards are or might be. Many today feel that such trust is both naive and misplaced.

Only Horace, the professional teacher, can prove such pessimism to be wrong. True, school people can try to avoid the critics once again, can go on the defensive. They can continue to sleep behind the walls of what in many communities is a de facto public school monopoly. They can avoid talking about high standards and what it really will take to reach them. They can let yet another testing scheme be inflicted on their students, one that they can mindlessly prep their students to manipulate and that will prove once again that poor kids score poorly and richer kids score better.

Or they can reach for better ideas—for new and better compromises—and for the political will to support them. The schools in the Coalition are embarked on this struggle. Theirs is difficult work: few of the influential public or critical policy makers have shadowed students recently, or carefully examined those tests whose scores they now believe are so important, or listened hard to the voices of the Horace Smiths. They lack anger about the most important things, about the neglect of young people and the waste represented by their schools. The remedies suggested (their rhetoric to the contrary notwithstanding) are often off the mark, insensitive to the social and economic realities in many communities, unfueled with resources, even fundamentally undemocratic. Most rarely go to the heart of the problem: the fundamental misdesign of schools and the instability of the families and communities from which the students come.

Some will say that high schools for the affluent appear to "work"; the graduates get into college. Why change anything? There is no sense even there of the grievous loss, the wasted time, the unintentional reinforcement of bad habits, the cynical treaty making, the hypocrisy, the intellectual sloppiness. And if schools for the affluent are OK, the political will to address the schools for everyone else is weak. So while the talk of reform is abroad in the land, the actuality of change—at the level of Horace Smith's classroom—is barely started.

And yet it *is* started. *I am Horace Smith,* many good people write. There are places—neighborhoods, districts, states—that support their schools' fundamental rethinking and consequent redesign, and the first graduates of those schools show the happy results. Even where venturesome school leaders have had setbacks, the trek, once started, appears to persist.

Change is slow. What comes first is thinking anew about learning and teaching, addressing those practices that bedevil Horace. From fresh thinking comes fresh design. People have to be persuaded. Policies have to be rethought, recrafted. Regulations have to be jettisoned or recast. Communities must be mobilized.

Happily, I can answer those *I am Horace Smith* letters today more easily than I was able to in the mid-1980s: a start *has* been made toward changing the compromises. I can connect the letter writers with like-minded colleagues, people who share the frustration and who have started their schools on the road to reform. One hopes that this company will become an army. One hopes that the public will be both patient and insistent that fundamental change is necessary. One hopes that political leaders will persevere and stay their course, that they won't reduce the school crisis to slogans or address it only from the outside, by merely juggling mechanisms for political control or imposing yet another layer of distorting tests. One hopes that some trust can spread through the system, and the respect that trust implies. And one hopes that through it all, the Horace Smiths will press ahead with their reforms and remain with their kids, keeping high their hopes for adolescents and for the freedom and richness of those students' minds.

Introduction

OF ALL the stages of life, adolescence is the most volatile—full of promise, energy, and, because of newly achieved freedom and potency, substantial peril. In its freshness, adolescence is attractive. In its enthusiasms, it can be, to older folk at least, exhausting. For most people, it is pivotal: it is the time of life when we find out who we are becoming, what we are good at, what and whom we like. What happens in these years profoundly affects what follows.

A society that is concerned about the strength and wisdom of its culture pays careful attention to its adolescents. Americans generously provide high schools to help these young citizens grow up well. Virtually all young people attend them, more or less regularly; they are a sturdy fixture of every American community. Because of their ubiquity and their importance for youth, high schools oftentimes are focuses of controversy—particularly so, it seems, in the early 1980s. Analysts of the American psyche may explain that we pick particularly on the schools when we're unhappy with ourselves in general (a perhaps unfair but safe bit of transference, as it were), but it may well be that the critical attention today paid to high schools is richly deserved.

It was with this belief that I and several colleagues in the late 1970s undertook to study American high schools. By training I am a historian and by recent experience a secondary school principal and teacher, and my approach over the last two years has been to read, to listen, and, above all, to visit—to try to understand the American high school by observing it firsthand. My purpose, and that of my colleagues and those who sponsored us, was ultimately to use this informed observation as the basis upon which to suggest improvements for these schools.

Curiously most of us, lay people and educators alike, tend to underrate teaching. We rarely underestimate the difficulties of learning. Having had to learn, we know that it is a complicated and unpredictable business. Likewise, the craft of provoking us to learn—the act of teaching—is itself complicated.

We can play at learning, without retaining much save the temporary pleasure of the play, and we can act the teacher, strutting expectable stuff in front of blackboards. Real learning and real teaching require more. Successful learning gives us that rush of confidence which comes from competence. We cannot fake it. Often it comes from a struggle, from hard reflecting, from trial and error, from considering the previously unconsidered. Sometimes it jumps out serendipitously, like the meant word in a crossword puzzle. Sometimes it is forced out by apprehension, by the fear that if we do not master this sequence of ideas, we will suffer a reduced respect from ourselves, our teachers, or our peers. Whether our learning comes from orderly revelation or serendipity or hard attention fueled with apprehension, we know that the process we went through to reach understanding is complex, subtle, often mysterious, and sometimes not much fun at all.

The experienced adult can reflect on his learning or lack of it. Why can't I get this point? Is there some other way to get at this problem? Why do others think that this task is so important: what do they see in it that I don't? We adults usually know how to organize and pace ourselves. If I stay at this another hour, I can piece it together. I need a break; my brain is sodden. I need quiet for this. Some soft rock or Rachmaninoff will help. We know from experience how our way of learning things differs from that used by others. She just hears their names and remembers them, but I have to write them down. He can concentrate with all those clacking typewriters around him, but I need quiet. With experience, we adapt

2

to things. Sometimes well, sometimes ineptly, we learn how to learn for ourselves.

But we are adults, experienced for the most part. Children, being inexperienced, neither know how to learn very efficiently nor are aware of how to reflect on their own knowing. Most children assume that knowledge just happens to them, that it is handed to them by some parentlike seer as if it were a peanut butter and jelly sandwich. Rarely are they asked *how* they learned something and how their way may be special. Thus, the teacher gets little help from his or her students: they are not apt at self-diagnosis nor much given to intellectual self-consciousness. (Indeed, most adolescents would gag at the thought that they should be "intellectually self-conscious.") As a result, the thoughtful teacher has to guess what is needed, for a class and for each individual in it, guess as to pace and style, pressure and patience.

Managing a high school classroom is a complex business, requiring judgment about adolescents as well as a sense of order, a firm grasp of the subject under study, and a thorough understanding about the accepted folkways of the craft. Irrespective of their credentials, teachers without judgment stumble. It is the heart of teaching.

And yet Americans underrate the craft of teaching. We treat it mechanistically. We expect to know how to teach fractions as though one needed only a formulaic routine to do so, a way to plug in. We talk about "delivering a service" to students by means of "instructional strategies"; our metaphors arise from the factory floor and issue from the military manual. Education, apparently, is something someone does to somebody else. Paradoxically, while we know that *we* don't learn very well that way, nor want very much to have someone else's definition of "service" to be "delivered" to *us,* we accept these metaphors for the mass of children. We thus underrate the mystery, challenge, and complexity of learning and, as a result, operate schools that are extraordinarily wasteful.

Not surprisingly, we also underrate teachers. We say, "Those who can, do; those who can't, teach." The parent confesses at a bar after work, "Our son David is just *temporarily* a schoolteacher, of course . . . He's earning the money he'll need for law school." The craft of keeping school is a subtle business requiring special kinds of judgment and patience, and thus special sorts of devoted and able practitioners, a notion lamentably far from the consciousness of most Americans.

This book urges renewed public attention to the importance of teaching in high schools and to the complexity and subtlety of that craft. While our system of schools contains many consequential characteristics—for example, the subjects of the curriculum, the forms of governance, the uses of technologies and teaching aids, the organization of programs for special groups—none is more important than who the teachers are and how they work. Without good teachers, sensibly deployed, schooling is barely worth the effort.

This is especially true in secondary education, where rapidly developing young people first face complicated issues that require careful reasoning. High schools exist not merely to subject the pupils to brute training—memorizing geometry theorems, dutifully showing up on time, learning how to mend an axle, reciting a passage from *Macbeth*—but to develop their powers of thought, of taste, and of judgment. High schools exist to help them with these uses of their minds. Such undertakings cannot be factory-wrought, for young people grow in idiosyncratic, variable ways, often unpredictably. Good teachers are essential to nourish this growth. It is their judgment and inspiration that can help young persons. No "system" or "school site leadership," no "treatment" or "intervention," no "innovative program," "approved textbook," or "curriculum guide" can overcome their influence, for good or ill. Learning is a humane process, and young humans look to those human elders with whom they are in daily contact for standards, for help, and as models. That is what teachers are for. This book, inevitably, is a celebration of their work. Equally inevitably, its primary recommendation is that Americans restore to teachers and to their particular students the largest share of responsibility for the latter's education.

This volume is one of several emerging from our five-year-long inquiry into adolescent education called A Study of High Schools. The present book concentrates on learning and teaching. A second, by Robert Hampel, consists of essays on the history of American high schools since 1940. A third, written by Arthur G. Powell, Eleanor Farrar, and David K. Cohen, carefully examines several critical themes arising in the world of fifteen high schools during the 1981–1982 academic year. The five of us, joined by Martha Landesberg and Patricia West-Barker and by a part-time field and research staff of some twenty individuals, worked in concert, even as our separate books present the interests of their individual authors.

A Study of High Schools was sponsored by the National Association of Secondary School Principals and the Commission on Educational Issues of the National Association of Independent Schools. Funding was provided by the Charles E. Culpeper Foundation, the Carnegie Corporation of New York, the Commonwealth Fund, the Esther A. and Joseph Klingenstein Fund, the Gates Foundation, and the Edward John Noble Foundation.

As readers will quickly observe in all our work, we have focused on the "triangle" of students, teachers, and the subjects of their study.[1] We know that the game of school learning is won or lost in classrooms, and we feel that America's present system of schooling makes winning often very difficult indeed. Any improvement in American high schools must take into account the stubborn realities of this triangle. Understand the triangle, and the subsequent necessary steps become clear.

A second reason for our focus is that other inquiries into secondary education have also been underway during the period of our work, several of which have usefully different, usually broader, perspectives than has ours. Thus, we chose to travel in a complementary way with them and to leave consideration of important issues beyond the scope of our work to them.

Looking only at high schools is distorting. The students come from somewhere—home and elementary and middle schools—and are going somewhere—to work, to college, to an independent life. Reference to these worlds before and after high school remains implicit in our work; we trust the reader appreciates the importance of these worlds. Since we could not inquire into everything at once, we chose here to look at the schooling of adolescents.

This big country contains numerous educational jurisdictions, with authority decentralized. Nonetheless, as one visits communities one is gradually struck by how *similar* the structure and articulated purpose of American high schools are. Rural schools, city schools; rich schools, poor schools; public schools, private schools; big schools, little schools: the *framework* of grades, schedules, calendar, courses of study, even rituals, is astonishingly uniform and has been so for at least forty years.[2] In most schools, I visited biology and social studies classes, and I could soon predict the particular topics under study during a given month in Bio I or U.S. History, whatever the school. While the texts had different covers and authors, their commonness was stunning. Given the extraordinary changes in American society and scholarship over the last decades and the remarkable diversity of American communities, the similarities among American high schools' purposes, structures, and procedures are fascinating. High school is a kind of secular church, a place of national rituals that mark stages of a young citizen's life. The value of its rites appears to depend on national consistency.

Among schools there was one important difference, which followed from a single variable only: the social class of the student body. If the school principally served poor adolescents, its character, if not its structure, varied from sister schools for the more affluent. It got so that I could say with some justification to school principals, Tell me about the incomes of your students' families and I'll describe to you your school.

Much has recently been made of an apparent splintering of American society, of a lack of a national consensus. This may be true in American politics, where special interest government has become more visible, if not more ubiquitous, than earlier, but it certainly is not true in American high schools. Tacit agreement exists as to the purpose of high school and how it is to be accomplished.

The lives of adolescents, whether from small towns or big cities or farms or suburbs, are profoundly affected by commonly observed and value-laden phenomena, from TV programs to advertisements to professional athletics to musical taste to what goes on in high school. Some of this commonality appears wrong-headed and dysfunctional, as I will presently argue; some is coarse, ungenerous, and simplistic. Looked at from a distance, the problem of American secondary education resides in its mediocre sameness rather than in fragmentation. Today we need no new consensus, but, rather, an agreement to help our adolescents break out of our existing mediocre harmonies.

This structural commonality among schools made our job somewhat easier. It would have been different a hundred years ago, when there was a bewildering variety of high schools, academies, lyceums, and colleges serving youth. The bureaucratic standardization of American education is now a fact; we have One Best System—in spite of the irrepressible individuality of adolescents and of the sharply etched discrimination between rich and poor.[3]

My colleagues and I visited dozens of schools. Although many of us have had substantial experience in school work, we wanted to look further, deeply and carefully, into a wide variety of institutions. The generosity of our supporting philanthropic foundations and the unstinting assistance of our two sponsoring associations made this possible. Most of my colleagues concentrated their watching and listening in fifteen schools, eleven public and four private, clustered around San Diego, Denver, Boston, northern Ohio, and southern Alabama. They gained there a special depth of understanding. My function was to gain breadth. During 1981 and 1982, I visited some eighty schools, starting during the summer of 1981 in Australia as a guest of that nation's Headmasters Conference and Association of Heads of Schools for Girls. In this country, I visited schools in fifteen states, in all quarters except the Northwest, Hawaii, Alaska, and Puerto Rico. Without exception, I was warmly greeted and generously helped.*

My argument in this book depends heavily on a series of word pictures drawn from these visits. I have used this approach to try to communicate to the reader—particularly the lay reader, to whom my work is especially directed—the essential "feel" of schools. What this device loses in precision I trust it will provide in a sense of the important, complicated daily-ness of the life of a school and its people.

The characters here portrayed are real people, and the places described are all actual places. With but a few, mostly personal, exceptions, however, I have masked true identities. It has been my experience that educators tend to ignore something not exactly on their own turf. "Oh, that's Lincoln High School," they say; "it can't apply to us." The points I am trying to make do in fact

---

* The names of these schools appear with other acknowledgments at the end of this volume.

extend beyond any one high school, and I wish no reader to be encouraged to think otherwise.

More important, brief portraits such as these inevitably distort. One can describe faithfully, but in making choices of what to represent, one inevitably shapes a point of view. While I have struggled to be fair, I want no person or school identified with a particular portrait. My purpose is not to tell their special stories, but to use aspects of their experience to make some useful general points.

Some of my actors are composites, a blending of people and places. Horace and Mark in particular are handled in this way. All their classes are "real" classes, but their juxtaposition is invented. For them, my device ends up somewhere between precise journalism and nonfiction fiction.

Although I have a historian's training and experience in higher education, my point of view throughout has been primarily that of schoolteacher and principal, roles that force on one an intense awareness of the frailties and strengths of individual human beings. There is bias here that I recognize—that the craft of teaching is both art and science, and that the poetry in learning and teaching is as important to promote as the purposeful. Social and behavioral science, usually driven by purposeful ends, has dominated the way contemporary Americans view and administer their schools. Such science undoubtedly has its contribution, but the humanities' place deserves fresh emphasis. We deal with adolescents' hearts as well as brains, with human idiosyncrasies as well as their calculable commonalities. If I err, I hope that it is toward the humanistic side.

Prologue
Horace's Compromise

HERE IS an English teacher, Horace Smith. He's fifty-three, a twenty-eight-year veteran of high school classrooms, what one calls an old pro. He's proud, respected, and committed to his practice. He'd do nothing else. Teaching is too much fun, too rewarding, to yield to another line of work.

Horace has been at Franklin High in a suburb of a big city for nineteen years. He served for eight years as English department chairman, but turned the job over to a colleague, because he felt that even the minimal administrative chores of that post interfered with the teaching he loved best.

He arises at 5:45 A.M., careful not to awaken either his wife or grown daughter. He likes to be at school by 7:00, and the drive there from his home takes forty minutes. He wishes he owned a home near the school, but he can't afford it. Only a few of his colleagues live in the school's town, and they are the wives of executives whose salaries can handle the mortgages. His wife's job at the liquor store that she, he, and her brother own doesn't start until 10:00 A.M., and their daughter, a new associate in a law firm in the city, likes to sleep until the last possible minute and skip breakfast. He washes and dresses on tiptoe.

Horace prepares the coffee, makes some toast, and leaves the house at 6:20. He's not the first at school. The custodians and other, usually older, teachers are already there, "puttering around," one of the teachers says.

The teachers' room is large, really two rooms. The inner portion, windowless, is arranged in a honeycomb of carrels, one for each older teacher. Younger or newer teachers share carrels. Each has a built-in desk and a chair. Most have file cabinets. The walls on three sides, five feet high, are festooned with posters, photographs, lists, little sayings, notes from colleagues on issues long past. Horace: Call home. Horace: The following students in the chorus are excused from your Period 7 class—Adelson, Cartwright, Donato . . .

Horace goes to his carrel, puts down his briefcase, picks up his mug, and walks to the coffee pot at the corner of the outer portion of the teachers' room, a space well lit by wide windows and fitted with a clutter of tables, vinyl-covered sofas, and chairs. The space is a familiar, comfortable jumble, fragrant with the smell of cigarettes smoked hours before. Horace lights up a fresh one, almost involuntarily, as a way perhaps to counteract yesterday's dead vapors. After pouring himself some coffee, he chats with some colleagues, mostly other English teachers.

The warning bell rings at 7:20. Horace smothers his cigarette, takes his still partly filled cup back to his carrel and adds it to the shuffle on his desk, collects some books and papers, and, with his briefcase, carries them down the hall to his classroom. Students are already clattering in, friendly, noisy, most of them ignoring him completely—not thoughtlessly, but without thinking. Horace often thinks of the importance of this semantic difference. Many adults are thoughtless about us teachers. Most students, however, just don't know we're here at all, people to think about. Innocents, he concludes.

7:30, and its bell. There are seventeen students here; there should be twenty-two. Bill Adams is ill; Horace has been told that by the office. Joyce Lezcowitz is at her grandmother's funeral; Horace hasn't been officially told that, but he knows it to be true. He marks Joyce "Ex Ab"—excused absence—on his attendance list. Looking up from the list, he sees two more students arrive, hustling to seats. You're late. Sorry . . . Sorry . . . The bus . . . Horace ignores the apologies and excuses and checks the two off on his list. One name is yet unaccounted for. Where is Jimmy Tibbetts? Silence. Tibbetts gets an "Abs" after his name.

Horace gets the class's attention by making some announcements about next week's test and about the method by which copies of the next play being read will be shared. This inordinately concerns some students and holds no interest for others. Mr. Smith, how can I finish the play when both Rosalie and I have to work after school? Mr. Smith, Sandy and I are on different buses. Can we switch partners? All these sorts of queries are from girls. There is whispering among some students. You got it? Horace asks, abruptly. Silence, signaling affirmation. Horace knows it is an illusion. Some character will come up two days later and guiltlessly assert that he has no play book, doesn't know how to get one, and has never heard of the plans to share the limited copies. Horace makes a mental note to inform Adams, Lezcowitz, and Tibbetts of the text-sharing plan.

This is a class of juniors, mostly seventeen. The department syllabus calls for Shakespeare during this marking period, and *Romeo and Juliet* is the choice this year. The students have been assigned to read Act IV for this week, and Horace and his colleagues all get them to read the play out loud. The previous class had been memorable: Juliet's suicide had provoked much mirth. *Romeo, I come!* The kids thought it funny, clumsily melodramatic. Several, sniggering, saw a sexual meaning. Horace knew this to be inevitable; he had taught the play many times before.

We'll start at Scene Four. A rustle of books. Two kids looking helplessly around. They had forgotten their books, even though in-class reading had been a daily exercise for three weeks. Mr. Smith, I forgot my book. You've got to remember, Alice . . . *remember!* All this with a smile as well as honest exasperation. Share with George. Alice gets up and moves her desk next to that of George. They solemnly peer into George's book while two girls across the classroom giggle.

Gloria, you're Lady Capulet. Mary, the Nurse. George, you're old man Capulet. Gloria starts, reading without punctuation: *Hold take these keys and fetch more spices Nurse.* Horace: Gloria. Those commas. They mean something. Use them. Now, again. *Hold. Take these keys. And fetch more spices. Nurse.* Horace swallows. Better . . . Go on, Mary. *They call for dates and quinces in the pastry.* What's a quince? a voice asks. Someone answers, It's a fruit, Fruit! Horace ignores this digression but is reminded how he doesn't like this group of kids. Individually, they're nice, but the chemistry of them together doesn't work. Classes are too much a game for them. Go on . . . George?

Come. Stir! Stir! Stir! The second cock hath crow'd. Horace knows that reference to "cock" will give an opening to some jokester, and he squelches it before it can begin, by being sure he is looking at the class and not at his book as the words are read.

The curfew bell hath rung. 'Tis three o'clock. Look to the bak'd meats, good Angelica . . . George reads accurately, but with little accentuation.

Mary: *Go, you cot-quean, go . . .* Horace interrupts, and explains "cot-quean," a touch of contempt by the Nurse for the meddling Capulet. Horace does not go into the word's etymology, although he knows it. He feels that such a digression would be lost on this group, if not on his third-period class. He'll tell them. And so he returns: George, you're still Capulet. Reply to that cheeky Nurse.

The reading goes on for about forty minutes, to 8:15. The play's repartee among the musicians and Peter was a struggle, and Horace cut off the reading-out-loud before the end of the fifth scene. He assigns Act V for the next period and explains what will be on the *Romeo and Juliet* test. Mr. Smith, Ms. Viola isn't giving a test to her class. The statement is, of course, an accusing question. Well, we are. Ms. Viola's class will get something else, don't you worry. The bell rings.

The students rush out as the next class tries to push in. The newcomers are freshmen and give way to the eleventh-graders. They get into their seats expectantly, without quite the swagger of the older kids. Even though this is March, some of these students are still overwhelmed by the size of the high school.

There should be thirty students in this class, but twenty-seven are present. He marks three absences on his sheet. The students watch him; there is no chatter, but a good deal of squirming. These kids have the Wriggles, Horace has often said. The bell rings: 8:24.

Horace tells the students to open their textbooks to page 104 and read the paragraph at its top. Two students have no textbook. Horace tells them to share with their neighbors. *Always* bring your textbook to class. We never know when we'll need them. The severity in his voice causes quiet. The students read.

Horace asks: Betty, which of the words in the first sentence is an adverb? Silence. Betty stares at her book. More silence. Betty, what is an adverb? Silence. Bill, help Betty. It's sort of a verb that tells you about things. Horace pauses: Not quite, Bill, but close. Phil, you try. Phil: An adverb modifies a verb . . . Horace: O.K., Phil, but what does "modify" mean? Silence. A voice: "Darkly." Who said that? Horace asks. The sentence was "Heathcliff was a darkly brooding character." I did, Taffy says. O.K., Horace follows, you're correct, Taffy, but tell us why "darkly" is an adverb, what it does. Taffy: It modifies "character." No, Taffy, try again. Heathcliff? No. Brooding? Yes, now why? Is "brooding" a verb? Silence.

Horace goes to the board, writes the sentence with chalk. He underlines *darkly*. Betty writes a note to her neighbor.

The class proceeds with this slow trudge through a paragraph from the textbook, searching for adverbs. Horace presses ahead patiently, almost dumbly at times. He is so familiar with the mistakes that ninth-graders make that he can sense them coming even before their utterance. Adverbs are always tougher to teach than adjectives. What frustrates him most are the partly correct answers; Horace worries that if he signals that a reply is somewhat accurate, all the students will think it is entirely accurate. At the same time, if he takes some minutes to sort out the truth from the falsity, the entire train of thought will be lost. He can never pursue any one student's errors to completion without losing all the others. Teaching grammar to classes like this is slow business, Horace feels. The bell rings. The students rush out, now more boisterous.

This is an Assembly Day, Horace remembers with pleasure. He leaves his papers on his desk, turns off the lights, shuts the door, and returns to the teachers' room. He can avoid assemblies; only the deans have to go. It's some student concert, in any event.

The teachers' room is full. Horace takes pleasure in it and wonders how his colleagues in schools in the city make do without such a sanctuary. Having a personal carrel is a luxury, he knows. He'd lose his here, he also knows, if enrollments went up again. The teachers' room was one happy consequence of the "baby bust."

The card game is going, set up on a square coffee table surrounded by a sofa and chairs. The kibitzers outnumber the players; all have coffee, some are smoking. The chatter is incessant, joshingly insulting. The staff members like one another.

Horace takes his mug, empties the cold leavings into the drain of the water fountain, and refills it. He puts a quarter in the large Maxwell House can supplied for that purpose, an honor system. He never pays for his early cup; Horace feels that if you come early, you get one on the house. He moves toward a clutch of fellow English and social studies teachers, and they gossip, mostly about a bit of trouble at the previous night's basketball game. No one was injured—that rarely happens at this high school—but indecorous words had been shouted back and forth, and Coke cans rolled on the gym floor. Someone could have been hurt. No teacher is much exercised about the incident. The talk is about things of more immediate importance to people: personal lives, essences even more transitory, Horace knows, than the odors of their collective cigarettes.

Horace looks about for Ms. Viola to find out whether it's true that she's not going to give a test on *Romeo and Juliet.* She isn't in sight, and Horace remembers why: she is a nonsmoker and is offended by smoke. He leaves his group and goes to Viola's carrel, where he finds her. She is put off by his query. Of course she is giving a test. Horace's lame explanation that a student told him differently doesn't help.

9:53. The third-period class of juniors. *Romeo and Juliet* again. Announcements over the public address system fill the first portion of the period, but Horace and a bunch of kids who call themselves "theater jocks" ignore them and talk about how to read Shakespeare well. They have to speak loudly to overpower the p.a. The rest of the class chatter among themselves. The readings from the play are lively, and Horace is able to exhibit his etymological talents with a disquisition on "cot-quean." The students are well engaged by the scene involving the musicians and Peter until the class is interrupted by a proctor from the principal's office, collecting absence slips for the first-class periods. Nonetheless, the lesson ends with a widespread sense of good feeling. Horace never gets around to giving out the assignment, talking about the upcoming test, or arranging for play books to be shared.

10:47, the Advanced Placement class. They are reading *Ulysses,* a novel with which Horace himself had trouble. Its circumlocutions are more precious than clever, he thinks, but he can't let on. Joyce is likely to be on the AP Exam, which will put him on a pedestal.

There are eighteen seniors in this class, but only five arrive. Horace remembers: This is United Nations Week at the local college, and a group of the high school's seniors is taking part, representing places like Mauritius and Libya. Many of the students in the UN Club are also those in Advanced Placement classes. Horace welcomes this remnant of five and suggests they use the hour to read. Although he is annoyed at losing several teaching days with this class, he is still quietly grateful for the respite this morning.

11:36. Lunch. Horace buys a salad on the cafeteria line—as a teacher he can jump ahead of students—and he takes it to the faculty dining room. He nods to the assistant principal on duty as he passes by. He takes a place at an empty table and is almost immediately joined by three physical education teachers, all of them coaches of varsity teams, who are noisily wrangling about the previous night's basketball game controversy. Horace listens, entertained. The coaches are having a good time, arguing with heat because they know the issue is really inconsequential and thus their disagreement will not mean much. Lunch is relaxing for Horace.

12:17. A free period. Horace checks with a colleague in the book storeroom about copies of a text soon to be used by the ninth-graders. Can he get more copies? His specific allotment is settled after some minutes' discussion. Horace returns to the teachers' room, to his carrel. He finds a note to call a Mrs. Altschuler, who turns out to be the stepmother of a former student. She asks, on behalf of her stepson, whether Horace will write a character reference for the young man to use in his search for a job. Horace agrees. Horace also finds a note to call the office. Was Tibbetts in your Period One class? No, Horace tells the assistant principal; that's why I marked him absent on the attendance sheet. The assistant principal overlooks this sarcasm. Well, he says, Tibbetts wasn't marked absent at any other class. Horace replies, That's someone else's problem. He was not in my class. The assistant principal: You're sure? Horace: Of course I'm sure.

The minutes of the free period remaining are spent in organizing a set of papers that is to be returned to Horace's third junior English class. Horace sometimes alternates weeks when he collects homework so as not totally to bury himself. He feels guilty about this. The sixth-period class had its turn this week. Horace had skimmed these exercises—a series of questions on Shakespeare's life—and hastily graded them, but using only a plus, check, or minus. He hadn't had time enough to do more.

1:11. More *Romeo and Juliet.* This section is less rambunctious than the first-period group and less interesting than that of the third period. The students are actually rather dull, perhaps because the class meets at the end of the day. Everyone is ready to leave; there is little energy for Montagues and Capulets. However, as with other sections, the kids are responsive when spoken to individually. It is their blandness when they are in a group that Horace finds trying. At least they aren't hell raisers, the way some last-period-of-the-day sections can be. The final bell rings at 2:00.

Horace has learned to stay in his classroom at the day's end so that students who want to consult with him can always find him there. Several appear today. One wants Horace to speak on his behalf to a prospective employer. Another needs to get an assignment. A couple of other students come by actually just to come by. They have no special errand, but seem to like to check in and chat. These youngsters puzzle Horace. They always seem to need reassurance.

Three students from the Theater Club arrive with questions about scenery for the upcoming play. (Horace is the faculty adviser to the stage crew.) Their shared construction work on sets behind the scenes gives Horace great pleasure. He knows these kids and likes their company.

By the time Horace finishes in his classroom, it is 2:30. He drops his papers and books at his carrel, selecting some—papers given him by his Advanced Placement students two days previously that he has yet to find time to read—to put in his briefcase. He does not check in on the card game, now winding down, in the outer section of the teachers' room but, rather, goes briefly to the auditorium to watch the Theater Club actors starting their rehearsals. The play is Wilder's *Our Town.* Horace is both grateful and wistful that the production requires virtually no set to be constructed. The challenge for his stage crew, Horace knows, will be in the lighting.

Horace drives directly to his liquor store, arriving shortly after 4:00. He gives his brother-in-law some help in the stockroom and helps at the counter during the usual 4:30-to-6:30 surge of customers. His wife had earlier left for home and has supper ready for them both and their daughter at 7:45.

After dinner, Horace works for an hour on the papers he has brought home and on the Joyce classes he knows are ahead of him once the UN Mock Assembly is over. He has two telephone calls from students, one who has been ill and wants an assignment and another who wants to talk about the lighting for *Our Town*. The latter, an eager but shy boy, calls Horace often.

Horace turns in at 10:45, can't sleep, and watches the 11:00 news while his wife sleeps. He finally drifts off just before midnight.

Horace has high standards. Almost above all, he believes in the importance of writing, having his students learn to use language well. He believes in "coaching"—in having his students write and be criticized, often. Horace has his five classes of fewer than thirty students each, a total of 120. (He is lucky; his colleagues in inner cities like New York, San Diego, Detroit, and St. Louis have a school board–union negotiated "load" base of 175 students.) Horace believes that each student should write something for criticism at least twice a week—but he is realistic. As a rule, his students write once a week.

Most of Horace's students are juniors and seniors, young people who should be beyond sentence and paragraph exercises and who should be working on short essays, written arguments with moderately complex sequencing and, if not grace exactly, at least clarity. A page or two would be a minimum—but Horace is realistic. He assigns but one or two paragraphs.

Being a veteran teacher, Horace takes only fifteen to twenty minutes to check over each student's daily homework, to read the week's theme, and to write an analysis of it. (The "good" papers take a shorter time, usually, and the work of inept or demoralized students takes much longer.) Horace wonders how his inner-city colleagues, who usually have a far greater percentage of demoralized students, manage. Horace is realistic: even in his accommodating suburban school, fifteen minutes is too much to spend. He compromises, averaging five minutes for each student's work by cutting all but the most essential corners (the *reading* of the paragraphs in the themes takes but a few seconds; it is the thoughtful criticizing, in red ballpoint pen in the margins and elsewhere, that takes the minutes).

So, to check homework and to read and criticize one paragraph per week per student with the maximum feasible corner-cutting takes six hundred minutes, or ten hours, assuming no coffee breaks or flagging attention (which is some assumption, considering how enervating is most students' forced and misspelled prose).

Horace's fifty-some-minute classes consume about twenty-three hours per week. Administrative chores chew up another hour and a half. Horace cares about his teaching and feels that he should take a half-hour to prepare for each class meeting, particularly for his classes with older students, who are swiftly moving over quite abstract and unfamiliar material, and his class of ninth-graders, which requires teaching that is highly individualized. However, he is realistic. He will compromise by spending no more than ten minutes' preparation time, on average, per class. (In effect, he concentrates his "prep" time on the Advanced Placement class, and teaches the others from old notes.) Three of his sections are ostensibly of the same course, but because the students are different in each case, he knows that he cannot satisfactorily clone each lesson plan twice and teach to his satisfaction. (Horace is uneasy with this compromise but feels he can live with it.) Horace's class preparation time per week: four hours.

Horace loves the theater, and when the principal begged him to help out with the afternoon drama program, he agreed. He is paid $800 extra per year to help the student stage crews prepare sets. This takes him in all about four hours per week, save for the ten days before the shows, when he and his crew happily work for hours on end.

Of course, Horace would like time to work on the curriculum with his colleagues. He would like to visit their classes and to work with them on the English department program. He would like to meet his students' parents, to read in his field, and, most important for him, to counsel students as they need such counseling one on one. Being a popular teacher, he is asked to write over fifty recommendations for college admissions offices each year, a Christmas vacation task that usually takes three full days. (He knows he is good at it now. When he was less experienced, the reference writing used to take him a full week. He can now quickly crank out the expected felicitous verbiage.) Yet Horace feels uneasy writing the crucial references for students with whom he has rarely exchanged ten consecutive sentences of private conversation. However, he is realistic: one does what one can and hopes that one is not sending the colleges too many lies.

And so before Horace assigns his one or two paragraphs per week, he is committed for over thirty-two hours of teaching, administration, class preparation, and extracurricular drama work. Collecting one short piece of writing per week from students and spending a bare five minutes per week on each student's weekly work adds ten hours, yielding a forty-two-hour work week. Lunch periods, supervisory duties frequently, if irregularly, assigned, coffee breaks, travel to and from school, and time for the courtesies, civilities, and biological necessities of life are all in addition.

For this, Horace, a twenty-eight-year veteran, is paid $27,300, a good salary for a teacher in his district. He works at the liquor store and earns another $8000 there, given a good year. The district adds 7 percent of his base salary to a nonvested pension account, and Horace tries to put away something more each month in an IRA. Fortunately, his wife also works at the store, and their one child went to the state university and its law school. She just received her J.D. Her starting salary in the law firm is $32,000.

Horace is a gentle man. He reads the frequent criticism of his profession in the press with compassion. Johnny can't read. Teachers have low Graduate Record Examination scores. We must vary our teaching to the learning styles of our pupils. We must relate to the community. We must be scholarly, keeping up with our fields. English teachers should be practicing, published writers. If they aren't all these things, it is obvious that *they don't care.* Horace is a trouper; he hides his bitterness. Nothing can be gained by showing it. The critics do not really want to hear him or to face facts. He will go with the flow. What alternative is there?

A prestigious college near Franklin High School assigns its full-time freshman expository writing instructors a maximum of two sections, totaling forty students. Horace thinks about his 120. Like these college freshmen, at least they show up, most of them turn in what homework he assigns, and they give him little hassle. The teachers in the city have 175 kids, almost half of whom may be absent on any given day but all of whom remain the teacher's responsibility. And those kids are a resentful, wary, often troublesome lot. Horace is relieved that he is where he is. He wonders whether any of those college teachers ever read any of the recommendations he writes each Christmas vacation.

Most jobs in the real world have a gap between what would be nice and what is possible. One adjusts. The tragedy for many high school teachers is that the gap is a chasm, not crossed by reasonable and judicious adjustments. Even after adroit accommodations and devastating compromises—only *five minutes per week* of attention on the written work of each student and an average of ten minutes of planning for each fifty-odd-minute class—the task is already crushing, in reality a sixty-hour work week. For this, Horace is paid a wage enjoyed by age-mates in semiskilled and low-pressure blue-collar jobs and by novices, twenty-five years his junior, in some other white-collar professions. Furthermore, none of these sixty-plus hours is spent in replenishing his own academic capital. That has to be done in addition, perhaps during the summer. However, he needs to earn more money then, and there is no pay for upgrading his teachers' skills. He has to take on tutoring work or increase his involvement at the liquor store.

Fortunately (from one point of view), few people seem to care whether he simply does not assign that paragraph per week, or whether he farms its criticism out to other students. ("Exchange papers, class, and take ten minutes to grade your neighbor's essay.") He is a colorful teacher, and he knows that he can do a good job of lecturing, some of which can, in theory at least, replace the coaching that Horace knows is the heart of high school teaching. By using an overhead projector, he can publicly analyze the paragraphs of six of his students. But he will have assigned writing to all of them. As long as he does not let on which six papers he will at the last minute "pull" to analyze, he will have given real practice to all. There *are* tricks like this to use.

His classes are quiet and orderly, and he has the reputation in the community of being a good teacher. Accordingly, he gets his administrators' blessings. If he were to complain about the extent of his overload, he would find no seriously empathetic audience. Reducing teacher load is, when all the negotiating is over, a low agenda item for the unions and school boards. The administration will arrange for in-service days on "teacher burnout" (more time away from grading paragraphs) run by moonlighting education professors who will get more pay for giving a few "professional workshops" than Horace gets for a year's worth of set construction in the theater.

No one blames the system; everyone blames him. Relax, the consultants advise. Here are some exercises to help you get some perspective. Morphine, Horace thinks. It dulls my pain . . . Come now, he mutters to himself. Don't get cynical . . . Don't keep insisting that these "experts" should try my job for a week . . . They assure me that they *understand* me, only they say, "We hear you, Horace." I wonder who their English teachers were.

Horace's students will get into college, their parents may remember to thank him for the references he wrote for their offspring (unlikely), and the better colleges will teach the kids to write. The students who do not get the coaching in college, or who do not go to college, do not complain. No one seems upset. Just let it all continue, a conspiracy, a toleration of a chasm between the necessary and the provided and acceptance of big rhetoric and little reality. Horace dares not express his bitterness to the visitor conducting a study of high schools, because he fears he will be portrayed as a whining hypocrite.[1]

I The Students

1

Five Adolescents

When I visit schools, I usually ask for a tour of the building and grounds, with a student as my guide. Often my request is granted. Sometimes one learns more about the guides than about the school plant, and one always finds out that the students are more complicated and interesting than even the most elaborate structures. Many of these young people are substantial individuals, Very Grown-Up, as unwittingly patronizing adults would say.

Two students, both seniors and elected officers, show up for my tour in a high school of a wealthy Midwestern suburb. Let's call them Janet and Will. Janet could have walked out of *Seventeen*. Pink oxford shirt, blazer, pleated skirt, loafers, hair combed and barretted: she is tall and pretty, and exudes assurance. She had been told the day before that she was to be tour guide for the visitor. Will is almost as preppy, chinos and all, but superficially less assured. His handshake has reserve in it, and he avoids looking me in the eye.

The school buildings are predictable, airplane-hangar-modern, set among lawns and asphalt parking lots, with the usual long halls flanked by built-in lockers and with classrooms on each side. Few students are in the passageways during classes, and all those we see make sure silently with body language that we know they have permission to be out of class. They move past us quickly, with purposeful steps and eyes straightforward.

Do my guides like their school? Oh, yes. All the students are happy. What makes this high school special? The people. They're friendly and get along. Do you mean kids don't get along in other high schools in town? No . . . but of course I've never been to Jefferson across town; that's a cliquish place. Everyone's friendly here. There are no cliques here? No. I protest: I don't believe it; surely the jocks are a recognizable clique, and the cheerleaders. (Laughter.) Oh, yes. (The boy speaking.) The athletes are a group. The smokers, too. The freaks. The brains. What about the preps? (More laughter, this time nervous.)

Why do you go to school? The question is unexpected; both are puzzled. The boy: To get into college. The girl agrees. We talk of their college hopes; each wants to enter a four-year college. Is there any other reason for going to school? Ultimately I pull what answers there are. To learn things. To have fun. Most of all, that's what kids our age do. What would we do if we didn't go to school?

The school has an open-campus policy, and students with free periods can go to the cafeteria, get a snack, gossip, study, or do all of these. My guides say they've heard that the cafeteria was wild in the early 1970s, with too much noise, litter, unpleasantness. Today, at least, the litter is still there, lying under the tables beside the rows of twitching Adidas, but the atmosphere is friendly-noisy, not challenging-noisy.

Janet is transformed as we enter the cafeteria. Hi, Jack. Hi, Susan. Will and I are quickly forgotten as she works the crowd, not so much politically pressing the flesh as orchestrating the giggle. She's pretty, and the boys look up, but it is the girls she talks with, even as she knows the guys watch her. Her face works constantly, and she swishes her hair, coveting sophistication.

Will stays with me, embarrassed. I am no less embarrassed. Are we supposed to follow our female leader through the room, are we to stand aside, or should we carry on our tour without her? I ask him solemn questions, about graduation requirements and the like. He gives me answers, presumably as accurate as he is diffident, but they are as forgettable as the questions themselves. When the awkwardness is too painful, I ask to see the gym. The two of us leave. Physical education classes are being held in the wide hallways, because it is raining outside. Ping-Pong, mostly desultory, proceeds. The gym is a basketball court, dividable in a number of ways. It is airy but has the familiar tang of dirty socks.

The school is largely on one level, with the principal academic departments occupying portions of each of several wings. As one wanders the corridors, it is easy to eavesdrop, and I and my guide peer into open classroom doors. Some rooms are quiet, with students writing or reading; in others the teacher is talking. Order prevails. Sometimes we hear a roomful of kids chattering among themselves. Such a class is not out of control, however; the gossiping may be nonacademic, but it circumscribes itself carefully. No sound of anger or fear or exaltation or clashing or disagreement or astonishment is heard. The tone is warm, happy without exuberance. If classroom sounds were colors, those in this school would be pastels.

I ask, Do you have a job after school? Yes, I work on lawns. Summer, too. Do most of your friends work? Yes, but it's tough in season. (Athletic teams practice after school.) For what do you use the money you earn? I save it for college. Really? You'll pay your own tuition? Oh, no, my parents will do that. But I've got to pay for my car. You own a car now? Yes. And the money you earn now pays for it? Yes.

We talk of student government. The girls hold most of the offices, and I ask why. He shrugs, claiming not to be able to explain. They always do, he says. I learn later from other students that girls hold offices because the offices are not perceived to be a very big deal. I am not sure what to make of that. What do the student officers do? We meet with the assistant principal. We appoint committees and coordinate the money-raising activities of clubs. We help school spirit. What's school spirit? He pauses over that question, since he is both very sure and not at all sure what it is. School spirit is yelling at football games against Jefferson High. Is school spirit the litter in the cafeteria too? He is uncomfortable now and says he has never thought about it that way before.

Are you eighteen yet? Yes. Did you register for the draft? Yes. Did all the guys register? Yes; it's the law, isn't it? Did any of the girls register? Perplexity. He is embarrassed, but more for me than for him. Girls don't have to register, you know. Yes, I know, but is that fair? Should you have to give up two years of your life and get shot at while the girls get ahead of you at law school? Yes, no. It's fair; fighting is man's business. It's unfair; we're all citizens. Couldn't some of your top female athletes fly bombers as adroitly as guys? Sure they could. Even better than some of the male "spazzes" in school? Yes, of course. But you say they shouldn't! No, women shouldn't have to fight. They have to be home with the children. Come on, men can raise children! Intense embarrassment. But they don't raise the children. And I wouldn't want to have a girl in a foxhole with me.

We agree that the topic is a complicated one. Did it come up in school when registration was first required by the federal government? No. Did any of the guys decide not to register? No, but some of them may have forgotten to. Did any teacher raise the issue, perhaps in social studies classes? No. Why so little talk of registration, a tough topic that clearly affects you? I don't know, but I've got to make my own decisions . . . We don't talk about things like that. What do you talk about? Oh, things. The pressure is beginning to show, and I ease off. His eyes still do not look at me, but the rest of him does.

Janet rejoins us. We discover her in a corridor, during a break between classes, talking to a boy painfully acned, a dermatologist's disaster. He is shorter than she, or at least appears so. As she talks with him her face is as tender as his eyes are adoring. Will says these two are "going out." She falls into step without embarrassment, and the two deliver me back to the principal's office. We four chat together, briefly, in his doorway. The talk is easy, assured, full of respect and good will on all sides. I thank the two students, and they depart. The principal says, They're nice kids. I agree.

It was different in an urban school district. I was there visiting a large, well-respected high school, the academic flagship of the system. The drab, boxy building was really a congeries of structures, additions made as the needs of the district expanded. It was set on a small park at the edge of the city; the trees round about were lush, softening the tatty look of the man-made constructions.

My request for a student-guided tour had been overlooked by the principal. We spent too long talking in his office, and it was midmorning before I was able to visit the biology and social studies classes that I had come to see. At luncheon, I pressed him once again about a tour, but it was not until the sixth period that he seriously set about providing for it. Where, though, was a student then to be found? He motioned me into the office of one of the assistant principals. Can you find Mr. Sizer a student to show him around the school? Of course; Pamela here can be the guide. The principal winced. Pamela, sulking in the corner, had been sent to sit in this office for lipping off to her typing teacher. The assistant principal, an assured, experienced woman, made it very clear to her boss that Pamela *would* do this. While his reluctance was painfully visible to us all, including Pamela, he agreed. Pamela, you'll give the *very* best tour *ever* given at Washington High School. Now Pamela winced. So did the assistant principal.

We shook hands. Hers was limp. Her distaste for this exercise was as bold as her principal's distaste for her conducting it. She was sixteen, an eleventh-grader. She was slight, Twiggy-skinny, but without the pallor of a true anorexic. She wore faded jeans, sneakers, a loose, embroidered, almost sacklike shirt. A twisted, soiled headband cinched her forehead. Attached to it, and spilling down her upper back, was a tassel of large feathers. We eyed each other; my coat and tie and tie clip and pocket watch and green bookbag were no less bizarre a uniform to her than her plumage was to me. The principal cooed as we started off, talking to me while looking at her. She's improving now. He was genuine; his remark was as well intentioned as it was patronizing. Pamela glared at him. The tension eased as soon as his door closed behind us.

She marched me down the hall, positively, even though she had no idea what she was to show me. Shortly: What do you want to see? You decide; you know the school. We continued to walk briskly to nowhere in particular, she providing no travelogue, no chatter. Finally I asked, What's special about this school? Pamela: How should I know? I haven't been to any other. She said this as a matter of fact, not pugnaciously. I tried fishing. Well, what's really good about this school? Pamela: Don't ask me that question. I don't like this school. Why? Her specific gripe was that she felt that all the adults assumed she would be like her older sister, who recently had left and who was a heavy drug user. I'm not a druggie, Pamela said, but they think I am. They think my sister is no good.

She went on, trying to articulate her resentments, but unable to do so very well. One strained out of her words her anger over what she felt were the patronizing, stereotyping attitudes of adults.

We were walking too briskly to eavesdrop usefully on teaching, and, furthermore, the classroom doors were all closed. However, one could see through the paned windows in the doors the teachers talking and the students writing. Pamela was still going fast to no place in particular. I suggested that we go outside and visit the athletic area and the physical education classes being held there. She quickly assented, grateful that I had given some direction.

The school was surrounded by fields and parking lots. The former were lumpy, with but scraggly grass in tufts. As this was the Southwest, even this green would probably be gone by June. One wondered how infielders plied their trade on these uncongenial fields. Flaccid softball was going on, girls only, with as much gossiping as throwing or hitting. The fielders stood clumsily with their gloves, balancing their weight awkwardly. Their attitudes at our distance said boredom and lack of interest. There was some shouting but no enthusiasm.

Pamela brightened up as we entered the sea of cars in the parking lots. She launched unasked into an exquisite disquisition on the sociology of the school as exhibited by cars driven, where the cars were parked, and what the drivers wore. The preppies drove Daddy's Le Mans and parked it over there. Preppies wore Topsiders, clean jeans or chinos, collared shirts emblazoned with alligators and other living things. Preppies are smart, Pamela said. They have special classes. Later I figured out that she meant Advanced Placement classes; the preppies were the set bound for four-year colleges.

The freaks. Pamela said she was a freak. That did not necessarily mean she was a habitual drug user. The freaks were those who conformed to nonconformity. Pamela's outfit was of their genre. They did not bring cars to school, nor did many even own them.

Pamela pointed to the lot that had older cars and a sprinkling of pickup trucks. These vehicles' drivers she called ropers, but she slurred the pronunciation so that it came out "gopers." Elsewhere, ropers are synonymous with cowboys. A goat roper is a cowboy who is also a jerk. Pamela's gopers said a bit about her view of the boot-and-worn-jean-wearing, tanned, noisy, physical kids in this group. Some at this school probably were farmers; most were not and just pretended they were. Adolescent Marlboros' ads.

Pamela was white. I asked of blacks and Hispanics. Did race cut across these groups? Somewhat, she said, especially if the kids were athletes. But mostly minority kids stayed by themselves. They didn't own cars.

Pamela wanted to be a model. Her stringbean look could have made the pages of *Vogue,* even if her current wardrobe would not. She loathed school. Would she drop out when she reached seventeen? No, she'd stay on and finish. Why, if school was so odious? She wanted the diploma so that she could get a job. What kind of a job? Any kind, typing, maybe. I took this opening to ask her about her altercation with the typing teacher; she would say only that the instructor kept riding her, and when she had had enough, she had told the teacher off, in colorful language. You hate school, and typing is hardly your favorite activity, and a typing job is what you see two years hence? Yes, because I need money so that I can leave home. I can't stand my mother.

On our return to the assistant principal's office, Pamela abruptly took her corner seat and resumed her sulk. I was an instant nonperson.

Louella and Margery were not guides at their inner-city Catholic high school. In fact, they were brand-new students there, even though this was February. I met them by chance when paying a visit to the school's guidance office, and I listened to their stories.

Each was fifteen years old, nominally in the tenth grade. One was white, the other black. Both came from very poor families. Both were skinny and looked more like older children than young women. Though they had met but ten days before, they were now fast friends.

In September, each had started at her neighborhood public high school, on opposite sides of the city, but had skipped classes almost from the first day. Within a few weeks, both were on the run, absent from home as well as school. Margery picked up with a long-distance trucker, and for over three months accompanied him on trips from this Midwestern city to places up and down the East Coast. Louella had been taken on by a pimp and added to his string of prostitutes. She had been beaten badly several times; her face showed disfiguring, fresh scars.

They giggled and squirmed during our talk, sometimes erupting with mirth, trying to cover it with hands over their mouths. They were not very articulate but were remarkably candid (and thus trusting), probably because Bill Conroy, a popular administrator, was with us for part of the conversation. They showed off for him shamelessly. Conroy described to me later the cruelties both of these girls had suffered in the preceding months. Think of all the most horrible things that could happen to teen-age girls under their circumstances, he told me, and you will still not complete the catalogue of horrors these waifs have experienced.

Behind the fifteen-year-old giggles were two very tough kids, street wise and, on occasion, surely petty thieves and perhaps even purse snatchers, muggers of much older, defenseless people. Both had mothers who struggled to help them. Indeed, it was the mothers' pressure that had gotten them to this private school, a place Margery said "is our last chance." How the tuition of $40 per week was to be covered, I never ascertained. Conroy merely said that it would be found.

Why had they come? I asked them. They could not directly explain, but it soon became clear that they had almost backed in, pushed by their mothers' desperation, dragged by their own inertia and by the pain that had followed their truancy of the previous autumn. They had no particular plans, but seemed disposed to settle in. Would they run away from this school? No, they said. (Conroy stayed deadpan: the odds were that they would.) Why not? I asked them. Both girls talked about how they liked the teachers, the warmth of the place, the fact that people seemed to accept them. The attitudes of the teachers toward them appeared crucial: that much—and it was genuine—came through the yarn these street kids were playfully spinning for the oddly serious visitor. I asked them what classes they had signed up for. They couldn't remember. They did remember luncheon, however, and left us, happily, for the cafeteria.

Adolescents, like these five young people and like all of humankind, are complicated. They come in all sizes and shapes. There are good ones and bad ones, saints and liars, bores and inspirers, quick ones and dullards, gentle ones and brutes. Besides their age, they have in common the vulnerability that comes from inexperience and a social status bordering on limbo. They are children, but they are adults, too. Many are ready and able to work, but are dissuaded from doing so. They can bear children, but are counseled not to. They can kill, and sometimes do. They can act autonomously, but are told what to do, with some orders, such as school attendance, having the force of law. They share the pain of a stereotype, of gum-chewing, noisy, careless, bloomingly sexual creatures who are allowed to have fun but not too much of it. When they raise hell, they win sobriquets like that applied by a Boston bus driver, "little maggots."[1] When they excel at some community service, such as sandbagging levees during a flood crisis, they win the surprised, happy plaudits of their elders.

We adults too easily talk of these adolescents as an undifferentiated blob of people, as a Client Group or an Age Cohort. We are quick to generalize about them—unless, of course, they are our own children. Then we feel the intensity of specialness; *these* young people are our own flesh and blood, each of unique promise. That Age Cohort we talk about professionally is full of *other* people's youngsters, grist to become Products of the System, faceless agents of national defense, social orderliness, and economic revival. We forget James Agee's quiet reminder that each child, ours and every other one, "is a new and incommunicably tender life, wounded in every breath and almost as hardly killed as easily wounded."[2]

After meeting and listening to hundreds of Janets and Louellas, Wills and Pamelas, and visiting the high schools that their communities or their parents have provided for them, I have fresh respect for the variety among young folk. Inevitably, though, I have looked for generalizations, for patterns among these many young people and among their schools, and it is these generalizations which inform this book. Schools should be designed to follow our conceptions of adolescence: one starts with the students.

My view is that American high schools today too readily stress the vulnerability and inexperience of adolescents and underrate the potency and authority that young people can exhibit. Many adolescents are awkward; so much in their lives is new. However, they can and often do act in consequential, "grown-up" ways, particularly if we encourage them to do so.

High schools must respect adolescents more and patronize them less. The best respect is high expectations for them, and a level of accountability more adult in its demand than childlike. We should expect them to learn more while being taught less. Their personal engagement with their own learning is crucial; adults cannot "give" them an education. Too much giving breeds docility, and the docility of students' minds is a widespread reality in American high schools. We adults should change our educational system where it rewards such docility, however benignly, and we should expect a great deal more from the beneficiaries of that system than we do today.

2

Diversity

ADOLESCENTS are most visibly and importantly classified by social class. Family income for Janet, Will, Pamela, Louella, and Margery makes a substantial difference in their behavior, in what is offered them in schools, and in how it is offered. One becomes sensitive to it in many ways, some very humble. For example, visit a school's cafeteria at lunch hour: How many students are wearing glasses or have the squint of inexperienced contact-lens wearers? More will be seen in wealthier neighborhoods than in those of poverty. There are fewer spectacles on poor kids—and it is not because their eyes are better. Listen to how staff responds to parents on the school's telephones: those of wealthier children are likely to be people who know how to apply pressure on the system and are therefore treated gingerly, respectfully. The parents of the poor can be patronized without penalty. Observe the social class backgrounds of students in a school's various academic and vocational "tracks": the honors programs serve the wealthier youngsters, and the general tracks (whatever their titles) serve the working class. Vocational programs are often a cruel social dumping ground. The exceptions to these characterizations are there, but they virtually prove the rule.

The sense of security of a Janet and Will contrast with the toughness of Louella and Margery. Children who grow up believing from their experience that their families—their worlds—will protect them have an ease and a settled quality about them. Teachers like it. These adolescents can afford to pay attention to the abstractions of school because they have little concern about their safety, health, or futures. They believe that they truly will live happily ever after; indeed, they often feel *entitled* to such a future.[3] There is a serenity about Janet and Will. Louella and Margery giggle, have fun, but they are hardly serene. They are watchful, and rank low those school routines which seem relatively unconnected with their immediate predicament. However richly they may dream about their futures, they know that they will have to scramble for what they get in life.[4]

Scramble though poor adolescents must, the schools that they attend are usually less favored than those of their wealthier age-mates. Christopher Jencks in 1972 estimated that the children of the wealthy have twice the number of dollars invested in their schooling as do the children of the poor, and there is no reason to believe that the gap has narrowed since that time.[5] For example, in one Midwestern metropolitan area typical of the country as a whole, in 1981–1982 the teacher-student ratio in inner-city high schools was 1:175; in the wealthier suburbs, 1:100; and in the independent country day schools, largely serving an affluent clientele, 1:60. The "feel" of schools enrolling poor children is different from that for the more affluent. One gets a sense of a more hectic, pressured atmosphere, less predictability, often more menace, often less arrogance and sense of expected entitlement.

The hard fact is that if you are the child of low-income parents, the chances are good that you will receive limited and often careless attention from adults in your high school. If you are the child of upper-middle-income parents, the chances are good that you will receive substantial and careful attention. The attitudes of various adults toward you will be very important. If you are a Chapter One child (family below the federal poverty line), many of your teachers, most of the adults in the street, and even your parents may deliberately tune their expectations for you to your current economic status in life. Most of this is realism that many Americans prefer to keep under the rug, of course: it is no easy task for the poor in America to break out, if they choose to, of their economic condition. But a change in status that is a matter of moderately poor odds becomes impossible when there is little encouragement for them to try.

I heard a veteran guidance counselor in a city secondary school that enrolled poor or working-class adolescents tell me of her academically most successful students and why she did not allow them to apply to any private colleges or competitive public colleges. They would meet fellow students there from wealthy homes, she explained, who may influence them to be disloyal to and uncomfortable in their own neighborhoods. Better that they go to college with their own kind, she argued.

Income and ethnicity overlap, of course. Statistically, if you are black or Hispanic, you are more likely to have a proportionately lower income than your white and Asian counterparts. Thus, your children are more likely to have no option other than to attend high schools where less attention is paid them than if you lived elsewhere. Furthermore, those schools will be less responsive to your involvement than if you were white or Asian. However, there are black and Hispanic youngsters in richly appointed and progressive schools, just as there are wealthy black and Hispanic families. And there are whites and Asians who are poor; indeed, the majority of the American poor are white.

Race and class snarl in many teachers' perceptions of students, leading to stereotypes. If you're black, you're poor. If you speak English haltingly, you're stupid. If you're white, you have a future. Blacks are basketball players. Blond is beautiful.

Class intrudes on academic achievement. Scholastic Aptitude Test scores generally mirror income ranking, for many obvious reasons.[6] Wealthier families can give their children more opportunities, the richer experience that helps with certain kinds of tests. Such families frequently value these tests highly and signal their concern to their offspring. They know, often better than many distracted low-income parents, what it takes to succeed at the tests.

Where low income and minority race overlap, as in our great cities, the effect is politically devastating. Where race and income do not drastically overlap, as in many smaller cities, the importance of race as a grouping device lessens, but does not disappear. Some of its edges soften. I spent an hour talking frankly with an interracial group in the large high school of a small, Southwestern city and found the relaxed candor of the young people striking, especially to an Easterner used to the inflammatory rhetoric of his city schools. The students bounced racial epithets—nigger, honky, spic—off each other with considerable humor. They lacked the tightened stomach muscles of their white listener, who was educated in these matters in the 1960s. The black students felt that adolescents of their race were "rougher on the street" than the whites, but that in school, behavior was similar across all groups. The blacks felt in this school (in contrast with that which Pamela attended) that the groupings of jocks, freaks, ropers, preppies, and the rest characterized the minority races as well as the majority. The court-forced integration in this city (the closing of the all-black high school and the merging of its students into the white school) was ancient history to these students. They agreed that the individual races do tend to congregate socially. Interracial dating is not the expectation, just a common and accepted exception. Given this fact, the complex sociology of adolescent life in that high school, and those like it, does emerge noticeably along racial lines.

One leaves visits to dozens of American high schools with the clear feeling, however, that race is a fixation of adults more than of the young and that class differences mean much more among adolescents. Again, class and race often overlap and affect one another. But the operative issues for students arise more from class behavior than from skin color. In Americans' paradoxical focus on race to obliterate racism, we may make more of it than it deserves. Awareness, fairness, yes. Obsession, no. But at the same time, we play the class issue at low volume. Americans find it embarrassing. The poor adolescent scrambles into adulthood, often taking risks and responsibilities never faced by his or her more affluent peers throughout their entire lives. Wealthier youths—the majority of the school population—have their protections built in; they are masked from many of the world's harsher realities. Because of the surroundings that forge them, modern adolescents differ more along income-class lines than along any other.

Class is only one expression of diversity, though the most important. Sometimes gender is significant. For example, in some families, the stress for success in school is greater on the boys than on the girls. Males do tend to score better than females in college-oriented tests, especially in senior high school. Sex stereotyping appears in course selections. Girls take domestic science, boys enroll in sheet-metal work. In some schools, one finds few girls in advanced mathematics or physics classes. Many schools formally endorse attitudes usually associated with males—competition, individualism, "toughing things out"—and give little support to attitudes more readily associated with females.[7] The pressures that followed the passage of Title IX, forbidding certain sorts of sex discrimination, have had notable effect in numerous schools, but many critics feel that a much greater distance has yet to be traveled. While this may be true, the fact remains that in most high school activities, young men and women are treated alike: the mathematics and French teachers' red pens fall equally on their tests. As American institutions go, high schools are less gender-biased than most others.

There are obvious differences among adolescents in intellectual quickness and energy, how "smart" they are. Some students catch on readily to school subjects, but their brothers or sisters mysteriously seem to learn more slowly, irrespective of effort. There may be genetic explanations for these discrepancies, as we are rapidly discovering. None of us learns precisely as any other does, and some of us respond better to the styles of teaching familiar in schools than do others. Some learn the same amount, but more slowly; others simply learn less. For some, there are low expectations: almost inevitably they learn less. Still others find formal learning irrelevant. "A large part of stupidity is just . . . chronic boredom, for a person can't learn, or be intelligent about, what he's not interested in, when his repressed thoughts are elsewhere."[8]

And so the categories of adolescence emerge unsatisfactorily. Income makes a difference, both in students' attitudes and those of their schools—some of the time. Families' aspirations for their sons tend to be higher than for their daughters—some of the time. Minority students, being disproportionately from lower income groups, score lower—some of the time. Some students are "smarter" than others some of the time, but we don't know quite why, certainly not in a way that allows us easily to correct for it. Accordingly, good teachers take note of these uneasy generalities, and then, freeing themselves as much as possible from the trap of stereotyping, deal with each student as an individual.

3

Commonality

A UNIFYING CHARACTERISTIC of adolescents is their common puberty—the physiological changes engulfing them and the psychic strains that attend these. If class separates adolescents from each other, rapid physical alterations separate this age group from all others.

Girls tend to start their pubertal growth spurt earlier than boys, even as early as eight years old. Boys rarely start the process before they are eleven, and most usually at thirteen; some may not begin until the age of sixteen. During this spurt, both boys and girls grow from two to five inches. Some parts of their bodies, such as hands, feet, and arms, grow faster than others, often giving a youngster an awkward, Woody Woodpecker look. Youngsters, particularly boys, eat more than they did before puberty. Watching a mob of fourteen-year-olds at fast food spots absorbing grease and sweets turns the adult stomach as much as it provokes his envy, because the bodies absorbing that punishment usually will remain sleek and hard. Growth requires endless nourishment, even of junk food.

These bodily alterations have an enormous effect on the souls within all that changing bone, flesh, and muscle. As he or she looks in a mirror, the young person properly asks, Is that I? Or is it some familiar but older person? Do I *like* that body there? Will anyone else like it? Can I adopt it and make it me? Hours of looking and primping and flexing and wondering and worrying over their bodies fill the lives of adolescents, as well they might. When one listens to the laments of fifty-year-olds morbidly worrying over a size 36 waist that has become a 38 or over a bit of wrinkle at the edge of an eye, one profoundly appreciates the scale of the concern that an adolescent feels. The disdain that many adults direct at adolescents' obsession with their physical selves is painfully unfair.

Some young people mock themselves deliciously. An Australian schoolgirl put it in a poem entitled "Wishful Thinking":

> Adolescence is looking into a mirror and wishing:
> Your feet were as small as your eyes
> Your eyes were as wide as the gap between your teeth
> Your teeth were as straight as your hair
> Your waist was as thin as your lips
> Your lips were as red as your nose
> And your nose was as small as your chest![9]

Given the scale of changes in how adolescents appear, it is remarkable how tolerant young people are of each other. This is not to say that there is not hazing: Shrimpy, Tubby, Fats, Zitface, and other imputable handles endure from generation to generation. It is only to note how much more there could be. And it is usually someone's well-intentioned auntie who says, My how you've grown! Or, You're becoming a real young man now! Most adolescents would prefer all kinds of gruesome tortures to such public attention to their growth.

Auntie's observation is apt, however, since the world outside a family or an age-graded school does not know a person's birth date and therefore responds to that individual according to how he or she looks. If you appear sophisticated to strangers, they will treat you as though you are sophisticated. If you're a thirteen-year-old girl with a fully developed body, men may try to pick you up, but if you're a string bean, sixteen, you'll hear few whistles. If you are a husky and bearded seventeen-year-old male standing before a judge, you may well get a tougher sentence than if you are still fuzzy-cheeked and an alto, though also seventeen. To the larger world, one is what one appears, whether six, sixteen, or sixty.

When teachers say, "Act your age," they most often mean, in fact, "Act the way you look." Few little guys are given positions of responsibility in schools.

This assumption that one is to be as one appears is difficult for many adolescents, because the change from child-seeming to adult-seeming can be abrupt. One day they tell you to eat up your carrots, and the next they don't bother to "card" you before serving you beer at a bar. There is also much painful anticipation. I know I'll grow some more, but how much? How much bustier will I become? Will I always be skinny? Adolescents know that their looks will change, but they have no way of knowing exactly how. For most of them, all this is heady stuff.

The psychologist Thomas Cottle listened to a sixteen-year-old Boston girl, Jeanne Melchione:

> I don't even know what people mean by adolescent. It seems to me people nowadays jump from being a child to being an adult . . . It's like going on an airplane. You can't tell anything is happening. You certainly don't know how fast you're going. You just sit there. Then they open the door and you're in a whole new place—or, anyway, you're supposed to be . . . It's hard to guess people's ages nowadays because everybody looks older; even if they don't, they act older. Everybody's acting one way or another. If you don't act you get lost . . .

Cottle appropriately titles his interview with Jeanne "Trying on Adult Masks."[10]

This acting, the trying on of older folk's masks, is another inevitable part of adolescence. The older one becomes, the more independence he or she is given. Some young people are on their own when they are very young. James Wilde wrote in *Time* magazine a celebrated, frightening portrait of "Baby Love," a fourteen-year-old "wolf in sneakers [who] inhabits . . . a Dickensian hell of cheap thrills, senseless deaths and almost unrelieved hopelessness." The boy "can barely read or write, even though he would have been in the seventh grade . . . He has been running wild so long now that he may be beyond redemption." Baby Love's acting, as Wilde reported it, was an overstated bit of braggadocio, full of angry menace.[11] Some other adolescents are sheltered by families or other institutions until they are almost twenty. I visited a boarding school for girls, set in a magnificent, fenced rural site in the foothills of mountains, where eighteen-year-old women were told what to wear, when to get up, when to study, when to eat, when to sleep. Whom they consorted with was carefully controlled. Baby Love was semi-literate, unschooled, and consorted with all manner of people; these young women were into calculus, John Updike, and conversational French. Baby Love survived by his wits; the women were naïve, but in the race of life they will probably excel. They have the right adult friends to protect them from any mistakes caused by their naïveté.

Not all adolescents on their own at a young age are poor, and not all cloistered children are wealthy. The restrictions on some children, particularly girls, of families of modest means can be very great. Many wealthier young people are as much on their own as Baby Love. The difference between him and them is not parental neglect or incompetence—those qualities seem fairly spread across the entire population—but, rather, is in resources. Baby Love had to hustle his drugs and steal his cars. The wealthier young person can obtain both with money provided by his family.

However, these young people are at the extremes. Most American fourteen-to-eighteen-year-olds inhabit more ambiguous worlds than the one that was theirs in childhood, when they were told what to do. Now they are often on their own. Many look adult and are treated as such, at least some of the time. Most adolescents, however, choose to continue accepting adult direction. For them the biggest problem is finding their own special place in their small world and learning both to protect it and to open it up to selected others. What is involved here is the skill of *reciprocity,* the business of accepting others and being accepted, of "making it" with peers and strangers. In the home, the young child had already made it, by definition. As the youngster grows up, as his parents are at a greater distance, and as the expectations of other adults include restraint and judgment autonomously grasped, the young person is on his or her own. It is a new experience to make up one's own mind. It is always easier to do what one is told. One is not troubled then by any agony of decision-making or procrastination, and if whatever is being done does not work, there is always someone else to blame. Being given class time or supervised study halls to complete one's homework is easier than being told only to get it done on one's own time. The latter often leads to no homework done. The supervised youth does the homework but may never learn the self-discipline that he will need in the future.

The reciprocity problem is more complicated when it extends beyond such straightforward matters as homework. The little child is told who his friends are; the adolescent picks his own friends. To get friends and to hold them is no easy task, as every adult knows from daily experience. It requires self-knowledge, decisions on how forward to be and when to be passive, and it demands the acceptance of someone else's agenda. One must be interested in what excites that other person, however far it may be from one's own affairs. True partnership occurs when something as inherently boring as another's relationship with her mother is in fact interesting to both daughter and daughter's friend. It takes a lot of living to get to that point. And, as the psychologist John J. Conger has pointed out, "being preoccupied with the self—a necessary developmental task of adolescence—is not usually the best prescription for a serious commitment to others."[12] One's understandable myopia, which is intensified by all the newness around one, makes empathy with others difficult.

"If adolescence is anything," Peter Davis wrote in his recent study of Hamilton, Indiana, "it is winning and losing. Grades, dates, sex, a driver's license, complexion, approval, graduation, scholarships, college admissions—success and failure looming on all fronts."[13] Most children have families that protect them from failure, but few adolescents, even those in the secure environments of boarding schools, have total protection. The process of learning how to position oneself in order to win or to thrive or to gain respect or to feel comfortable is a part of adolescence. Some young people are as gawky at learning this as they are physically graceless.

Above all, the process is new, as new as one's fledgling beard or filled-out body. Being on one's own is as exhilarating as it is frightening. Growing autonomy has growing loneliness as its handmaiden. One learns to make it privately, and many of the signals of failure—reprimands, rebuffs, insults, being ignored—are harsh.

It takes time to sift through these issues and, if one has friends, time to talk them through. What strikes many adults as superficial gossip is, for those adolescents engaged in it, the embarrassed, embarrassing process of learning how to sort out their places in their group. It sounds superficial, because these young people have no experience at it. Their humor, much of it a gross cliché, reflects their rawness. What is predictable banality to adult ears is fresh stuff to theirs. They call it "hanging out."

Hanging out is gossiping, seeing and being seen. Older folk do it in restaurants, bars, and the Places to Be. Adolescents have their own places. In some communities it is a corner or a particular store. In my very small hometown, it is a stretch of stone wall backing on the local cemetery, down from the general store and across the street from the post office. Fast food restaurants are often hangouts, sometimes in a cluster or a strip, if cars are available. Some adults find these adolescent congregations menacing, because of their inevitable noisiness, colorful posturing, and false self-assurance. Sometimes they *are* menacing: a terrorizing gang is a gathered group of friends gone vicious.

Although violent crime committed by youths decreased somewhat in the late 1970s, 50 percent of all arrests were of people under twenty-five.[14] Most were males. Petty crimes against property, such as shoplifting, are still common. Like the use of illicit drugs, such crime is exciting, a new experience. And as with the presumptive adolescent alcoholic, for whom too much liquor is not *his* problem, the petty thief can see few consequences for his felonies. He is, very simply, inexperienced. The wealth of those of his felonious friends not yet caught seems a more persuasive life style than studying about paramecia in school or taking a job as a dishwasher's assistant.

Vandalism, so mindless to middle-class adult eyes, is more excitement. Trashing for the sake of trashing. Leaving one's mark. One high school principal who was struggling to keep graffiti off his school's walls placed the blame on the students' lack of self-esteem. They are everywhere treated as nothing, as dirt, he argued. Their painted scrawls, nonsense ideographs, for the most part, were a statement of existence. Kilroy was here.

Most adolescents are neither criminals nor vandals. And most criminals are not adolescents. For every dollar lost to shoplifters of all ages, $15 is stolen from companies by their adult employees.[15] Most gatherings of adolescents, the hanging out at the fried chicken stand, are as awkward and ill focused as they are raucous, and it is awkwardness, the gawky inexperience, that especially marks the adolescent age group.

Inexperience provokes fear and withdrawal and frustration, whether that greenness is suffered by a fifty-year-old facing his first proctoscopy, a thirty-year-old entering a foreign country whose language is unfamiliar, or a fourteen-year-old taking out a locker for the first time in a gymnasium. In each instance, one does not know exactly how to respond and, while one hopes his nervousness is invisible, he is sure everyone is looking at him. The nurses are too efficient. One does not ask them what lies ahead. Nonchalance is vital. The natives talk fast and are impatient. Barely familiar older boys walk about barely clothed, roaring at one another and slamming locker doors. Teachers earlier known in chemistry classrooms to be decorous now bark coarsely at the noisemakers. *Shut up,* you goddam animals. It is all very confusing.

On the other hand, most adults tread familiar ground. They have taken a train or plane or bus. They have opened a bank account. They have made love. They know how a car reacts when one of its tires blows. They have been in a hospital. They have taken Achievement Tests. They have sought and landed jobs. They know how to hold a cigarette. They have friends whom they know well, and many know how to keep up a conversation, however trivial. Others know how not to be afraid in fearful places. Most adolescents know none of these. So much of their lives, even the routines, is new. There is stress in that.

Bigger, older, more mature, more sophisticated, is better, or so our society signals. The big boys, the Brooke Shieldses, the fifteen-year-old mathematics wizards get the acclaim. Young people feel the pressure to get on with life. They want to have sex to have had sex; virginity for some is like a festering appendix, something to get out and over some time. They want to have tried things, to have experience in adult ways. Experimentation is not all pain, of course. There is adventure here, "the unspoiled sense of possibility that characterizes teenaged Americans at their freshest."[16] The American Walkabout is subtle, implicit, but ultimately perhaps more stressful than the Australian aboriginal version. Adults help little to ease the stress, but add much, through their voyeurism, to the pressure. The fumblings of young people are a source of amusement, titillation, and sanctimoniousness. The First Time. They're too young. They shouldn't. They're *growing up*.

Not surprisingly, sex is especially potent for adolescents. Puberty spawns arousal, and all the excitement, guilt, pleasure, and fear that go with it. When I was a high school principal, I often threatened, but fortunately never had the courage, to put a sign on my desk: HIGH SCHOOL IS HORMONES. The aphorism sums up all too well many charged, awkward confrontations with students.

American attitudes toward sexuality have changed since the 1960s, and the effects on young people have been substantial. "Adolescent attitudes and values regarding sex and sexual behavior itself are changing dramatically, although the extent of the change varies widely from one segment of the youth population to another . . . Greater sexual freedom [is likely to be] the most enduring residue" of the 1960s.[17] In general, attitudes have liberalized more rapidly among economically privileged and highly educated people than others, particularly as they affect women. Almost half of all sixteen-year-old boys and a third of the girls have had sexual intercourse. The figures for nineteen-year-olds are almost three-quarters for boys and three-fifths for girls. Out-of-wedlock births to adolescents have soared.[18]

I stood by the front door of a middle-sized Eastern inner-city high school and met two fifteen-year-old mothers, each of whom lived on her own. One, a white, had had a child by a black father and been banished by her community; she was accepted, more or less, in an otherwise all-black public housing project. She was the only white living there. In a Western, rural, and church-dominated community, I heard an honest, agonized argument between the principal and the district's superintendent over whether 10 percent or only 5 percent of the high school's girls were pregnant each year. I met a seventeen-year-old mother of three in a heavily Catholic Southern community. I talked with four pregnant girls in the common room set aside for their special use in an urban high school.

Two were close to term, one achingly great with her child. They giggled and chatted like the fourteen- and fifteen-year-olds they were, seemingly remote from the situation in which they and their children would soon find themselves. The statistics about child-parents are troubling enough; the poignance is increased when one meets them and gets to know them as individuals.

The issue of adolescent sexual activity is everywhere. Given the prominence that sex is given in books and movies, from *Lolita* to *Fast Times at Ridgemont High,* the freedom that most young people have for privacy, and the awesome silence of most adults outside and inside schools about the obligations that accompany sexuality and the biological ability to create new life, it is a wonder that the problem is not greater.

Many adults are alarmed by all this pubescent sexual activity. The fears are understandable but overdrawn, and the truth is probably closer to the whimsical essays of Delia Ephron (the author of *Teenage Romance; or, How to Die of Embarrassment*) than to the movie *Taxi Driver.* Many adolescents parade their new sexuality. The choreography in a high school hallway during a break between classes is colorful, with awkward strutting, overdressing or underdressing for effect, hip swinging, hugging, self-conscious and overenthusiastic joshing, little bits of competition clumsily overexpressed.

Two eleventh-graders are on an outdoor basketball court, behind the high school gym, otherwise alone. It is vacation, and the weather is warm. He is shirtless, in jeans and sneakers. She is wearing shorts and an oversized man's shirt with its tails tied under her breasts, presumably to accentuate them. They are shooting baskets, he showboating his torso and hook shot simultaneously, she hanging back. She is a lithe athlete, but shows off her ability only when he is not looking. She climbs on his shoulders, and they stumble about, as he balances and she tries to sink the basketball. Their banter is of trivialities. Shortly, she leaves him taking shots, gets on a motorbike parked nearby, and runs it around the court, behind and in front of him, slowly, with a weaving front wheel. More banter. More display. Look at me, each body says, while their talk is of nothing. Finally they drive off, with her in the driver's seat (the bike is presumably hers), and with him holding on behind. The oversized shirt is untied and left loose before he grasps her waist.

In all, it is sensuous, innocent, clumsy, hilarious, universal. This encounter is more the norm than this same pair motorbiking to a secluded beach to couple on a blanket, but both are common. One's first sex is both exciting and scary. Today's adolescents experience it earlier than did their parents and grandparents, which for some surely adds to its frightening and guilt-provoking qualities. Others today may take it as casually as they do the bland nakedness of the models in *Playboy* and *Playgirl.*

Barely behind sex on the list of new experiences are the use and misuse of alcohol and drugs. In a nation awash in alcohol, this is no surprise. If an adult orders a drink at a restaurant to land a business deal, he gets a tax break. Mom and Dad never give a party without liquor, and they have been known to have a shot even before the guests arrive, to ease their preparty panic. Over 70 percent of the high school class of 1981 had consumed alcohol during the thirty days prior to a recent government survey.[19] Most school people rank alcohol—and alcoholism—as the most troublesome problem of this sort. To many adolescents, marijuana, rather than booze, is especially cool, and it often provides weak and uncertain youngsters with an illusion of sought-after power and confidence. It is inexpensive, easily hidden, makes one feel good, and has the extra spice of being both illegal and something that makes adults uptight. The Gallup organization reports that illicit drugs are seen by the general public as the number three problem (after discipline and lack of financial support) in the public schools, though overall drug use has in fact decreased since 1978.[20] A 1980 study revealed that almost half the high school seniors reported using marijuana during the previous year; slightly over a third of the students had done so during the immediately previous month. Almost 10 percent of these seniors were daily pot users. Thirty-nine percent reported using additional illicit drugs.[21]

Even if sex, alcohol, and illicit drugs represent visible and controversial aspects of adolescence, they do not, mercifully, represent the whole experience of growing up. Adults tend to be pathological about them. They are Sins, and represent Dangers for Youth. We dwell on them at the expense of other concerns, matters such as generosity and responsibility. Perhaps adults shy away from these topics out of fear that their adolescent children may change the conversation. Can an ungenerous and irresponsible adult culture long get away with preaching virtue to its young?

Eighty years ago, most adolescents had far more sustained contact with both older and younger people than do today's youth. The separateness and the specialness of adolescence were less attended to. Furthermore, the social expectations for younger folk were clearly etched, with likely behaviors and careers prominently set before the young person, whether rich or poor, rural or urban. There were few models of living different from those of the youth's immediate surroundings, whatever they were. They were sometimes constricting, but the signposts were there.

It is different in the 1980s, an age of international life styles insinuated into millions of living rooms by television. The signals for young people must be confusing. Be healthy, but smoke tobacco. Don't have sex, but be sexy. Be a good boy, but boys should be boys. America is a land of immigrants, but keep those black Haitians out.

Added to this is the lessened cohesion of the family. A greater percentage of adolescents live in single-parent homes than in the recent past. Most parents, male and female, together or apart, are in the labor force, also a phenomenon of the last twenty years. Parents are not at home as much, it seems, not available to chat, to show easy interest in the youngsters, or to be useful models for them. This "break-up of the American family" has been much chronicled, and too much can be made of it; but the fact that modern adolescents are more on their own than earlier generations in this century is inescapable.

In all, there is no lack of evidence of the potential for confusion of young people. However, contrary to much conventional wisdom, most American adolescents handle it much as their predecessors did, by turning to their parents—however much or little at home— and by charting their futures within predictable environs.[22] The attitudes of parents and their expectations for their children are very powerful influences indeed, far more powerful than many weary, confused mothers and fathers of adolescents may realize.

The rituals of school also reflect adolescents' conventionalism, because, after home, school is the most dominant institution in an adolescent's life. Homecoming. The football game with the arch rival. Honors assemblies. Proms. Pep clubs. Kings and Queens. Being a Senior. Graduation, with caps and gowns. Prizes. These various rites are surprising both for their pervasiveness and for their venerability. Contemporary students are inventing few new rituals; they honor the old, however awkward in some abstract sense these may be. (A few sophisticated kids perversely honor traditions by mocking them; they dare not ignore them, however.) Some are very expensive. The principal of a city high school whose students are from working-class homes estimated the outlay per couple for the senior prom to be $200. The girls buy evening gowns; the boys rent their outfits and limousines. Their big bash was in a rented function room, not even in the school gymnasium. Many hard-earned student dollars went into the brief, utterly predictable ritual, a ritual, however, that filled an important psychological need for the participants, a rite of passage.

And so, in their inexperience, adolescents look for models to copy, their elders or their peers, their teachers or folk heroes and heroines. However, *they* will do the choosing from among these models: they are adult enough for that. They are impressionable, but also autonomous; the two are not contradictory. Because of the fluid, ambiguous nature of this stage of life, the persuasive influence of parents and teachers is especially potent—far more than in college or graduate school. The practical implications of the mixture of dependence and autonomy that is adolescence have been well summarized by a lawyer, Franklin Zimring. "How do we train young people to be *free?*" he asks. "If the exercise of independent choice is an essential element of maturity, part of the process of becoming mature is learning to make independent decisions. This type of liberty cannot be taught; it can only be learned." Adults can help this learning, in powerful ways, by example, by being honest, by trusting young people, and by giving them the compliment of both asking much of them and holding them accountable for it.

"Our authority over our adolescent children is tenuous. As a matter of sensible political science, we should attempt to exercise that authority in a visibly credible manner. Candor and consistency may make the high school principal's life harder, but this may be the last best hope for the legitimate authority he needs if the high school is to remain a viable educational institution." In a word, we shouldn't pander to youth. We should show them respect by expecting much of them and by being straight—and part of being straight is telling them that they are still inexperienced and therefore must share their freedom with older people until they have learned the dimensions of liberty. Zimring summarizes adolescence as a "learner's permit."[23]

Even the most effective parent or teacher stumbles when asked precisely what is meant by "learner" and by "permit." It all depends on the child and the situation. One cannot shield an adolescent from all risk and hurt; to do so would be to deny that young person the essential opportunity to learn through failure. Thus, adult wisdom runs, curiously, to apparent inconsistency: effective adults change their attitude and rules (insofar as they can enforce these) as the learner learns. The absence of permanent absolutes—Regulations—can seem a waffle or a walk down both sides of the street. In fact, constancy is there in the process: I'll give you all the rope that I think you can handle. Most adolescents most of the time accept this learner's permit argument; indeed, many welcome it. Some reject it out of hand, because they see any rope to be all theirs. All adolescents reject it some of the time, inevitably as a part of their own learning. Wise teachers and parents wait, explain, encourage, criticize, love, and explain again. There is no more difficult teaching job than that of helping an adolescent into adulthood. Few jobs are more thankless and few more rewarding.

4

Docility

I WANT hungry students, the teacher said.

What do you mean by hungry? Kids who want to learn. Kids who aren't afraid to ask questions. Kids who try the hard problems. Questers.

Oh, you mean the smart ones. No. Not at all. You don't have to be smart to be hungry, and there are plenty of high scorers around here who aren't hungry. A lot of the honors students aren't questers. They dodge the hard problems, the hard courses, to keep their averages up. They con the colleges with this, too.

Not always. O.K., not always. The smart kids *are* easy to teach. But the kid who's fun to teach is the questing one, the kid who wants to know why.

You like him because he lets you show off that you can field all his questions. O.K., fair enough. But it's that kid who will be the self-starter, the person who'll do new things. He'll be a leader. That hunger is in his nature. He'll be the better citizen than the selfish grade grubber of a kid who just coasts through. A great school would be one made up of only hungry kids. (And I, a school principal quietly sitting in, add, And of hungry teachers.)[24]

The line of argument pressed by this teacher is not only a good but a critical one. Although the society, in the academic arena at least, officially rewards only the student with high performance on conventionally accepted tests, some teachers and parents hanker for more than that. They respect the young person who, while paying close attention to the details of the material being studied, tries to arrange them in new ways, ones that do not necessarily fit the approved solution. It is the student who finds a roundabout but ingenious way to solve a word problem in algebra. Or it is the pupil who sees an unexpected connection between a name and a foreign word. Why, for example, was the Faust of legend and of Goethe given as a name the German for "fist"? It is the budding historian who, after reading in the textbooks that Jefferson and John Adams stood at opposite political poles in the 1790s, discovers that in later life they became close correspondents. For this student the shape of the men's harmonies may be more important than their familiar differences. It is the student who insists that his metalwork is precise to a bare millimeter, when rougher work might do. It is the student who is neither afraid to move a discussion of a worldly matter to a spiritual concern, nor embarrassed to probe issues that reach beyond the immediate. It is the young person who tries again and again to get exactly right something that is important to him.

In another sense, the hungry student has critical radar, the ability to spot the inaccurate, meretricious, or inane. He is the person who tries to find new truth. "Our intellectual history is a chronicle of the anguish and suffering of men who tried to help their contemporaries see that some part of their fondest beliefs were misconceptions, faulty assumptions, superstitions, and even outright lies," Neil Postman and Charles Weingartner recently wrote.[25] Of course, one has to understand well the old truth before rejecting it, a step that many self-styled revolutionaries fail to take. At his or her best, the hungry student is the constructively skeptical student.

Above all, the hungry student is active, engaged in his or her own learning. It is that quality which is most appealing to many teachers. The student takes the initiative and works at teaching himself.

Lamentably, far too few modern American adolescents are hungry students. No more important finding has emerged from the inquiries of our study than that the American high school student, *as student,* is all too often docile, compliant, and without initiative. Some who have initiative use it to undertake as little engagement as possible with school. They await their education and take in such of it that interests them. Such students like to be entertained. Their harshest epithet for a teacher is "boring." Nonetheless, and paradoxically, students do accept the boring classes, as a price that the school sets. There are too few rewards for being inquisitive; there rarely is extra credit for the ingenious proof. The constructive skeptic can be unsettling to all too many teachers, who may find him cheeky and disruptive. Questing can be costly.

Ironically, most adolescents are not docile on their jobs, away from school—and the majority of high school–age young people now are working or are searching for work during the academic year. A 1980 survey showed that "nearly three-fifths of the sopho-mores interviewed and over three-quarters of the seniors interviewed had either worked for pay or were looking for a job."[26] All adolescent groups were involved—males and females equally, the college preparatory students almost as frequently as the vocational-technical students, the children of the rich as well as the children of the poor. The jobs they hold are unskilled or semiskilled and usually "dead end," though this last characteristic little offends these young workers, because they see their employment as temporary, a way to earn their own pocket money. It is the pay from these jobs that fills the gas tanks of all those cars in the parking lot of Pamela's school. The adolescents work as fast food chefs and servers, delivery boys and girls and salespeople. Some carry heavy responsibilities and hours. I met an honors track senior who worked over forty hours per week as head chef in a French restaurant. I heard about the joys and sorrows of being the $8.00-an-hour lead salesperson in a shoestore.

A visit to any suburban mall in the late weekday afternoon or on a Saturday introduces one to the local high school population: as many sell as buy. There is colorful, energetic bustle, for example, in an ice cream store, where uniformed sixteen-year-olds slop jim-mies on towering cones, make change, gossip, negotiate dates, and watch the scene in the mall's corridors alongside. There is no docility here, and the purpose for the activity is as clear as it is primitive. The kids get the money that frees them from parental allowances, and they get a kick out of being even marginally important, selling something to someone. All this job-related energy of so many students apparently does not affect their academic record; as a careful survey reports, "Working during high school appears to have virtually no effect on grade point average."[27]

The contrast between the energy on the jobs and the lassitude in classrooms is striking. What is so sad about docility in school is not only that it is so pervasive, but that it is a condition of long standing. John Dewey warned about it. David Riesman and Edgar Friedenberg looked for yeasty, "counter-cyclical" young people in the 1950s. Paul Goodman, James Coleman, and Postman and Weingartner continued the search in the 1960s.[28] Charles Silberman, in his thorough study of the schools in the late 1960s, pinpointed the problem in the central chapter of his book *Crisis in the Classroom,* which he titled "Education for Docility." He argued that the students quickly learn what it takes to survive in school, and that is to conform to what the system and its teachers want. "The most important strategy for survival is docility and conformity," Silberman asserted. "Docility is not only encouraged but frequently demanded, for teachers and administrators seem unable to distinguish between authority and power." The students accept the power. "The tragedy is that the great majority of students do not rebel; they accept the stultifying rules, the lack of privacy, the authoritarianism, the abuse of power—indeed, virtually every aspect of school life—as The Way Things Are."[29] A colleague, Peter Holland, recently told me that, if anything, the situation has worsened since the 1960s. "The schools may be anaesthetizing the students . . . [There's] not enough stimulus."[30] In visiting high schools, Holland, a former physics teacher and principal, noticed especially the increasing blandness of debate clubs and student newspapers. Many schools are quiet, apparently happy, orderly, but intellectually dull. They are not provoking, stimulating places, and their students are not hungry. A Hamilton, Ohio, athletic coach is quoted to the effect that schools allow students "to practice stupidity as long as they don't become discipline problems. They get good at dumbness."[31] David Seeley sadly sums up his view: "Education has become a massive process for producing passive minds."[32]

The consequences of this passivity are troubling. I saw it clearly with Will; his well-meant but unexamined and sloppy responses to my simple questions were inexcusable for such an obviously alert and advantaged young person. Will's intellectual softness is, alas, familiar, both in casual conversation like ours and in more formal academic matters. Add together all the Wills, and you get a distressing picture. Although America, among developed nations, ranks "first on measures of resources and resource allocation [for schooling], we are currently not first on any measures of intellectual achievement . . . Our mean scores placed us in the bottom half of the rank-order distributions thirteen times and in the top half only six times."[33] This record of American students in competition with their foreign peers is worrisome, particularly given the scale of our investment in education.

The most thorough national investigations of student mastery are those carried out by the National Assessment of Educational Progress, which conducts regular cycles of achievement testing with tens of thousands of schoolchildren. Some of the recent findings about American seventeen-year-olds—high school seniors—are revealing.

First, from a 1977–1978 survey in mathematics: over 90 percent of the seventeen-year-olds could handle the processes of addition, subtraction, and multiplication; three quarters of them could correctly multiply 671 by 402. However, 20 percent could not add 3.57 and 1.2. Less than a third could find 4 percent of 75.

> Only . . . forty percent at age seventeen realized that if one picks a marble from a bag containing eight red marbles, seven green marbles, and six blue marbles, the marble picked is most likely *not* red . . . About sixty percent of the [thirteen- and seventeen-year-old] teenagers knew that the sides of a square are of equal length . . . and almost seventy-five percent of the seventeen-year-olds could calculate the area of a rectangle, given its length and its width. Yet, only . . . forty-two percent of the seventeen-year-olds could successfully figure the area of a square when the length of only one side is given.[34]

From tests in the social studies given in the middle and late 1970s: almost a third of seventeen-year-olds were unaware that the United States and Russia were both rich in natural resources. Two-fifths failed a routine question on the causes of the American Revolution, and almost a third did not know that the legislative branch of government passes laws.[35]

From a 1981 review, "Reading, Thinking, and Writing": some 10 percent of seventeen-year-olds could not really read at all. Many of those who could read could not "use" their reading.

> The most significant finding from this assessment [the researchers wrote] is that while students learn to read a wide range of material, they develop very few skills for examining the nature of the ideas that they take away from their reading. Though most have learned to make simple inferences about such things as a character's behavior and motivation, for example, and could express their own judgments of a work as "good" or "bad," they generally did not return to the passage to explain the interpretations they made.[36]

What is especially troubling is the low level of their reasoning skills, the abilities of analysis and synthesis. While students seem to be improving in rote-level, concrete learnings—vocabulary recognition and, in mathematics, simple addition, for example—their ability to think critically and resourcefully is lamentably weak and is continuing to weaken.

> Between 1970 and 1980, both thirteen- and seventeen-year-olds became less likely to try to interpret what they read and more likely to simply make unexplained value judgments about it. One way of characterizing the change during the seventies is to say that seventeen-year-olds' papers became somewhat more like thirteen-year-olds' papers.[37]
>
> [The NAEP researchers sum up as follows.] Quality of life is directly tied to our ability to think clearly amid the noise of modern life, to sift through all that competes for our attention until we find what we value, what will make our lives worth living. What we value is seldom on the surface and, when it is found, can seldom be defended from the incursions of the trivial without sustained efforts to understand it more deeply . . . . A society in which the habits of disciplined reading, analysis, interpretation and discourse are not sufficiently cultivated has much to fear.[38]

5

Incentives

IF WE AMERICANS agree that the habits of clear, resourceful, and useful thinking must be cultivated more effectively than they are now, we must ask how it can be done. The secret lies in providing *incentives,* in our making these habits more desirable for adolescents than the alternatives. Given the susceptibility of most young people to strong persuasion by their elders, this can be readily done, though some traditional structures and attitudes will have to change. For most adolescents, two incentives are dominant. They want the high school diploma, and they want to respect themselves and be respected. High schools will be effective to the extent that they design their policies and practices around these two powerful stimuli.

Most adolescents attend school for a collection of reasons, not very well defined in their minds. Most powerful is tradition: one goes to high school because that is what one does from the age of fourteen to seventeen. Furthermore, the alternatives to school are not attractive. In some communities, one not in school is disparagingly called a "dropout" and is ridiculed. (In others, where truancy is widely accepted, the reverse may be true: cutting school may be cool, a rite of passage in its own way.) For many, school is the social center, where one meets one's friends. The price of the party is going to class. Some schools elaborate this "fun" image. The hoopla around the nonacademic accoutrements of school-going—sports rivalries, proms, clubs, sororities and fraternities, beauty contests, and the rest—shows the extent of nonacademic lures to school. In many communities, these incentives are very powerful, often exaggerated by the adults who enjoy the community spectacles that go along with many of them.

That high school leads somewhere is also well understood by most adolescents. Several have written to us about it.* A tenth-grader at a city high school in the West, the son of a college professor: "By going to school and learning of man's past experiences, we can apply those experiences today." A sixteen-year-old, the daughter of a commercial artist and a secretary: "In an ideal situation, high school provides the challenge necessary to spark incentive, as well as a somewhat buffered environment in which the student can mature intellectually in preparation for higher education."

The seventeen-year-old son of a truck driver and factory worker, at an inner-city parochial school, put it very practically:

> I have a long way to go . . . but here's what I'm going to do. First thing I would finish high school. If you don't, you would not find a decent good paying job. Young people today don't know what it is like if you quit school and you'll sit around the house all day and do nothing. People will think of you as some kind of bum when you can't find a job with out your high school diploma and you'll just walk the streets with no where to go . . .

A tenth-grade girl from a Midwestern high school, the daughter of a dispatcher and a housewife, put it less specifically, but with faith and trust:

> A lot of kids are dropping out of school, not because their dumb, just because they think it's cool. They get a job and think they have got it made. This is not true. Education is the best thing they can get. If they drop out they will never know what they could have been, what they could have done . . .

* I have left these testimonials as I received them, misspellings, grammatical problems and all. They speak for themselves.

Another tenth-grader from the same school put her investment not only in practical but also in very personal terms:

> My education is important to me, because I want to be able to get a decent job. I want to have a nice feeling about myself. I also want people to think more of me because I think they will need to know what you are like if you are smart or dumb. I also think you will get further if you had your education.

Her view is especially poignant: this youngster is totally deaf and has had a struggle with schooling. She wrote further, "Now I can hardly hear at all. I lip read. I am also good at that. People treat me like I don't belong in this world but I am only human please remember that . . ." Apparently some teachers had earlier forgotten. School is for rememberings such as this, she wisely implies; it is not only a preparation for something in the future.

Many of the students who wrote to us felt that their peers did not understand the importance of investing their time in education. A seventeen-year-old girl from a suburban public high school wrote of this, and exhibited again a profound faith in schooling:

> Priorities pertaining to the insecure high school girls in my school deal mainly with blow drying their hair in the morning, looking beautiful before school and never being seen shoveling snow or mowing a lawn. My priorities start with school. I believe school is very important . . . Grades nine through twelve are the most crucial grades since most future decisions are based upon the performance of the student during these four years. If you compare these four years to the amount of years the average person lives, it does not seem like a very big sacrifice to put your best effort into school. It almost seems selfish to waste a mind.

And for some, the experience of high school is less one of preparation than of epiphany. From a regional high school in an Eastern industrial area, a young man wrote to us:

> I am here to get a good Education and to get prepared for life most blacks couldn't go to school because they wern't

alowed to Read or write but times have changed and i feel
that my teacher have taught me a skill and a trade i'll never
forget plus i will always remember the teachers that open my
eyes and showed me how important an Education is, and if
my teacher's didn't care they would not have keep telling me
to striegen up. i was a kid that everybody wanted me out of
school but because i was always fighting I didn't care if i got
suspendent, But i met a teacher that was determen to teach
me manners and a trade at the same time but what did i do,
i treated him like everybody els no respect, But he didn't go
for that, he put me in my place like no other man has done
since my father left and it realy opened my eyes and showed
me how impoertant school was an i'll never forget my wood
[working] III teacher in my life.

As always, there are exceptions, the adolescents who are not
convinced that sticking it out at school will in fact help them very
much. Many of these—often minority youths from low-income backgrounds who attend marginally effective schools—are quite correct
in their analysis.

For at least half of the American students, the lure of higher
education is a powerful incentive to stay in secondary school. If
the colleges to which they aspire set significant and substantive
admissions requirements, the students will work to achieve them.
One can see the power of the incentive that college admission often
provides by observing during the course of a student's senior year
what happens when a college tells him he is admitted: he may
then simply stop working. Teaching honors track seniors in the
fall term is very different from teaching them in the spring. In
the fall, the senior's concern is to get into the college or university.
In the spring, after admission to college is settled, it is to have a
party and, if white, to get a tan.

Ironically, the popularization of American higher education may
have weakened the strength of college admissions as an incentive
for adolescents. If one could merely attend school and still get a
place in college, why work very hard? As soon as higher education became something to which any citizen around the age of
eighteen was entitled, it lost its power to affect what happened in
high school. Open admission to college may have been necessary,

owing to the inadequacy of schooling for some young citizens and the consequences of rigid age-grading, but it has been a mixed blessing.

What is completely clear, however, is that most students see the *diploma* as their high school goal, the passport to their next stage of life. The way to receive it, they now know, is to serve time, to be in attendance the requisite number of weeks in the requisite courses. One thereby amasses "credits," which ultimately "earn" the diploma. *Attendance* is the way it is done.

If a school awarded the diploma whenever a student reached the agreed-on level of mastery at the completion of a student's study rather than after four years of attendance and the collection of credits, the effect on student behavior would be dramatic. That is, we should use the incentive that the diploma provides as a means to improve students' learning. Award it only when there is a clear exhibition by the student that such learning has been mastered. Be less concerned about *means,* such as mere attendance or how many years a student has been at school. Place the emphasis on ends, on exhibited *mastery.*

This approach would give the students a clear, academically substantive goal, the obviously appropriate priority.

It would usefully undermine the tyranny of age-grading: a student can elect to exhibit his mastery when he is prepared to do so, not just when his birthday signals that he "ought" to be ready. It would give an incentive to the students' learning on their own and would reward those who do. It would eliminate the painfully distorting counting of Carnegie units, where equally useful but very different enterprises—physical education and physics, for example—are equated, usually on an "hours-attended" basis.

It would ensure sustained attention to key subjects and topics, a major improvement over the current system, where a student can drop a subject, such as mathematics, when the credits are earned, perhaps even in the tenth grade. Two years later, the diploma—presumably a symbol of a mastered general education—is awarded to a seventeen-year-old who probably has forgotten, because of disuse, much of mathematics.

For teachers, the need to create the mechanisms for students to exhibit their mastery will force into the open the myriad questions of academic priorities that now lie buried under the political neutrality of the credit-collection system.

The practical problems that follow from this modest change of goals from attendance to exhibited mastery are substantial. Fair tests are difficult to prepare.[39] Not everyone shows off best on a single test, and the exhibitions would have to be designed to let the students show what they know, rather than what they do not know. Arranging for a variety of ways for students to show their accomplishments will take imagination, and a variety of examinations and exhibitions will be necessary for reasons of fairness. All of this will take time, and time is money. Credit-counting may be financially cheap; educationally, it is very costly.

The most important person in an adolescent's life is himself or herself. While that is true of most people of all ages, it is especially true of those in their teens, a time of rapid change and of shaping an identity. Self-absorption is the rule; deserved self-esteem, not surprisingly, is the most powerful positive attribute an adolescent can hope for.

I was forcefully reminded of this truism after spending a day visiting a juvenile prison. Actually, it was a holding tank for boys and girls, between the ages of ten and fifteen, waiting for trial or for sentencing, youngsters who either had no parent or guardian willing to post the $25 bail or were accused of such violent crimes as to preclude temporary release. Most were barely literate and most seemed in subdued shock in their lock-dominated surroundings and highly regimented routine. A learning center was provided for them, with the teachers planning work for the youngsters individually, day by day. What did these kids, most of whom were male and black or Asian, have in common? I asked. All the adults with whom I spoke reported similarly: *bitterness,* because many kids just like them were still at large, and because getting caught and locked up was more a matter of bad luck than of justice; and *lack of self-esteem.* These young people hated themselves, I was told, and saw no purpose in investing in themselves. They took risks that anyone with even a marginal stake in a future would avoid. Their reconstruction, the teachers told me, would start only when they believed even a bit in their ability to make it on their own. The hard stares and the swagger of some of the boys masked their lack of assurance. They were dangerously tough because they were not tough enough. Irony attends a lack of self-esteem.

Get a person to believe in himself and give him a powerful incentive to learn, and the results can be striking. I saw a simple example of this while serving in the army during the 1950s. At that time, one needed a high school diploma or its equivalent in order to become a sergeant. An able but stolid and aloof corporal commanded one of our gun sections, holding effectively a position usually assigned to a sergeant first class. He had, according to his records, dropped out of school at the ninth grade; he had a measured I.Q. of around 90, and the scores from other tests taken on his enlistment early in the Korean War were equally low. He was black and came from a poor (and probably poorly schooled) rural area. He knew, and the battery commander made it clear to him, that if he passed the army's high school equivalency examination, the sergeant's stripes—and salary and special living quarters that went along with them—would instantly be his. The commander signaled clear confidence in this soldier: *of course* he could pass the tests. He was doing the work of higher-ranking men now, wasn't he? The corporal joined classes provided by the army and passed the examination within three months.

The keys held by the battery commander here were an expressed belief in the ability and worth of the corporal and personal interest in him as an individual. The message wasn't that all corporals could qualify; it was that *this* corporal could. Once that honest signal was received and understood by the young soldier, his self-esteem soared. He knew that someone he respected believed in him and gave him responsibility. The ultimate educational effect was dramatic.

Adolescents have far more power than they display, or are asked to or are expected to display, in most schools. We assume they will be truant, late, irresponsible—and that prophecy is self-fulfilling. We assume they cannot figure things out for themselves, so we tell them things. Paradoxically, we are conspirators, often with them, in their dependence. Happy dependence is a pleasant state for many adolescents. If little is asked of them, their risk of failure is likewise small. Yet one has limited self-esteem in that dependent state. Most adolescents know they can do more.

No one is flattered more than when his help is solicited. People, adolescents included, respond to challenge, and they feel personal esteem when their power is recognized and sought. A school which assumes that students will respond to challenge, rather than shrink from it, will be effective.

A principal of a large urban high school had all his security guards removed as the result of financial cutbacks. He turned to the members of his army Junior Reserve Officers Training Corps (JROTC) unit. Would they, he asked, see whether they could solve the school's security problem? They responded with a plan that they carried out, and the number of incidents (most of which were caused by outsiders entering the school on illegal or disruptive business) decreased over the days when hired security officers manned the halls. This principal, it should be noted, did not ask his JROTC students to undertake more than they could accomplish. For example, he did not expect them to control serious violence among students, but merely to report it to the assistant principal. The learner's permit status of adolescents *was* recognized, but they *were* given a considerable amount of autonomy and responsibility. The effect on the self-esteem of those in the JROTC unit was visible, and their loyalty to the school enhanced.

There are parallels in the academic side of school. None of us learns what we think we can't learn. Others' belief in our power gives us power. Being asked to teach ourselves gives us confidence that we can learn. Although a teacher must not overshoot an adolescent's reach, his request that the young person take charge of himself or herself is a powerful stimulus.

Finding the right way to elicit each student's self-esteem requires knowing each student. It follows that the more the high schools *personalize* their work with students, the more effective they will be. We all work best for people we respect; we study well in school for teachers we admire; we admire and respect those teachers who know us as individual, worthwhile people.

A good teacher will often speak of getting a student "to work for me." He does so by knowing that student well enough to appreciate his or her strengths and weaknesses and by having the flexibility to allow the student to follow his or her strengths at his or her own speed. Will and Pamela and Louella would respond to attention, and each would flourish with different kinds of teaching. If each of them, especially Pamela, is given a significant part in choosing his or her kind of learning, so much the better.

Personalization absolutely implies options for students, different ways and settings for differing individuals. While total personalization is practically impossible, much is clearly attainable within the kinds of constraints usually found in many high schools. The biggest hurdle will be adult attitudes, particularly those that confuse standardization with standards. Today, we so often hear: Everyone must go to class exactly as often as everyone else. Being absent is always bad. Every sophomore must take Biology I. Such edicts defy the diversity among students and are thus stunningly wasteful. They also throw away the possibility of the gains in motivation possible when the students themselves have a chance to program some important part of their lives in school.

Every adult likes to be respected and enjoys being given responsibility. Truly controlling one's destiny is a powerful attraction. Adolescents are no different from us in this respect. Therefore, set them a clear goal, give them some sensible guidance—the rules attendant on owning a learner's permit—and put the burden of learning on them. Such responsibility will liberate energy now lost because of the impersonality and the patronizing inherent in the lock-step routines of many schools.

I talk with Horace Smith of this concern for incentives, these notions of awarding diplomas only on the basis of exhibited mastery and of provoking students' self-esteem by giving them responsibility. His first reactions are familiar: You'll lose kids. There will be chaos. Tests don't work. Too many kids just want fun, not mastery of the stuff of school. There isn't time.

Yes, we'll lose kids. The ones bucking the system could find it easier to evade learning. But they do that now. And I say *could,* because a school could tie freedom to mastery along the way. That is, the better the performance, the greater the latitude given a student. Make mastery a precondition of freedom.

We've tried that, and it doesn't work very well, Horace complains.

No, I counter, we haven't tried it. Almost no school that I've seen gives mastery more prominence than it gives its routines. Very few high schools ever give their students a *clear* long-term academic goal and an equally clear signal that it's the student's responsibility to get there. We teachers are too nice: we test the kids, and take the blame if they fail. We constantly give them second and third chances, mollycoddle them.

Horace snorts. You've been reading Dickens. You want to savage the kids.

No, I just want to respect their potency and their self-respect. There's plenty of patronizing in our excessive direction of adolescent students, and they quite properly resent it.

Perhaps, Horace concedes. Tests? They're clumsy instruments, often riddled with discrimination.

I agree: Tests, or any exhibition of mastery (I prefer that positive term, the student's opportunity to show off rather than his trial by question), are troublesome mechanisms. But the alternative to them—no basis to describe or assess what school is for—simply is worse. A sensible school would have a variety of means for exhibition—timed tests, essays, oral exams, portfolios of work. Yes, these will take hundreds of faculty hours to prepare and monitor. However, I persist, those hours are better so spent than continuing with the known inadequacies of the status quo.

The waste represented by Horace's compromise—his precarious balance of what is needed for the students and what he has time and energy to give—is demonstrably large. Horace hates to admit that some sort of change is necessary, major change. He hates his compromise, but he is comfortable with the familiar routines, however inadequate. The fear that another practice might be even more inadequate makes him chary. Furthermore, he thinks that agreeing with me will demean him. He's proud and stubborn, good qualities for a teacher. But they make change exceedingly difficult, especially when the change may further threaten his already compromised self-esteem.

II The Program

1

What High School Is

MARK, sixteen and a genial eleventh-grader, rides a bus to Franklin High School, arriving at 7:25. It is an Assembly Day, so the schedule is adapted to allow for a meeting of the entire school. He hangs out with his friends, first outside school and then inside, by his locker. He carries a pile of textbooks and notebooks; in all, it weighs eight and a half pounds.

From 7:30 to 8:19, with nineteen other students, he is in Room 304 for English class. The Shakespeare play being read this year by the eleventh grade is *Romeo and Juliet*. The teacher, Ms. Viola, has various students in turn take parts and read out loud. Periodically, she interrupts the (usually halting) recitations to ask whether the thread of the conversation in the play is clear. Mark is entertained by the stumbling readings of some of his classmates. He hopes he will not be asked to be Romeo, particularly if his current steady, Sally, is Juliet. There is a good deal of giggling in class, and much attention paid to who may be called on next. Ms. Viola reminds the class of a test on this part of the play to be given next week.

The bell rings at 8:19. Mark goes to the boys' room, where he sees a classmate who he thinks is a wimp but who constantly tries to be a buddy. Mark avoids the leech by rushing off. On the way, he notices two boys engaged in some sort of transaction, probably over marijuana. He pays them no attention. 8:24. Typing class. The rows of desks that embrace big office machines are almost filled before the bell. Mark is uncomfortable here: typing class is girl country. The teacher constantly threatens what to Mark is a humiliatingly female future: "Your employer won't like these erasures." The minutes during the period are spent copying a letter from a handbook onto business stationery. Mark struggles to keep from looking at his work; the teacher wants him to watch only the material from which he is copying. Mark is frustrated, uncomfortable, and scared that he will not complete his letter by the class's end, which would be embarrassing.

Nine tenths of the students present at school that day are assembled in the auditorium by the 9:18 bell. The dilatory tenth still stumble in, running down aisles. Annoyed class deans try to get the mob settled. The curtains part; the program is a concert by a student rock group. Their electronic gear flashes under the lights, and the five boys and one girl in the group work hard at being casual. Their movements on stage are studiously at three-quarter time, and they chat with one another as though the tumultuous screaming of their schoolmates were totally inaudible. The girl balances on a stool; the boys crank up the music. It is very soft rock, the sanitized lyrics surely cleared with the assistant principal. The girl sings, holding the mike close to her mouth, but can scarcely be heard. Her light voice is tentative, and the lyrics indecipherable. The guitars, amplified, are tuneful, however, and the drums are played with energy.

The students around Mark—all juniors, since they are seated by class—alternately slouch in their upholstered, hinged seats, talking to one another, or sit forward, leaning on the chair backs in front of them, watching the band. A boy near Mark shouts noisily at the microphone-fondling singer, "Bite it . . . ohhh," and the area around Mark explodes in vulgar male laughter, but quickly subsides. A teacher walks down the aisle. Songs continue, to great applause. Assembly is over at 9:46, two minutes early.

9:53 and biology class. Mark was at a different high school last year and did not take this course there as a tenth-grader. He is in it now, and all but one of his classmates are a year younger than he. He sits on the side, not taking part in the chatter that goes on after the bell. At 9:57, the public address system goes on, with the announcements of the day. After a few words from the principal ("Here's today's cheers and jeers . . ." with a cheer for the winning basketball team and a jeer for the spectators who made a ruckus at the gymnasium), the task is taken over by officers of ASB (Associated Student Bodies). There is an appeal for "bat bunnies." Carnations are for sale by the Girls' League. Miss Indian American is coming. Students are auctioning off their services (background catcalls are heard) to earn money for the prom. Nominees are needed for the ballot for school bachelor and school bachelorette. The announcements end with a "thought for the day. When you throw a little mud, you lose a little ground."

At 10:04 the biology class finally turns to science. The teacher, Mr. Robbins, has placed one of several labeled laboratory specimens—some are pinned in frames, others swim in formaldehyde—on each of the classroom's eight laboratory tables. The three or so students whose chairs circle each of these benches are to study the specimen and make notes about it or drawings of it. After a few minutes each group of three will move to another table. The teacher points out that these specimens are of organisms already studied in previous classes. He says that the period-long test set for the following day will involve observing some of these specimens—then to be without labels—and writing an identifying paragraph on each. Mr. Robbins points out that some of the printed labels ascribe the specimens names different from those given in the textbook. He explains that biologists often give several names to the same organism.

The class now falls to peering, writing, and quiet talking. Mr. Robbins comes over to Mark, and in whispered words asks him to carry a requisition form for science department materials to the business office. Mark, because of his "older" status, is usually chosen by Robbins for this kind of errand. Robbins gives Mark the form and a green hall pass to show to any teacher who might challenge him, on his way to the office, for being out of a classroom. The errand takes Mark four minutes. Meanwhile Mark's group is hard at work but gets to only three of the specimens before the bell rings at 10:42. As the students surge out, Robbins shouts a reminder about a "double" laboratory period on Thursday.

Between classes one of the seniors asks Mark whether he plans to be a candidate for schoolwide office next year. Mark says no. He starts to explain. The 10:47 bell rings, meaning that he is late for French class.

There are fifteen students in Monsieur Bates's language class. He hands out tests taken the day before: *"C'est bien fait, Etienne . . . c'est mieux, Marie . . . Tch, tch, Robert . . ."* Mark notes his C+ and peeks at the A— in front of Susanna, next to him. The class has been assigned seats by M. Bates; Mark resents sitting next to prissy, brainy Susanna. Bates starts by asking a student to read a question and give the correct answer. *"James, question un."* James haltingly reads the question and gives an answer that Bates, now speaking English, says is incomplete. In due course: *"Mark, question cinq."* Mark does his bit, and the sequence goes on, the eight quiz questions and answers filling about twenty minutes of time.

"Turn to page forty-nine. *Maintenant, lisez après moi . . ."* and Bates reads a sentence and has the class echo it. Mark is embarrassed by this and mumbles with a barely audible sound. Others, like Susanna, keep the decibel count up, so Mark can hide. This I-say-you-repeat drill is interrupted once by the public address system, with an announcement about a meeting for the cheerleaders. Bates finishes the class, almost precisely at the bell, with a homework assignment. The students are to review these sentences for a brief quiz the following day. Mark takes note of the assignment, because he knows that tomorrow will be a day of busy-work in French class. Much though he dislikes oral drills, they are better than the workbook stuff that Bates hands out. Write, write, write, for Bates to throw away, Mark thinks.

11:36. Down to the cafeteria, talking noisily, hanging out, munching. Getting to Room 104 by 12:17: U.S. history. The teacher is sitting cross-legged on his desk when Mark comes in, heatedly arguing with three students over the fracas that had followed the previous night's basketball game. The teacher, Mr. Suslovic, while agreeing that the spectators from their school certainly were provoked, argues that they should neither have been so obviously obscene in yelling at the opposing cheerleaders nor have allowed Coke cans to be rolled out on the floor. The three students keep saying that "it isn't fair." Apparently they and some others had been assigned "Saturday mornings" (detentions) by the principal for the ruckus.

At 12:34, the argument appears to subside. The uninvolved students, including Mark, are in their seats, chatting amiably. Mr. Suslovic climbs off his desk and starts talking: "We've almost finished this unit, chapters nine and ten . . ." The students stop chattering among themselves and turn toward Suslovic. Several slouch down in their chairs. Some open notebooks. Most have the five-pound textbook on their desks.

Suslovic lectures on the cattle drives, from north Texas to railroads west of St. Louis. He breaks up this narrative with questions ("Why were the railroad lines laid largely east to west?"), directed at nobody in particular and eventually answered by Suslovic himself. Some students take notes. Mark doesn't. A student walks in the open door, hands Mr. Suslovic a list, and starts whispering with him. Suslovic turns from the class and hears out this messenger. He then asks, "Does anyone know where Maggie Sharp is?" Someone answers, "Sick at home"; someone else says, "I thought I saw her at lunch." Genial consternation. Finally Suslovic tells the messenger, "Sorry, we can't help you," and returns to the class: "Now, where were we?" He goes on for some minutes. The bell rings. Suslovic forgets to give the homework assignment.

1:11 and Algebra II. There is a commotion in the hallway: someone's locker is rumored to have been opened by the assistant principal and a narcotics agent. In the five-minute passing time, Mark hears the story three times and three ways. A locker had been broken into by another student. It was Mr. Gregory and a narc. It was the cops, and they did it without Gregory's knowing. Mrs. Ames, the mathematics teacher, has not heard anything about it. Several of the nineteen students try to tell her and start arguing among themselves. "O.K., that's enough." She hands out the day's problem, one sheet to each student. Mark sees with dismay that it is a single, complicated "word" problem about some train that, while traveling at 84 mph, due west, passes a car that was going due east at 55 mph. Mark struggles: Is it $d = rt$ or $t = rd$? The class becomes quiet, writing, while Mrs. Ames writes some additional, short problems on the blackboard. "Time's up." A sigh; most students still writing. A muffled "Shit." Mrs. Ames frowns.

"Come on, now." She collects papers, but it takes four minutes for her to corral them all.

"Copy down the problems from the board." A minute passes. "William, try number one." William suggests an approach. Mrs. Ames corrects and cajoles, and William finally gets it right. Mark watches two kids to his right passing notes; he tries to read them, but the handwriting is illegible from his distance. He hopes he is not called on, and he isn't. Only three students are asked to puzzle out an answer. The bell rings at 2:00. Mrs. Ames shouts a homework assignment over the resulting hubbub.

Mark leaves his books in his locker. He remembers that he has homework, but figures that he can do it during English class the next day. He knows that there will be an in-class presentation of one of the *Romeo and Juliet* scenes and that he will not be in it. The teacher will not notice his homework writing, or won't do anything about it if she does.

Mark passes various friends heading toward the gym, members of the basketball teams. Like most students, Mark isn't an active school athlete. However, he is associated with the yearbook staff. Although he is not taking "Yearbook" for credit as an English course, he is contributing photographs. Mark takes twenty minutes checking into the yearbook staff's headquarters (the classroom of its faculty adviser) and getting some assignments of pictures from his boss, the senior who is the photography editor. Mark knows that if he pleases his boss and the faculty adviser, he'll take that editor's post for the next year. He'll get English credit for his work then.

After gossiping a bit with the yearbook staff, Mark will leave school by 2:35 and go home. His grocery market bagger's job is from 4:45 to 8:00, the rush hour for the store. He'll have a snack at 4:30, and his mother will save him some supper to eat at 8:30. She will ask whether he has any homework, and he'll tell her no. Tomorrow, and virtually every other tomorrow, will be the same for Mark, save for the lack of the assembly: each period then will be five minutes longer.

Most Americans have an uncomplicated vision of what secondary education should be. Their conception of high school is remarkably uniform across the country, a striking fact, given the size and diversity of the United States and the politically decentralized character of the schools. This uniformity is of several generations' standing. It has, however, two appearances, each quite different from the other, one of words and the other of practice, a world of political rhetoric and Mark's world.

A California high school's general goals, set out in 1979, could serve equally well most of America's high schools, public and private. This school had as its ends:

- Fundamental scholastic achievement . . . to acquire knowledge and share in the traditionally accepted academic fundamentals . . . to develop the ability to make decisions, to solve problems, to reason independently, and to accept responsibility for self-evaluation and continuing self-improvement.
- Career and economic competence . . .
- Citizenship and civil responsibility . . .
- Competence in human and social relations . . .
- Moral and ethical values . . .
- Self-realization and mental and physical health . . .
- Aesthetic awareness . . .
- Cultural diversity . . .[1]

In addition to its optimistic rhetoric, what distinguishes this list is its comprehensiveness. The high school is to touch most aspects of an adolescent's existence—mind, body, morals, values, career. No one of these areas is given especial prominence. School people arrogate to themselves an obligation to all.

An example of the wide acceptability of these goals is found in the courts. Forced to present a detailed definition of "thorough and efficient education," elementary as well as secondary, a West Virginia judge sampled the best of conventional wisdom and concluded that

> there are eight general elements of a thorough and efficient system of education: (a) Literacy, (b) The ability to add, subtract, multiply, and divide numbers, (c) Knowledge of government to the extent the child will be equipped as a citizen to

make informed choices among persons and issues that affect his own governance, (d) Self-knowledge and knowledge of his or her total environment to allow the child to intelligently choose life work—to know his or her options, (e) Work-training and advanced academic training as the child may intelligently choose, (f) Recreational pursuits, (g) Interests in all creative arts such as music, theater, literature, and the visual arts, and (h) Social ethics, both behavioral and abstract, to facilitate compatibility with others in this society.[2]

That these eight—now powerfully part of the debate over the purpose and practice of education in West Virginia—are reminiscent of the influential list, "The Seven Cardinal Principles of Secondary Education," promulgated in 1918 by the National Education Association, is no surprise.[3] The rhetoric of high school purpose has been uniform and consistent for decades. Americans agree on the goals for their high schools.

That agreement is convenient, but it masks the fact that virtually all the words in these goal statements beg definition. Some schools have labored long to identify specific criteria beyond them; the result has been lists of daunting pseudospecificity and numbing earnestness. However, most leave the words undefined and let the momentum of traditional practice speak for itself. That is why analyzing how Mark spends his time is important: from watching him one uncovers the important purposes of education, the ones that shape practice. Mark's day is similar to that of other high school students across the country, as similar as the rhetoric of one goal statement to others'. Of course, there are variations, but the extent of consistency in the shape of school routine for a large and diverse adolescent population is extraordinary, indicating more graphically than any rhetoric the measure of agreement in America about what one does in high school, and, by implication, what it is for.

The basic organizing structures in schools are familiar. Above all, students are grouped by age (that is, freshman, sophomore, junior, senior), and all are expected to take precisely the same time—around 720 school days over four years, to be precise—to meet the requirements for a diploma. When one is out of his grade level, he can feel odd, as Mark did in his biology class. The goals are the same for all, and the means to achieve them are also similar.

Young males and females are treated remarkably alike; the schools' goals are the same for each gender. In execution, there are differences, as those pressing sex discrimination suits have made educators intensely aware. The students in metalworking classes are mostly male; those in home economics, mostly female. But it is revealing how much less sex discrimination there is in high schools than in other American institutions. For many young women, the most liberated hours of their week are in school.

School is to be like a job: you start in the morning and end in the afternoon, five days a week. You don't get much of a lunch hour, so you go home early, unless you are an athlete or are involved in some special school or extracurricular activity. School is conceived of as the children's workplace, and it takes young people off parents' hands and out of the labor market during prime-time work hours. Not surprisingly, many students see going to school as little more than a dogged necessity. They perceive the day-to-day routine, a Minnesota study reports, as one of "boredom and lethargy." One of the students summarizes: School is "boring, restless, tiresome, puts ya to sleep, tedious, monotonous, pain in the neck."[4]

The school schedule is a series of units of time: the clock is king. The base time block is about fifty minutes in length. Some schools, on what they call modular scheduling, split that fifty-minute block into two or even three pieces. Most schools have double periods for laboratory work, especially in the sciences, or four-hour units for the small numbers of students involved in intensive vocational or other work-study programs. The flow of all school activity arises from or is blocked by these time units. "How much time do I have with my kids" is the teacher's key question.

Because there are many claims for those fifty-minute blocks, there is little time set aside for rest between them, usually no more than three to ten minutes, depending on how big the school is and, consequently, how far students and teachers have to walk from class to class. As a result, there is a frenetic quality to the school day, a sense of sustained restlessness. For the adolescents, there are frequent changes of room and fellow students, each change giving tempting opportunities for distraction, which are stoutly resisted by teachers. Some schools play soft music during these "passing times," to quiet the multitude, one principal told me.

Many teachers have a chance for a coffee break. Few students do. In some city schools where security is a problem, students must be in class for seven consecutive periods, interrupted by a heavily monitored twenty-minute lunch period for small groups, starting as early as 10:30 A.M. and running to after 1:00 P.M. A high premium is placed on punctuality and on "being where you're supposed to be." Obviously, a low premium is placed on reflection and repose. The student rushes from class to class to collect knowledge. Savoring it, it is implied, is not to be done much in school, nor is such meditation really much admired. The picture that these familiar patterns yield is that of an academic supermarket. The purpose of going to school is to pick things up, in an organized and predictable way, the faster the better.

What is supposed to be picked up is remarkably consistent among all sorts of high schools. Most schools specifically mandate three out of every five courses a student selects. Nearly all of these mandates fall into five areas—English, social studies, mathematics, science, and physical education. On the average, English is required to be taken each year, social studies and physical education three out of the four high school years, and mathematics and science one or two years. Trends indicate that in the mid-eighties there is likely to be an increase in the time allocated to these last two subjects. Most students take classes in these four major academic areas beyond the minimum requirements, sometimes in such special areas as journalism and "yearbook," offshoots of English departments.[5]

Press most adults about what high school is for, and you hear these subjects listed. *High school? That's where you learn English and math and that sort of thing.* Ask students, and you get the same answer. High school is to "teach" these "subjects."

What is often absent is any definition of these subjects or any rationale for them. They are just there, labels. Under those labels lie a multitude of things. A great deal of material is supposed to be "covered"; most of these courses are surveys, great sweeps of the stuff of their parent disciplines.

While there is often a sequence *within* subjects—algebra before trigonometry, "first-year" French before "second-year" French—

there is rarely a coherent relationship or sequence *across* subjects. Even the most logically related matters—reading ability as a precondition for the reading of history books, and certain mathematical concepts or skills before the study of some of physics—are only loosely coordinated, if at all. There is little demand for a synthesis of it all; English, mathematics, and the rest are discrete items, to be picked up individually. The incentive for picking them up is largely through tests and, with success at these, in credits earned.

Coverage within subjects is the key priority. If some imaginative teacher makes a proposal to force the marriage of, say, mathematics and physics or to require some culminating challenges to students to use several subjects in the solution of a complex problem, and if this proposal will take "time" away from other things, opposition is usually phrased in terms of what may be thus forgone. If we do that, we'll have to give up colonial history. We won't be able to get to programming. We'll not be able to read *Death of a Salesman*. There isn't time. The protesters usually win out.

The subjects come at a student like Mark in random order, a kaleidoscope of worlds: algebraic formulae to poetry to French verbs to Ping-Pong to the War of the Spanish Succession, all before lunch. Pupils are to pick up these things. Tests measure whether the picking up has been successful.

The lack of connection between stated goals, such as those of the California high school cited earlier, and the goals inherent in school practice is obvious and, curiously, tolerated. Most striking is the gap between statements about "self-realization and mental and physical growth" or "moral and ethical values"—common rhetoric in school documents—and practice. Most physical education programs have neither the time nor the focus really to ensure fitness. Mental health is rarely defined. Neither are ethical values, save at the negative extremes, such as opposition to assault or dishonesty. Nothing in the regimen of a day like Mark's signals direct or implicit teaching in this area. The "schoolboy code" (not ratting on a fellow student) protects the marijuana pusher, and a leechlike associate is shrugged off without concern. The issue of the locker search was pushed aside, as not appropriate for class time.

Most students, like Mark, go to class in groups of twenty to twenty-seven students. The expected attendance in some schools, particularly those in low-income areas, is usually higher, often thirty-five students per class, but high absentee rates push the actual numbers down. About twenty-five per class is an average figure for expected attendance, and the actual numbers are somewhat lower. There are remarkably few students who go to class in groups much larger or smaller than twenty-five.[6]

A student such as Mark sees five or six teachers per day; their differing styles and expectations are part of his kaleidoscope. High school staffs are highly specialized: guidance counselors rarely teach mathematics, mathematics teachers rarely teach English, principals rarely do any classroom instruction. Mark, then, is known a little bit by a number of people, each of whom sees him in one specialized situation. No one may know him as a "whole person"—unless he becomes a special problem or has special needs.

Save in extracurricular or coaching situations, such as in athletics, drama, or shop classes, there is little opportunity for sustained conversation between student and teacher. The mode is a one-sentence or two-sentence exchange: *Mark, when was Grover Cleveland president?* Let's see, was 1890 . . . or something . . . wasn't he the one . . . he was elected twice, wasn't he? . . . *Yes . . . Gloria, can you get the dates right?* Dialogue is strikingly absent, and as a result the opportunity of teachers to challenge students' ideas in a systematic and logical way is limited. Given the rushed, full quality of the school day, it can seldom happen. One must infer that careful probing of students' thinking is not a high priority. How one gains (to quote the California school's statement of goals again) "the ability to make decisions, to solve problems, to reason independently, and to accept responsibility for self-evaluation and continuing self-improvement" without being challenged is difficult to imagine. One certainly doesn't learn these things merely from lectures and textbooks.

Most schools are nice places. Mark and his friends enjoy being in theirs. The adults who work in schools generally like adolescents. The academic pressures are limited, and the accommodations to students are substantial. For example, if many members of an English class have jobs after school, the English teacher's expectations for them are adjusted, downward. In a word, school is sensitively accommodating, as long as students are punctual, where they are supposed to be, and minimally dutiful about picking things up from the clutch of courses in which they enroll.

This characterization is not pretty, but it is accurate, and it serves to describe the vast majority of American secondary schools. "Taking subjects" in a systematized, conveyer-belt way is what one does in high school. That this process is, in substantial respects, not related to the rhetorical purposes of education is tolerated by most people, perhaps because they do not really either believe in those ill-defined goals or, in their heart of hearts, believe that schools can or should even try to achieve them. The students are happy taking subjects. The parents are happy, because that's what they did in high school. The rituals, the most important of which is graduation, remain intact. The adolescents are supervised, safely and constructively most of the time, during the morning and afternoon hours, and they are off the labor market. That is what high school is all about.

2

Purpose: Mind and Character

LATE-TWENTIETH CENTURY high schools deserve a more appropriate purpose than a warmed-over version of principles promulgated in 1918. We are no longer in the early twentieth century, needing an institution that provides a comprehensive set of experiences to prepare adolescents for a newly modernized state. We live today, crowded together, in a culture overloaded with information, surfeited with data and opinions and experiences that we pump up with the buttons on our TV sets, home computers, telephones, and word processors. The world around us, for good or ill, is a more insistent, rich, and effective provider of information than was our grandparents'. Education's job today is less in purveying information than in helping people to use it—that is, to exercise their minds.

An earlier day may have required that we create an institution to fill a full range of needs, to provide the comprehensive objectives that are now so deeply ingrained in American tradition. Today we need to ask what special role schools should play among the extraordinary sets of educating influences around and available to the modern American adolescent.

One purpose for schools—*education of the intellect*—is obvious. The other—*an education in character*—is inescapable.

No other institution in the culture is solely devoted to developing mental powers, and the existence both of powerful means of psychological and political influence through the organized media and of an intellectually complex culture and economy amply justifies, and indeed compels, a focus on the effective use of one's mind. Furthermore, intellectual training is eminently "useful": it opens means to educate oneself in any sphere of interest or importance. Without it, one is crippled. With it, one can gain, on one's own, that comprehensive learning which so attracted our predecessors.

Questions of conduct and of rights and obligations inevitably arise in all institutions, including schools. If one is to get along, one has to have rules. Some things go; some things do not go. On these issues, this person will decide. On those, someone else will be the judge. High schools are full of people, most of them inexperienced individuals trying to discover their own rules and those of others. This activity of discovery is inevitable, and it can be either ignored, which leaves the process in anarchy or agony, or confronted, which takes time and imagination. Useful and sensitive confrontation about conduct can help lead a student to an understanding of restraint and of action and to know when each is appropriate. That is, it can assist in the development of the student's character.

Obviously, American high schools must reconcile their practice and their philosophy, and find convincing rationales for both. One cannot proceed with this process, however, without addressing the issue of compulsion. What learning can the state properly demand of its citizens? How should that demand be exercised? Indeed, *should* there be a common learning among Americans, a set of skills and attitudes and beliefs that all share? If this common learning does not readily arise from private choice—that is, skills and beliefs that emerge consistently from the informal family and neighborhood structures of the country—how should it be mandated?

While there may be a certain, theoretical contradiction between a state which asserts that it exists at the pleasure of the governed, who have important rights as autonomous individuals, and a state which requires that all individuals understand and believe certain things and act in certain ways, it is fanciful to argue that the state has no claims on the minds and actions of its citizens. The real issue is *what* claims and how they are to be met.

The essential claims in education are very elementary: literacy, numeracy, and civic understanding. Literacy means more than merely skills in decoding words. It means the ability to comprehend and to understand ideas and arguments to a degree that allows an individual to use them. Literacy implies clear thought; that is, one must read easily and sensitively enough to comprehend at least the basic arguments presented by contemporary political and social life. Without that ability and the correlative ability to present such arguments oneself orally and in clear writing, a citizen cannot fully participate in a democracy. Any community that expects collective, affirmative government requires a literate citizenry.[7]

Numeracy means the ability both to use numbers, arithmetically and algebraically, and to understand the concepts, relationships, and logic embedded in mathematical thought. A modern citizen cannot make critical judgments without these skills.

Civic understanding means a grasp of the basis for consensual democratic government, a respect for its processes, and acceptance of the restraints and obligations incumbent on a citizen. These restraints and obligations are eloquently summarized in the Bill of Rights. One need go not much further: if all American citizens had mastered at the least the complex principles there, this would be a more just society.

The foregoing three desiderata are neither surprising nor threatening. They are the chestnuts of American educational thought. They can be taught, and they can be learned. Indeed, few Americans, if sensitively taught, could not grasp them by early adolescence.

Although these three claims of the state are minimal, they should be maximal, as well. They provide the essential context for responsible citizenship and government. Since democracy could not long survive without them, it is reasonable for the state to insist on their mastery and to tax its citizens to ensure that each citizen has the means to gain their mastery. However, beyond these three elements, the claims of the state have far less merit. The state has no right to insist that I be "employable" on its terms of what a "career" may be. That is my private matter, and I take the risk that no one will purchase the services that I prepare myself to offer. The state has no right or obligation to tell me how to spend my leisure time. I can enrich myself and the state if I am cultured, but it is unreasonable of the state to impose on me its own definition of culture. As long as my style of life and values do not impinge on those of others, I should have the sovereign right to be what I want to be, including a slob. Beyond expecting me to be sensitive and responsive to legal and constitutional principles that allow freedom, the state has no claim whatsoever on my beliefs or character. Beyond expecting rudimentary civility, the state has no subtle or not-so-subtle right to shape my personality.

This is not at all to say that it may not be in the interest of the state to *assist* me, if I wish, to become employable, to enjoy culture and leisure, and to develop myself fully. It would not be at all unreasonable for the state from time to time to try to *persuade* me to turn in some particular direction, to become, say, a scientist, if scientists were needed, or to be aware of high culture. This persuasion could be in the form of financial incentives or aid, with no comparable aid provided by the state for what it may consider to be less important fields. But it would be an unacceptable abridgment of my freedom if the state prevented me from pursuing a line of endeavor I chose, whatever its priority in the eyes of the state (other than one that is obviously antisocial, such as professional terrorism).

The implications of this principle of the state's minimal and maximal claims are substantial. On one hand, the state has, for its own reasonable protection, the obligation to see that each citizen is literate, reasonably adept with numbers, and aware of his civic obligations. Whatever the cost, it must be paid. On the other hand, the state has no right whatsoever to compel a citizen to attend school once those minima are demonstrably reached nor the right to compel her or him to learn anything else. Encouragement, yes. Opportunity, yes. Mandate, no.

Americans must come to terms with the limits on compulsion, on the minimal reasonable claims of the state on the time and minds of young citizens. Not surprisingly, those who are eager for the state to mandate the entire high school program are those in power at a given moment. Compulsion is fine as long as *we* do the compelling, of things to *our* taste. In this country, the powers that be are in the habit of adding things beyond the minima. For example, we insist on people being physically fit, according to the state's definition of fitness. (Absurdly, this all plays out as mere attendance at ill-defined physical education classes.) Some states insist that their young citizens study their state's history, which may be good for local pride, but as it is usually taught, it rarely has much to do with civic understanding. Others require courses on the "free enterprise system" or, as the state of Maine does, on "principles of morality and justice and a sacred regard for truth, love of country, humanity, a universal benevolence, sobriety, industry and frugality, chastity, moderation and temperance, and all other virtues that ornament human society."[8] The temptations to extend this list beckon every special interest lobby.

Some today, with earnest good intentions, urge that a common core of subjects be legislated for high school students. Depending on one's point of view, much of this certainly is nice. Laudable or not in the abstract, however, if it is mandatory, it is an abuse of state power, an excessive reach of political authority. Again, the state is fully justified in providing it at public expense, if it wishes, and prescribing it for certain certificates and diplomas that citizens may voluntarily choose to earn.

Some others say that an adolescent should have a "high school experience," something that is inherently a Good Thing, an experience that teaches young people to "get along with others." Proponents of this view offer no evidence for support of their argument for mandatory "residence" at a school. This is prudent on their part: there isn't any. Most real reasons for enforced attendance actually turn on the need to preserve adults' jobs. Compulsory attendance in an educational institution should cease when a young citizen demonstrates mastery of the minima, and most young citizens should master those minima before senior high school. As a result, schooling for most adolescents would be voluntary. Few would be compelled to attend high school, though a prudent state would vigorously encourage it. High school would be an opportunity, not an obligation.[9]

One usefully starts analysis of the implications of a fresh purpose for high schools—an education of mind and character—by returning to Mark's world and looking carefully at the course of study his school has placed before him. One lowers himself gently into the cauldron of polemics called the "high school curriculum." Not only is this curriculum the usual rubric by which high school is defined—the place where you take math and English and health and those sorts of things—but the subjects' labels, and what lies behind them, tend to be the focus of reformers' attention. They are therefore controversial.

My argument here starts with an explanation of how the curriculum means quite different things, depending on one's position in a school—whether one is a theorist, a principal, a teacher, or a student. I will challenge the prevalent belief in "coverage," that the course of study which spreads over many areas is necessarily better than a more modest one. I will then turn to an analysis of a curriculum and its pedagogy, using the simple distinctions between skills, knowledge, and understanding that were recently sketched by Mortimer Adler in his *Paideia Proposal.*[10]

My basic conclusion is contained in the aphorism "Less is more." I believe that the qualities of mind that should be the goal of high school need time to grow and that they develop best when engaging a few, important ideas, deeply. Information is plentiful, cheap; learning how to use it is often stressful and absolutely requires a form of personal coaching of each student by a teacher that is neither possible in many schools today nor recognized as an important process.

For centuries, concerned scholars have asked what knowledge is most worthy, what schools should provide for the discipline and furniture of the student's mind, the skills he requires, and the substantive knowledge that he should grasp. Their answers, accepted even in our day, have often been elegant and have always been urgent. With few exceptions the assumption has been that the children of whatever time have poor discipline and little mental furniture. Typically, the scholar-planner surveys knowledge and categorizes it in such a way that it can be organized for teaching. This categorization is really an effort at distillation. What is the important framework of what is known and knowable? What of this is to be mastered by the young?

Nineteenth-century scholars, such as Yale's president Jeremiah Day, whose conceptions of discipline and furniture had great impact on the antebellum American college, presumed that a scholarly individual working alone, a person like one of them, could evolve these categories and draft the catechisms that would flow from them.[11] Due to the expansion of scholarly knowledge, to the growing and becoming humility of scholars, and to the increasingly sharp delineation of areas of knowledge into "subjects" or "disciplines," twentieth-century categorizers of the subject matter appropriate for advanced schooling have usually worked in committees, with the task of outlining the substance of the curriculum delegated to experts, subject by subject. The overarching frameworks now usually represent configurations of these subjects, the particular differences among various models being represented primarily by the time allotted to each.

This task of categorization fascinates scholars. It is fun to do. It allows a committee of academics to go back to its subject's roots, to debate what is fundamental, what is nice but secondary, and what is ornamental. It forces the group to do what its members tried to do, awkwardly, as beginning graduate students: to figure out the nature of their disciplines. Finally, creating an agreed-on outline is pleasing and reassuring.

The task of professional curriculum specialists is to orchestrate these outlines, to fashion them into a reasonable whole. This is usually expressed in terms of classes per week; that is, in time. The politics of this fashioning is usually fierce, and the consequence is ordinarily an overfull menu for teachers and students. At its best, the curriculum is a set of objectives that includes lists of skills, knowledges, and attitudes to be learned by the student, and detailed courses of study, subject by subject—a blend of priorities that are finely tuned and interrelated.

Few high school teachers have much awareness of this tuning and interrelationship. In good schools, the rationale is usually written out and made available for all to see, but few pay much attention to it, both because most curriculum statements are written in unspecific, and thus not very useful, language, and because there are few sanctions for not taking the schoolwide goals seriously. The academic momentum in most high schools is found in the particular departments, not in any central curriculum office, and the program of importance to a teacher is the work to be done in his or her subject. Other departments, if they appear to encroach on that department's time, are perceived as the enemy. In those schools—disproportionately, independent schools—where the overall curriculum is debated and voted on by a school's faculty as a whole, one can clearly see this conflict.[12] The issues are ones not of general education but of specific education, each specialty jockeying for the student's time. Not all of this jockeying is bad, because it has the effect of forcing departments to articulate, and thus to think through, what the ends and means of their subjects are. If a science department is going to bid to take more of the students' time, it must have a rationale more powerful than those of other departments, though votes, much as those in elected legislatures, tend ultimately to be political logrolling.

And so the high school teacher looks at the curriculum through the special lens of his or her subject. Within it, the familiar questions of discipline and furniture are again raised, with due deference to the promulgations of such higher authorities as systemwide curriculum directors, state mandates (such as for a course in United States history or government), and the indirect but often quite powerful pressures of scholars in their fields (for example, the professional scientists' call for instruction in computer techniques to be part of mathematics courses). A teacher or teachers sit down and look at the "time" they have and the textbooks required and available. They then slice the subject matter into even smaller pieces, down to clusters of days ("units") and individual days ("the daily lesson plan"). Sometimes central authorities do this detailed planning for the teachers, though my experience in observing classes suggests that these promulgations from "downtown" are usually as well ignored as they were well intended. However planned, the ultimate breakdown of each subject into daily lessons is largely cast in terms of material to be covered: introductory explanations of the binomial theorem, Act I, Scenes 2 and 3 from *Lear,* the Lincoln-Douglas debates, the characteristics of colloids, the adjusting of carburetors, the rules in volleyball. As this process of reduction to a class-by-class plan proceeds, the distance of each bit of planned instruction from the overall curriculum objectives of the high school, and often even of the department, get ever more remote, sometimes completely out of sight. If one looked at a coral reef made up of individual lesson plans, one might be hard pressed to recognize a curricular atoll shaped as originally intended.

This dysfunction between overall intentions and the reality of a teacher's progress day by day is not the result of a conspiracy. It merely reflects the fact that schoolwide curricular goals have far less claim on most teachers' professionalism than do the subjects that in college they were prepared to teach. There are few significant pressures operating in most high schools to encourage coherent collective work, and in few schools is there any time set aside for teachers to collaborate or to know what is happening in other classrooms, even those staffed by colleagues in the same department. The focus on content—we'll cover *Lear* during the first ten teaching days of October—is the only truly practical coordinating device that a department chairperson has when his or her teachers have but a few dozen minutes a week to discuss their collective work. The curricular world of a typical high school teacher is a world in a particular department, dominated by a sequence of things to be covered, week by week, day by day, very privately in particular classes.

This series of things to be covered is what hits Mark, the student. Unlike Jeremiah Day, or the general curricular specialist or the individual teacher, he can rarely make any sense of the whole. He does not know enough. The sequence of daily lessons and units follows no logic with which he can be expected to be familiar. The more cosmic concerns—the epistemologies, the designs for the disciplining and furnishing of the mind—usually are at a level of abstraction beyond his ken or his interest. Furthermore, few teachers bother to try to explain to him the broad reasons. His duty is to accept what is offered, on faith.

Consequently, the student sees the curriculum neither as a coherent whole nor as a set of academic imperatives arising from a cluster of subjects. The key question is more often "What do we have to know for the test?" than "What should we know?" And what is to be tested is usually factual material: what *is* in Act I, Scenes 2 and 3, of *Lear*. The teacher makes such an assignment because the claims on the sequence of classes he or she has just taught are less those of general qualities of mind than those of immediate specifics. Mastery of these specificities is what leads to a high academic record. As Jerome Bruner has explained, "The assignment of grades in school typically emphasizes the acquisition of factual knowledge, primarily because that is what is most easily evaluated; moreover, it tends to emphasize the correct answer, since it is the correct answer on the straightforward examination that can be graded as 'correct.' "[13] Thus, most high school students perceive the course of study to be a large collection of unambiguously specific data to be memorized and sometimes manipulated. While the data within some subjects, such as well-taught mathematics, may emerge with some sort of internal rationale, other data may seem disembodied and therefore inert. So I know that Franklin Roosevelt launched the New Deal; so what? These data may make good sense to the curriculum planner or to a teacher in a discipline, but they often appear inchoate to even the eager student and senseless to the docile student, save as grist for the examinations that ultimately provide credit toward a diploma.

Ask the graduate five years out about his or her high school years, and you will hear a recitation of specific incidents and descriptions of people. Few of the incidents took place as part of the regularities of a particular class. What made them memorable was their irregularity in a school world that valued consistency, predictability, and order. It is the people who are most remembered, the teachers, each usually disconnected from his or her subject. Few graduates can remember the books they read or the papers they wrote; few could pass the final examinations they took as high school seniors, because they have forgotten the specificities that got them through earlier. Was Roosevelt the New Deal or the Fair Deal? How *do* you use log tables? When they recall important things, these most usually center on personalities, those of teachers and other students. They had learned skills, of course, but the acquisition of these provokes little retelling. What sticks most indelibly are factors wholly absent from grand curricular and departmental plans: the character of the people at their high school and the unusual incidents experienced there.

In spite of this incongruity between philosophy and practice, one watches and listens in schoolrooms and sees and hears torrents of facts: formulae, procedures, lists, dates. They pour out of every classroom. Introductory biology classes teach the names of all the central branches of the plant and animal kingdoms. Chemistry labors through the elements. English covers the plots of stories and plays of major writers. Mathematics covers the basic procedures of the generally accepted core of the subject: arithmetic, algebra, geometry. History goes from the pharaohs to the latest election. The awesome bulk of a typical world history textbook is deadening and its myriad end-of-chapter questions daunting. Would anyone not in school pick up and read such a weighty tome? (Not students' parents, a point the young poignantly notice.) Who can retain all those facts, usually assembled by a committee of authors, which is evidence enough of the vast scale the volume represents? The exercise of memory and understanding implied by such books chills the hardiest of budding scholars.

The load of data purveyed in a typical high school year is staggering. Just because the facts roll out, of course, does not mean that they are either understood or retained. Most are ignored. A few may be deliberately identified as vital for the various tests, but many, if not most, of these facts mean little to the student.

Israel Scheffler made the good point that

> it does *not* follow that the student will *know* . . . new facts simply because he has been *informed* . . . Knowing requires something more than the receipt and acceptance of true information. It requires that the student earn the right to his assurance of the truth of the information in question. New *information,* in short, can be intelligibly conveyed by statements; new knowledge cannot.[14]

Almost fifty years before Scheffler wrote (and Scheffler was paraphrasing St. Augustine, who died in A.D. 430), John Dewey argued similarly:

> When education, under the influence of a scholastic conception of knowledge which ignores everything but scientifically formulated facts and truths, fails to recognize that primary or initial subject matter always exists as matter of an active doing . . . the subject matter of instruction is isolated from the needs and purposes of the learner, and so becomes just a something

to be memorized and reproduced upon demand . . . Only in education, never in the life of farmer, sailor, merchant, physician, or laboratory experimenter, does knowledge mean primarily a store of information aloof from doing . . . Knowledge which is mainly secondhand, other men's knowledge, tends to become merely verbal.[15]

In 1853, Charles Dickens saw as much, in a mocking way. His *Hard Times* opens, in a well-known section entitled "Sowing," with these famous words of Master Thomas Gradgrind, murderer (Dickens says) of the innocents: "Now, what I want is Facts. Teach these boys and girls nothing but Facts. Facts alone are wanted in life. Plant nothing else, and root out everything else . . . Stick to Facts, sir!"[16] By 1929, Alfred North Whitehead was saying the same thing, but in gentler form. "In the history of education, the most striking phenomenon is that schools of learning, which at one epoch are alive with a ferment of genius, in a succeeding generation exhibit merely pedantry and routine. The reason is, that they are laden with inert ideas. Education with inert ideas is not only useless: it is, above all things, harmful." He continued with an oft-quoted assertion: "Education is the acquisition of the art of the utilization of knowledge."[17] Jerome Bruner, writing in 1960, put it most simply. "The first object of any act of learning, over and beyond the pleasure it may give, is that it should serve us in the future. Learning should not only take us somewhere; it should allow us later to go further more easily."[18] Learning is not most accurately described as belonging to *us* in general; it must belong to *each* of us, as individuals. We can all be informed, but it is up to each one of us to know. To know facts is to have used them. As an ancient Chinese saying puts it, "I hear and I forget, I see and I remember, I do and I understand."

It takes time to *do* things, to use them in order to know them. Purveying information takes a fraction of that time. If there is pressure in a high school to cover ground, more time is spent informing and less on the process of individual knowing. The facts tumble forth.

The teacher in an inner-city high school's tenth-grade social studies class had chalked a time line on the blackboard, and the seventeen students present were copying it down when I arrived at this classroom, five minutes after the start of the period. The teacher was an energetic, articulate young liberal; he told me that thirty-five youngsters were assigned to this class and that this attendance of under 50 percent was about par for the course. He motioned me to a seat at the back of the classroom, next to a noticeably bright-eyed and trimly dressed boy, who sat intently working, his books and other academic accoutrements arranged around him. From his neatly labeled notebook, I learned that his name was Dennis. It was a warm day, and the windows were open. The clatter of the busy street just below and the faint redolence of engine exhaust were unremitting. The students in attendance were scattered around the room, most of them at desks along the side and back aisles.

The time line was roughly drawn and confusing to read. It started, as best I could ascertain, at 2300 B.C. and ran to the present. After some conversation about a recent TV documentary unrelated to the time line and carried on as the students were supposedly copying the material on the blackboard, the teacher turned and started working through the diagram, largely by means of questions that he asked and, after a pause, answered himself. The items singled out for inclusion on the chart had much to do with cities—the first in China, the first to install community plumbing ("2000 B.C."), "the founding of Mehenjo [sic], India" . . . He went on: "Rome starts to show up in seven-fifty B.C. . . ." There was "the golden age of Athens . . . Rome is now growing . . . Greece is basically in power." Some detours were tolerated, such as a disquisition on the use of horses in China, the fact that horsemeat is today a staple of dog food, and that many poor humans therefore eat horsemeat. There were details about "the great sewer of Rome," which was "only in the rich section." One student asked whether unicorns existed (I could see no reference to them on the time line); the teacher mentioned seeing a TV program in which unicorns' existence had been bruited, but asserted that as far as he knew "none are running around." In another context the class was told to "remember: this country acts on one key principle—make money." The only technically apt question from a student had to do with the great fire of Rome (which was on the time line). For how long had it burned? The teacher did not know the answer, and he acted embarrassed. He shouldn't have. Even Will Durant would not have been able to field every specific question that might have arisen from that time line.

I watched the students work at their copying, which took the full class period and was done concurrently with the teacher's lecturing and questioning. Some students were diligent; others whispered and passed notes. However, all had some sort of paper in front of them, on which they were, more or less, recording the diagram. There seemed to be no uniformity of note-taking or notebooks; some of the pieces of paper being used were tattered. One could guess that most of these "notes" would be lost before nightfall.

Dennis' bright eyes deadened as the class proceeded. His paper was as neat as his haircut and tennis shirt, but it was clear that he could barely write. It was as though he were copying nonsense ideographs. He persisted for a while and then slowly sank, head downward, asleep, propped up by his over-eight-hundred-page world history textbook, virtually none of which he could either read or understand. Roman fires and sewers, Chinese horses, Indian cities, dates B.C. and A.D., were light years from this youngster. Morpheus put him out of his misery.

With exactly ten minutes remaining, the teacher abruptly switched topics, to a required drill on a test question shortly to be asked on the new city proficiency examination. The topic was automobile accidents; the text was the pamphlet on driving behavior issued by the state department of motor vehicles. The teacher read the story of an accident and described the actions of a family involved in it. He then asked the students whether the family members had done the "correct" things, taken the "correct" steps. The students were engaged in this, and some half of them offered to answer the questions. Dennis woke up. The bell rang.

In his essay on the aims of education, Whitehead asked himself "how in our system of education we are to guard against . . . mental dryrot." He answered, "We enunciate two educational commandments. 'Do not teach too many subjects,' and again, 'What you teach, teach thoroughly.'"[19] In the light of this sensible stricture, one can fruitfully look at the subject matter of high school, the ideas, skills, and facts that are presented. One should do so humbly, recognizing that the student is the crucial actor. Whether we adults like it or not, he or she decides what has been purveyed and how it has been transformed in the purveying. Fascinating though the exercise of agenda-setting may be for academics, the assignment of areas of study and "subject matter content" in the abstract has limited utility. It is important, but never an end in itself. It is merely a point of departure.

3

Skills: The Importance of Coaching

AS PART of his *Paideia Proposal,* Mortimer Adler made a useful distinction between three spheres of learning: the development of intellectual skills, the acquisition of knowledge, and the enlargement of understanding of ideas and values.[20] These three spheres overlap, obviously, but they provide a sensible way to enter the complex labyrinth of the course of study.

"The skills to be acquired," Adler wrote, "are the skills of *reading, writing, speaking, listening, measuring, estimating,* and *calculating.*" I would add *seeing.* The visual, especially in our day, is as important as the "linguistic, mathematical, and scientific skills" that Adler highlighted.[21] While subject to moderately different definitions, these eight skills seem widely acceptable as staples of schooling at all levels, kindergarten through the university.

How one employs those skills is itself an intellectual craft. The different operations we use are numerous but so often employed as to be taken for granted. If young people are not taught these operations directly, their instincts save them, to some degree. However, reliance on instinct can be wasteful. Basic reasoning is usefully taught directly.

Take an exercise in inquiry—a common sequence of coming to know that humans use—and carefully pull apart its several steps. One starts, say, with *observation.* What is that? What is there?

What is this object or idea that I am trying to use or to understand? Perceiving it—seeing it, hearing it, imagining it in one's mind's eye—can be accomplished superficially or thoroughly. Seeing a problem accurately is a crucially important first step in its solution, obviously. An old friend of mine, a former physics teacher, tells of the exercise he gave his students on their first day of class. He issued each of them a wax candle and a match, told them to light the candle and then carefully observe it, and finally write down everything they saw. The mysteries of a commonplace flame slowly emerged, and the limitations of the naked eye were revealed. It was a memorable exercise, an antidote to careless observation.[22]

Ethnographers have long shown how observation can be systematic. Legal experts have demonstrated how a question and the way it is cast—in effect, how it has been observed—is the heart of much law. Observing is something we all do, but can be taught to do better. Whether one is observing a candle or a classroom, much of the trick is to decide what to record, which of the myriad data that one picks up is so important that its image should be retained. Inevitably, every person creates a screen through which impressions are strained. That is why people who observe the same candle describe it differently, even if they have made heroic efforts to eradicate any sort of editorializing. The flaming wick is ultimately described in different ways by different people. Each person's motives for looking will vary, also affecting observation. A student needs to be aware of these inevitable and important discrepancies and to gain not only self-consciousness in selecting from his observations but also some sense of how to hold his biases at a proper distance and some skill in selecting and arranging the words, orally and on paper, that accurately convey what he intends.

An educated person knows the difference between observation and inference, and the uses of each.[23] One can observe that a disproportionately high number of fatal accidents involve teen-age drivers, and hypothesize that because they are inexperienced drivers, teenagers get into a disproportionate number of fatal accidents. One can observe that a Gertrude Stein poem is in blank verse, and infer what she may have meant by the words in that poem. Everyday experiences show how important this distinction is. SAT scores have gone up two points. Some then hypothesize that because SAT scores have gone up, high schools must be getting tougher. The first statement is an observation, and the second a conclusion (of substantial dubiousness) drawn from the observation. Sloppy people confuse the two. Schools should help their students not to.

Sometimes the object being observed is another person's talking or writing. One needs to learn how to observe this object in such a way that one can express it in his own words. This form of precise writing helps a student gain skill at describing abstractions—another person's rendering of his observations of a candle—and leads him toward the skill of expressing his own abstractions, descriptions of his own ideas as he observes them.

Listening to someone talk and recasting later in one's own words what was heard can involve more than mere listening. An assignment was given a class of seniors (by a veteran principal who had continued part-time, regular English teaching) to listen to a speech given at the school by a distinguished citizen and then to write a paper, *not* on what the man said, but on what "messages" he gave beyond his speech, in ways other than talking. The problem was to observe and describe the speaker's visible signals—the way he stood, his frowns, his apparent concerns, his attitudes toward (perhaps) young people. The exercise was an exquisite one of observation and a demanding one of exposition.

To be successful, description has to be understandable to someone else. Definitions have to be precise, in a commonly shared terminology (words, numbers, or other symbols). Thus, the writing of one's own ideas must at some point be a disembodying exercise. The writer must stand apart from the observer, though they are one, and represent faithfully what he sees. This sounds easy, but teachers endlessly hear themselves saying, "But, George, what do you *mean?*" George may have an idea in there, an apt observation, but he cannot unlock it. Or he may have an imperfect idea, the beginning of a conception, in his head, one that needs further consideration. Whether the problem is merely one of unlocking George's idea or of helping him to shape it, the skill can be taught—and learned.

Much complex thinking requires *memory,* most usually of a temporary sort. Most important reasoning requires juggling variables, and in order constantly to work with them, one has to have them in mind. For example, observe that wilting cauliflower plant. I can describe it. I can also describe the physical condition of the soil, the mineral content of the soil, the frequency and amount of rain and of artificial watering, the existence or nonexistence of parasites that may enjoy feeding on cauliflower plants, the amount of sunny weather, the extent of shade in which the cauliflower plant finds itself, the variety of seed from which the plant sprung, and more. In order to find a way to keep that plant from wilting any further, I need to examine and analyze each of these variables, separately and in combination. I have to remember what the variables are.

Humans have long used crutches for their limited memories. Writing replaced the arduous and chancy task of passing down traditions by memorizing oral stories. Note cards, notebooks, flash cards, TelePrompTers, are all memory-easing devices. The computer extends our memory to a wondrous degree. With its banks at our disposal, filled by us with multitudes of data too numerous to put into our human memory, we can juggle variables to an extent heretofore unthinkable.

Yet we do not walk around with computers on our hips, and most decisions are too trivial to justify working up a computer program and are simple enough to be addressed with but a few variables. One can learn to solve such problems from the experience of living, but schools can help adolescents to do it efficiently. Many people would see that wilting cauliflower and pour water on it, neither cognizant of explanations other than parching for its sad state nor able to sort out the other options.

One can learn how to remember things. A list with some sort of internal logic is easier to recall than a list of random words or numbers. A person remembers a list that he prepares for himself better than a list someone has prepared for him. "Ownership" of an idea—the ability to retrieve and use it—assists in its retention. Schools should provide students with experience with their memories.

Observing a condition, accurately describing it, and getting mental control of its complexities and variables, bring one to a next stage, that of *analysis and resolution.* This involves the crafty art of getting rid of the silly variables. A Chrysler Cordoba is not a better car because it has a name reminiscent of old Spain. Analysis also involves identifying and ordering the most important aspects of a problem.

It involves identifying what is still unknown or unknowable. (Maybe the packet of cauliflower seeds was flawed.) It then involves drawing inferences. (Perhaps the fact that I planted this cauliflower in hard clay is why it wilts.) And in this process of using one's imagination, one tries one idea, then another, a sequence of trials and errors, cuts and fits. It involves simple logic arising from one's theory. (If I carefully loosen up the soil around this plant and add peat moss, then it may be restored to health.) It may involve inductive reasoning. (Given this constellation of facts about this plant, other plants, and this garden, it seems likely that this theory about gardens—that vegetables grow poorly in shaded, clay-soil sites—may be plausible.) And it may involve deductive reasoning. (These other cauliflowers, precisely similar in most respects to the wilted one, but clearly different in that they were planted in rich loam in a sunny area, seem to be doing better, leading me to predict a successful crop from them.) And it may involve the extension of deduction into a hypothetical realm. (If next year I move my garden to a sunnier site, add special nutrients to the soil, and use a different strain of cauliflower seeds, one more suited to this climate, then I will, in all likelihood, gain a magnificent crop.)

Employing the jargon of logic and practicing what some call "critical thinking" can be intimidating. Effective people, however, use the processes for which these are the labels all the time, in all sorts of combinations, and apparently by instinct. Of course, instinct is not the most of it, at all. One learns these processes, and schools can make this learning efficient. To do so, they must make them explicit and have the students practice with them, as with any skill.

It is in this context that one sees the special importance of writing. One learns complex thinking by practice. There are few certain, easily applied rules for effective thinking; there are, rather, principles with which one wrestles. No subject matters or situations are ever precisely the same, and no two people ever see an issue—even the same simple flaming candle—in quite the same way. The way one learns to think well is through disciplined, self-conscious trial and error. One thinks, one imagines, one analyzes those ideas, one tests them, and then thinks again. Obviously, unless one has a record of the sequence of one's thoughts, it is difficult to review or analyze them after the fact. A written essay is such a record, and it stays, indelible and unchanging, allowing for dissection. B. F. Skinner has said that learning is behaving; the written record of that behavior is the tracks of the unfolding ideas exposed.[24] For this reason, exercises in writing should be the center of schooling. Those who treat writing merely as a form of casual communication, perhaps to be replaced in this modern world by the telephone, miss the point. Writing is not only an end in itself; it is a means by which a person can delve into his or her mind.

Then in the sequence of thinking there is *application,* the synthesis of the analyzed elements, options, or variables. Application implies *use,* "doing" the idea. Nothing sets learning more firmly in our minds than its use. (What teacher would not admit that he *really* understood his subject only after he had had to teach it?) Given all this review of my wilting cauliflower, what will I now do? This stage is painful for many. We are less vulnerable when we are merely kicking around the options, without ever coming to any conclusion. I could water the cauliflower, but on the other hand a bit of mulch might just help. Most of the time, whether with quiet decisions or cataclysmic ones, we can rarely predict precisely what will happen. A decision involves a leap of faith, in gardening and in all sorts of situations, humble and not so humble. We decide that the problem of a balky engine is in the carburetor, but in replacing that part we cannot be 100 percent sure that the automobile will now assuredly purr. Harry S Truman and his Manhattan Project personnel were not at all certain the Hiroshima bomb would in fact go off, nor were they precisely sure what would happen if it did. Resolution and action involve risk. Students in good schools face this all the time. What is the answer—*your* answer—to this mathematical problem? There is no "right" answer to the character of Willy Loman, but what is *your* reading of him? There is no "right" way to categorize people, but what is *your* best assessment of a useful typology of this school's student body? One learns to take a stand.

Learning to estimate—to make a shrewd guess—assists this process of coming to conclusions. It is most visibly helpful in mathematics. You don't know the precise answer yet, but in what range would it likely be? With what we now know, it is difficult accurately to categorize this situation, but what are the likely limits of the probabilities? Some teachers resist encouraging estimating, thinking it mere guessing. And guessing, they reason, is what schools are trying to lessen. However, there is an obvious, important difference between making a random guess and positing an informed estimate. The latter is a critical skill that we all need.

Thinking, of course, is rarely as neat as this observing-recording-imagining-analyzing-resolving paradigm suggests. Nor does all useful thinking flow in such a step-by-step sequence; indeed, most complex thinking forms a loop, each "conclusion" provoking one's imagination toward fresh observations. Throughout, we use our intuitions. Jerome Bruner, among psychologists the most persuasive advocate of intuitive thinking, put it well in his *Process of Education:*

> In contrast to analytic thinking, intuitive thinking characteristi-
> cally does not advance in careful, well-defined steps. It tends
> to involve maneuvers based seemingly on an implicit perception
> of the total problem . . . Usually intuitive thinking rests on
> familiarity with the domain of knowledge involved and with
> its structure, which makes it possible for the thinker to leap
> about, skipping steps and employing short cuts in a manner
> that requires a later rechecking of conclusions by more analytic
> means . . . Unfortunately, the formulation of school learning
> has somehow devalued intuition.[25]

Schools that always insist on the right answer, with no concern as to how a student reaches it, smother the student's efforts to become an effective intuitive thinker. A person who is groping to understand, and is on a fruitful but somewhat misdirected track, needs to learn how to redirect his thoughts and to try a parallel but somewhat different scheme. Simply telling that person that he is wrong throws away the opportunity to engage him in questions about his logic and approach. Well-directed questions by teachers can promote ever more effective intuition, albeit often by a process that is difficult to ascertain. Nonetheless, like aspirin, whose precise functioning we do not understand, it works.

Schools value strictly orderly thinking. The computer, with its special form of algorithmic "reasoning," reinforces this predilection. Some adults in schools dismiss all other kinds of thinking as playing around, making mudpies. For them, intuition and imagination are not really serious pursuits. The trial-and-error procedures involved are messy. Accordingly, they get short shrift in far too many schools, with sad costs to the individuals and their communities.

In sum, these skills—reading, writing, speaking, listening, measuring, estimating, calculating, seeing—and the basic modes of imagining and of reasoning should be at the core of high school work. They should pervade all subjects offered and be visibly and reviewably part of the school program.

How are skills learned? By experience. How, then, are they best taught? By *coaching*.

I, the teacher, can tell you rules for writing—grammar, forms of felicitous phrasing, types of argument. I can show you examples of good and bad writing, and with the aid of an overhead projector I can demonstrate for you how to analyze a piece of work. However, until *you* write and I criticize *your* writing, your expository skills and the thinking behind them lie latent. You may know in the abstract about how to write, but you don't know in practice how to do it, at least not very well.

So it is in athletics. I can tell you how to throw the javelin. I can show you movies of people throwing the javelin, and I can analyze these movie athletes, the good and the bad. All this does help you become a javelin thrower. But until you pick the instrument up and hurl it, the whole process is an abstraction. Until I can point out your particular failings and skills (ideally, on a videotape playback), I cannot help you very much to become a competent javelin thrower. You throw. I criticize, suggesting some possible improvements. You throw again. And again I criticize. This is how skills in a strong athletic program are shaped. The analogies to intellectual training are powerful and apt. (Ironically, it is the athletic coach, often arrogantly dismissed by some academic instructors as a kind of dumb ox, unworthy of being called a real teacher, who may be a school's most effective teacher of skills.)

One fall I had an eleventh-grade girl named Susan, newly arrived at our school, enroll in my advanced history class. She had transferred to our school from a suburban public high school of substantial reputation, and on this basis she had convinced her adviser that her enrollment in what was primarily a seminar for seniors was appropriate. One of the key, culminating exercises in this course was the writing of a fifteen-to-twenty-five-page analytic paper. As even the swiftest scholars in my classes had had little experience in handling an assignment of such scope, I described the exercise at considerable length at the start of the course and announced that each student, by the middle of the term, was to turn in an outline of what he or she proposed to do. The students usually greeted the prospect of such a paper with apprehension and peppered me with dozens of questions. Susan, however, kept still.

On the day the outlines were due, none came from Susan, and at the end of class I asked her why. Consternation, embarrassment, welling tears. I suggested that we talk about it, later and privately, when other students could not eavesdrop. When we did meet, the problem spilled out. She had never before been asked to identify a topic, frame a question, develop a theme, and analyze it on paper, at least in any sophisticated form. In effect, she had never been asked to write a serious essay. She didn't know how to start, but she was stubbornly, if tearfully, game to try. We started to talk about possible topics, with my asking about her interests in the area of the course and her answering. Some possible subjects emerged. We recorded them on a blackboard. I showed her some easy ways to outline an argument. I suggested that she draw up outlines for two or three of the topics and then make a second appointment.

Susan returned in three days with one topic, the one she most cared about, fully worked out. I asked her to copy it on the blackboard, and then we went at it, I questioning and suggesting, she suggesting and rearranging. Sections of the planned paper were moved forward and back, lines of argument were arranged, areas where she needed to do some library research uncovered. We talked for about twenty minutes; then she copied down the final diagram from the blackboard and promised to work over a fresh draft and give it to me. It arrived the next week, wooden, unimaginative, but sturdy.

In this course, my colleagues and I always urged students to turn in a first draft of a paper for our review. Indeed, we told them that we would read and criticize several drafts, if these were responsibly done, with all final papers ultimately to be held to the same standard. That is, if a student wanted help, he or she could start early, turn out more drafts, and get them criticized, thereby benefiting from them without risk of penalty. This gave the students an incentive to take advantage of our coaching. In Susan's case, I insisted on seeing a first draft. It came in, a bit later than it should have. I read it, wrote comments and suggestions on it, and talked with her privately for ten minutes. It was as wooden as the outline, but still sensible and sturdy. Her final essay was some twenty pages long and solidly done, a thoroughly satisfactory paper. Without coaching, however, it would never have been done at all. The distance between a paper in the abstract and her paper assigned in my course had been too great, and her apprehension (and self-inflicted humiliation in a course shared with some loud-mouthed, confident-seeming students) was paralyzing. My total time spent in coaching her individually and reading her work was barely more than fifty minutes, spread over a period of three weeks. It was well-spent, crucial time for her development, both as a young student and as a person whose confidence had been shaky.

In this personal example, one can note some conditions critical for coaching. There was agreement on and understanding between teacher and student about the academic task that the paper represented. The student was as keen to succeed at it as she was frightened by it. However, it was not wholly out of her reach. Most important, she had time during her school day to connect with me, I had time to connect with her, and there was a free place, with a blackboard, for the consultation. Few teachers and few students, alas, have such luxuries. *Coaching absolutely requires them.*

4

Knowledge: Less Is More

THE SECOND SPHERE of learning discussed in the *Paideia Proposal* is the acquisition of knowledge, the things a student learns to know. The United States Constitution, what it says. The nature of the arguments in the Federalist Papers, what some of the dilemmas of popular democracy are. How the heart works, and what hurts it. The character of Iago and other archetypes. That the product of whatever number and zero is always zero.

The pedagogy here is *telling*. Teachers explain things; they, textbooks, films, and analogous paraphernalia furnish information. If students are interested and orderly (often a tall order for adolescents), many can be taught at once, in lecture theaters. Telling is cost effective, far more so than coaching. That is why it is so popular in schools.

The extent of items worth knowing is infinite and would be ordered differently by different people. A person interested in computer programming would want to know more mathematics and logic than would a prospective home economist, whose interest would lean in the directions of biology and social science. How to select is a critical issue.

As I have earlier pointed out, administrators usually finesse the issue of course content selection in high schools by adopting the conventional frameworks of subjects and not thereafter paying much attention to what is in fact offered within each. The central office administrators or school principals may assert that their schools "require four years of English." However, if one asks, "*What* English?" the answers flow slowly indeed, usually prefaced with the sensible observation that that is an issue for the teachers to decide. So one then asks the teachers and often gets a jumble of answers, the confusion sometimes explained away by the need for each teacher to teach from his or her strength, to cover ground familiar to each (again, a sensible argument, within limits), and by the lack of time provided by the school for the English teachers carefully to decide what they will do (an argument often unhappily true).

There are four general things that one can say about the choice of subject matter in high schools. First, if students have yet to meet fundamental standards of literacy, numeracy, and civic understanding, their programs should focus *exclusively* on these. Some critics will argue that the school must go beyond these subjects to hold the interest of the pupils. However, doing so would be a disservice to the students; a fourteen-year-old who is semiliterate is an adolescent in need of intensive, focused attention. Furthermore, most typical high school subjects require these fundamentals as preconditions. One cannot study history very well if one cannot read, nor can one get far in algebra if one cannot add or subtract. And furthermore, these three basic areas can be taught with all sorts of materials appropriate for the interest of older students. To say that reading, ciphering, and learning about practical government are somehow beneath a young teen-ager is absurd, an evasion by people who cannot see the importance of adapting the curriculum and the school to the student, rather than the reverse. The common practice of handing an eight-hundred-page world history textbook to tenth-graders like Dennis, who can barely read at all, is as cruel as it is wasteful.

Second, choices are matters of taste and of the priorities sensed at a particular time. Only a hundred years ago much of the academic establishment had great doubt about the importance in secondary school studies of physical and biological science and of modern languages and little doubt about the central role of Latin and Greek. What is essential to one time may be anachronistic to another. Yet some cultural traditions doggedly persist. *Huckleberry Finn* may be banned in some quarters, but as a staple of high school work it has persevered. So has Shakespeare. The causes of the Civil War. The various "systems" of the human body. Fractions. The momentum behind these and many other academic traditions is substantial. Few communities could break from them, even if determined pressure groups tried to force them to do so.

Given these conditions, the questions about choice of material then shift to a second level, to subject matter about which there is less traditional consensus. *Catcher in the Rye* or *Silas Marner?* Calculus or probability and statistics? Organic or inorganic chemistry? An outside reading assignment by Howard Zinn or one by Oscar Handlin? Mandatory instruction in birth control? The Bible as literature or as a holy book? Happily, few communities can achieve a consensus on these kinds of issues. American values vary too richly for that. Such being the case, what do schools do? The only sensible answer is for them to make choices available, to give students, teachers, and their families the opportunity to follow their preferences. There are limits here, obviously, especially in small communities, but reasonable compromises are possible. The alternative—a course of study mandated as the result of decisions reached through special interest politics and unrelieved majority rule—is both insensitive educationally (no one of us, including an adolescent, learns much from things that, forced on us, we resent) and un-American (the tradition of minority rights is an important aspect in American liberty).

A third consideration in the choice of subject matter is that it should support the students' learning of skills. An English program that assigns only short stories would give students little scope either in learning to observe and analyze a variety of means of written expression or in exploring models for them to use in their own writing. A science course, built on sheer memory work, that never gives examples of or experience in scientific inquiry would be as stunted as a course that engages in some sort of disembodied, abstract problem-solving that demands of the students no command of precise knowledge.

The fourth consideration is that the subject matter chosen should lead somewhere, in the eyes and mind of the student. This means that it must connect to wherever that student is rooted—his experi-

111

ence—and that it promise to take him toward an important place. It must be ultimately useful and patently interesting to him, at the time it is learned and in the future.

Setting a beginning algebra student a problem that requires a quadratic equation for its solution is shortsighted, to say the least. One should not assign the prologue of the *Canterbury Tales* in Middle English to a group of hostile ninth-graders who are reading at a fifth-grade level. One should not assign Nancy Drew novels to twelfth-grade students ready for the English Advanced Placement Examinations of the College Board. However, and unfortunately, if one has a student who is doggedly dutiful and wants to do well, one can assign him either Chaucer in the original or Nancy Drew novels and get away with it, at least in the sense that the student will go along with the teacher. The cost will be that if the assignment is inappropriate, he may not learn much. Dutiful students, determined to earn their diplomas and eager to please their teachers and parents, will wade through what to them is irrelevance, though this exercise tests their loyalty, frustrates them, sends them a false signal about the subject under study, and wastes their time.

A teacher should try to start where the student is. This imperative is susceptible to misinterpretation and, as a result, ridicule. A mean-minded cynic may say, "The kids are interested only in sex and rock music, so you should assign *The Joy of Sex* and take field trips to hear the Grateful Dead." He may go on: The kids are soft, they just want easy things, like comic books. If you push them, they won't be interested. The only interested student will be the unchallenged student.

Like most criticism, even of the extreme kind, there is some truth in this. Like adults, many adolescents *are* interested in sex and rock, as well as in a lot of other things. Much of great literature is about sex, and its ordinary handmaiden, love; and rock connects readily with a full world of music. Sex and rock or love and art? A teacher does not have to be tasteless or frivolous when dealing with these themes. There is plenty of love and sex in *Romeo and Juliet* and plenty of wonder in all forms of music.

Aha! says the cynical critic, but how do I get sex and rock into my mathematics class? You don't, obviously. However, it goes without much saying that adolescents are interested in many, many things besides sex and rock, and you will have to find and use these. Sometimes it is not easy. The more abstract the subject, the more difficult is the task of connecting it to students' experience.

Some teachers face hard odds. I observed an instructor of English in a juvenile prison. His class of eight youngsters ran in age from the early teens to probably eighteen, but only one or two of the boys present were minimally literate. All were hostile, wary, defeated. The teacher knew that the one subject that interested them the most—beyond even sex and rock or what have you—was themselves. They would struggle with words as long as those words were autobiographical. Accordingly, he had distributed forms for simple personal résumés, and asked the students to fill them in. Most tried, painfully. So they did work at writing; if they stayed with this teacher long enough, they would have moved to autobiographical sentences, then paragraphs.[26]

Our cynical critic's second objection was that students do not like to be challenged. No one of any age likes his word rejected, his motive questioned, or his solutions proved inaccurate. But most people want to be taken seriously and to enjoy the sweetness of success at something they believed they could not do. That is, they like to meet challenge. Most people will accept and use criticism if they can see some point in it (I believe that I will swim faster if I change my stroke as you request) and if they know the criticism is of their actions and not of themselves as people (your backstroke is terrible, but you're O.K. as a person). The implications of this are as simple to say as they are often hard to do. Stretch a student, but not so much that he will repeatedly fail. If he can see that he is getting somewhere, he will accept your challenges.

Holding a student's commitment requires convincing him that the subject matter over which he is toiling is genuinely usable—if not now, then in the future. There is a limited amount he can master, so the material given him should be that which provides or can provide needed knowledge in the future. It must, in a word, be generative. One learns something in order to learn more. One studies *Plessy* v. *Ferguson* not because it happened as much as because it raises continuing issues about equality and because the way one analyzes this Supreme Court case may apply to analyses of future Supreme Court cases. Learning something simply because it is there is nice but barren. Whitehead felt that much in the curriculum of his day was there because it was there, and for no other reason. He spoke of

> the fatal disconnection of subjects which kills the vitality of our modern curriculum. There is only one subject-matter for education, and that is Life in all its manifestations. Instead of this single unit, we offer children—Algebra, from which nothing follows; Geometry, from which nothing follows; Science, from which nothing follows; History, from which nothing follows; a Couple of Languages, never mastered; and lastly, most dreary of all, Literature, represented by plays of Shakespeare, with philological notes and short analyses of plot and character to be in substance committed to memory. Can such a list be said to represent Life? [27]

Jerome Bruner has made a strong case for "structure" as the basis for generative subject matter. He argued that "grasping the structure of a subject is understanding it in a way that permits many other things to be related to it meaningfully. To learn structure, in short, is to learn how things are related." He presented his point in several ways. "Understanding fundamentals makes a subject more comprehensible . . . A good theory is the vehicle not only for understanding a phenomenon now but also for remembering it tomorrow."[28] If we have a general pattern in mind, we can recall its various pieces more readily than if we have merely a random list of such pieces. Structure moves beyond memory: "An understanding of fundamental principles and ideas . . . appears to be the main road to adequate 'transfer of training.' "[29] Learn how a system works in general, and you can easily estimate how particular examples of that system operate. A clear example of this is found in the theorems of geometry, but the principle applies widely.

All this is readily believable. Give me a useful law, a student will agree, and I can apply it to specific situations in the future. But teaching fundamentals can be difficult, because their structure is often abstract. One therefore starts with the specifics, with stories out of which will eventually emerge the structure of plot and form. One gets students to "mess around" with batteries, bulbs, and wires before giving them the theories of electric conduction.[30] The laws evolve from experience with the specifics, and the specifics may have an intrinsic interest that will catch and hold the attention of students.

Anything in life can be used as the stuff of learning, or at the very least as an entry to the stuff of learning. So-called vocational education should be looked at from this point of view. There are those who say that all training for specific jobs should be removed from the course of study. People must at some point learn the specifics for their jobs, it goes without saying, and with few exceptions the most common, efficient, and up-to-date way of providing training is on those jobs.[31] The focus of schools should be on general intellectual powers—which are, after all, an important aspect of vocational preparation, for more than entry-level skills. It is nonetheless important to state that training in school for specific jobs may be the most efficient means of connecting the lives of some students to the more abstract employment of a mature mind.

All subject matter should be fuel for the travel to more subject matter. The details of every school curriculum must meet this test. There are few universal answers, though. How subject matter is generated depends on where a *particular* student or group of students is. The construction of the subject matter of any curriculum is a task of cabinetmaking, not of prefab carpentry. The pieces *have* to fit the conditions peculiar to each school. Master plans for cities, states, and the nation that standardize instruction are certain to be inefficient: no one set of procedures can conceivably serve most students well.

5

Understanding: The Importance of Questions

THE THIRD SPHERE of learning described in the *Paideia Proposal* is understanding, the development of powers of discrimination and judgment. In a way, this sphere overlaps the other two. The skills of analysis, of estimation, and of observation, and a grasp of generative subject matter, all demand judgment. Yet there is more to the process of understanding. One can deductively prove that some things are true and others are false. One can predict that in, say, three out of four instances, such-and-such will happen. But one cannot ascertain, as a universal matter, that some quite different things are good or bad, better or worse. Which is "better" for a proven purpose, United States–style constitutional federalism or United Kingdom–style parliamentary democracy? Why may Woody Allen's *Annie Hall* be a "better" or "worse" movie than *Gone With the Wind?* When is euthanasia acceptable? No teacher can give a student precise answers to such questions, as sure, for example, as that the speed of light is faster than the speed of the fastest tortoise that ever lived.

When issues of this sort, humble or not, arise in everyday life, which is frequently, the best one can hope for, before reaching a conclusion, is that all the key questions have been asked. Is the person for whom euthanasia is suggested in a coma? Mentally incompetent? Clear-minded? Is a question of suicide or solicited murder one about which a terminally ill person can be judicious?

Schools can help students gain experience in asking such questions and get them in the habit of doing so. Sometimes the issues come from daily life. So you think Pamela is a freak and therefore no good. Why? What's a freak? Do you know she's a druggie? Are all druggies bad? Is it any of your business to judge her? And so forth. More elevated are aesthetic judgments, why *Antigone* may tell us more about human fundamentals than does *General Hospital.*

There is much that must be tentative in this sphere. There are no secure rights or wrongs and therefore there can be no true/false or multiple-choice tests. Furthermore, people, including adolescents, may protest, with a good deal of justice, that they are entitled to their own opinions. It takes courage to agree with that and in the same breath insist that their personal opinions must emerge from a process of rigorous, thorough self-questioning. Asking questions of someone about his judgments may provoke deep anger, since those questions may invade the person's possibly ill-considered but emotional values. A person who holds an opinion in high passion may be a person who has some illogic or prejudice to hide. One treads this turf cautiously, but good teachers must so tread. It is not to tell the person what to believe as much as it is to habituate him to asking tough questions before he constructs the belief.

Opportunities spring up almost daily. Mr. Suslovic, Mark's social studies teacher, was using the incident at the basketball game, albeit clumsily. Many flow from literature and works of art. The problematic character of Hemingway's old fisherman, the releasing exuberance of *Messiah,* the terror in a Kollwitz print: such are the stimulations toward learning that good teachers put before students.

Understanding is more stimulated than learned. It grows from questioning oneself or from being questioned by others, such as teachers. Questioning is a far more difficult form of pedagogy for teachers than are coaching and telling, because it is the least predictable. Coaching for skills is usually focused on a piece of work that gives it clear limits, and the teller can control his material. If I'm lecturing on life in the Northern States during the Civil War and feel poorly informed about how the costs of the conflict were being met, I can tread lightly on that financial ground and concentrate on the details of the military campaigns. In a discussion, however,

I have no such luxury, even if I am the prime questioner. A sequence of questions may force me to discuss the Northern war debt, the various and often unsalubrious moneymen, and Lincoln's economic tightrope. Questioning develops its own pattern. A teacher cannot be sure how it may twist or turn, because it depends on the students' perceptions of the topic under debate.

In my twelfth-grade history classes, my college-bound, largely upper-middle-income students regularly stumbled over and were disturbed by the issue of social class. I had discovered that an early chapter in Edward Banfield's *The Unheavenly City,* entitled "The Imperatives of Class," was a good reading assignment to set off a consideration of the concept.[32] It is a challenging piece, arguing that "class" is most usefully defined on the basis of people's behavior in regard to their own futures. An upper-class person invests against distant, often abstract goals, Banfield contends; he may, for example, engage in many years of costly, grinding education in order eventually to become a surgeon. If the interest rates are right, an upper-class person will tie his spare money up in a four-year certificate of deposit to gain a substantial ultimate profit. A lower-class person, on the other hand, lives for the present. If school is not fun, play hookey. If you have money, spend it. Banfield argues not that all people who have low incomes are "lower class," but that most of them are. Their behavior inevitably leaves them so. Banfield's chapter paints with subtleties and several key reservations, but the foregoing blatant summary is what my students generally remembered.

Inevitably some of my students arrived at class angry. I would start by asking them for definitions of social class. The largest percentage of the students would keep very quiet: "social class," surprisingly, is a concept rarely studied seriously in high school. Then some constructive soul would proffer the notion that class was related to income, with rich folk being upper class and poor folk being lower class. Is that Banfield's definition? I would ask. No. Well, what is it? At this point, some student would explode. (I must have taught the lesson this way over a dozen times, and an exploder was always there.) It isn't right to classify, particularly the way Banfield does. Why not? It puts people into boxes. It sets up harmful stereotypes. It hurts people. I don't want anyone to put me into some kind of a pigeonhole. The exploder would almost always cause the other, silent ones to complain: It isn't fair. It's un-American.

I would counter: What about the jocks and the freaks and the nerds and the preppies that you all label here at school? Nervous laughter. Is *your* "class" system fair? I'd ask. No, some would say. You mean it isn't accurate? Yes, it's accurate. I would continue: Is it classification on the basis of people's behavior? Yes. Is that fair? Yes. No.

Someone at that point would ask why it is necessary ever to have categories. Why run the risk of harmful stereotyping? Why, indeed, I would reply. My students would ultimately stumble back to Banfield to see whether a characterization of clusters of individuals did or did not help them, at a general level, to understand how groups of humans seemed to interact and get on with their lives.

Throughout this exercise, my role was that of questioner, never teller. The objective was to provoke the students to see an important idea in its complexity and to develop an understanding of it. As with coaching, classes for questioning must be small.[33] A large class means that students are just an audience. A student's judgment is poorly honed if he merely listens to a dialogue between a teacher and a fellow student. Questioning requires a seminar format, a circle of fewer than twenty people. There must be give-and-take, with the teacher being a participant as well as leader and in no sense a source of "answers." Again, and alas, seminar formats, with classes of twenty or fewer students, are simply impossible in some schools, with the result that the effective teaching of a student to make judgments never takes place.

6

Character: Decency

No school can dodge the issues raised by the conduct and interactions among its students and teachers, however sticky these issues may be. Students learn much from the way a school is run.

The principal at the underfinanced and troubled city school that I visited was a resourceful man, proud of his ability to keep going within a system that neglected his school. The classroom and hallway walls of the building needed paint, window frames were rotting, ceiling tiles had broken away. A recently repaired roof was already leaking; even an amateur could see how sloppily the job had been done. But the principal, a determined white man in a now all-black school, kept things going. He took me on a tour of his building, and while he was telling me of the games he had to play with the "downtown" authorities over his budget, we happened on the school nurse. He asked her to tell me of a recent incident—and proceeded to do so himself, as an example of how one has to husband a school's limited monies.

It seemed that a girl student had fainted in class and had been carried, semiconscious, to the nurse's station by other students. Apparently she had recently had an illegal, botched abortion and was bleeding. The nurse called the principal, saying that the young student needed to be taken to a hospital at once. The principal told her that nothing should be done until the parents were called.

The nurse got on the telephone, but there was no answer at the parents' home. She tried the grandparents. Again, no answer. The nurse repeatedly insisted that the young student be sent immediately to the hospital, but the principal knew that if anyone on the school staff called the ambulance, the school would be charged for it. However, if the school called the police and if the officers replying to the call felt that the student needed to go to the hospital, they would telephone for the ambulance, and the police department would be billed. So the principal told the nurse to call the police. She did. The officers came, observed the young person, and called an ambulance.

The school had avoided a financial charge. The youngster had waited for an hour, bleeding on the nurse's cot, before being taken away to the hospital. The principal had an unhappy story about modern management necessities with which to inform the visitor. The nurse said nothing. What the young student's friends learned from this episode is sad and ugly.

Any school of integrity, public or private, secular or religious, should try to help its students become decent people. This is an appropriately limited objective: the values that a young man or woman learns to adopt should come from many quarters, among which the family is prominent and the school of lesser influence. *Decency* denotes satisfaction of a widely understood and accepted standard and, as such, it is limited. Going beyond such a threshhold standard—that is, setting schools on a course to turn out philosopher-kings or moral revolutionaries—is as repugnant as it would be impossible.

Decency in the American tradition (obviously the creation more of our Judeo-Christian than of our republican tradition) comprises fairness, generosity, and tolerance. Everyone should get a fair shake. People who are in trouble or who for whatever reason are weak deserve a special hand; the big guys should not force their way on the little guys. It is difficult to imagine a citizen who would seriously quarrel with any school that tried to stand for these values and to persuade its students to make these values operative parts of their character. At the same time, it is difficult to find many schools today that both formally articulate decency as an aim and precisely outline how the students can achieve it.

While most high schools' formal statements of purpose identify "ethical conduct" and "citizenship" as goals for their schools, they shy away from specific programs toward these ends or even from carefully defining the words these statements employ. When pressed, many public school people assert that "morals" are not the schools' business but, rather, that of the family. The probable inconsistency between this assertion and the goal statement of their schools is dismissed with a shrug. Private school people, particularly those in church schools, tend to be more aggressive about the goal, though for many of them the line between religious doctrine and ethical conduct is seriously blurred, begging clarification.

Sorting out the problems associated with schooling and character illumines the reason that Americans have long favored silence or at least ambiguity on these matters.[34] Nonetheless, the fact is that one goes to school in order to *change,* whatever metaphor—growth, maturation, socialization—one uses. A student is to be different as a consequence of the experience. I often started my own courses for high school seniors by telling them explicitly that my purpose was to make them different, in effect to alter them. Their reaction was a mixture of indignation and incredulity. They resented my objective, missing the point that my only function as a teacher was to extend their knowledge and thus "change" them, and they could not believe the baldness of my assertion. They usually pushed me and howled a bit about it, not fully sure of the extent to which I might be putting them on. They were unused to being bluntly told what a teacher's objectives were. Ultimately, they agreed that maybe it *would* be O.K. for me to try to change them, but I ought to keep it quiet.

Knowledge, skills, and understanding do affect personality: there is no escaping this fact. No one remains unaffected when one gains new insights and new competences and thus new confidence. For schools to pretend somehow that they are merely in the business of filling independent and autonomous skulls with benign and neutral substance is silly. There are many influences on the development of a young person's personality, of course, and school is only one. But it can be a powerful one, especially for people who are inexperienced and often uncertain of their values—and many adolescents certainly exhibit these vulnerabilities. An honest school faces the issue of how it wishes to affect personalities, what values it wishes to promote or at least to live by in school.

Some will say that the school should seek nothing even as bland as "decency" and should promote only open-mindedness, attitudes of questing, dispassion, and concerned neutrality. However, a wholly open mind is dangerous, and probably unattainable in any case.[35] What a teacher selects to "tell" in a class is an exercise in values. If one refers in a social studies lesson to Native Americans as "them" and implies that the first settlers of the American West were Europeans, one is saying a great deal. Describing the Indians as the (likely) first of many human immigrants to these continents sends a quite different message. The way a biology teacher treats life in class— whether, for example, live frogs are purchased and pithed in quantity for students to dissect—signals important values. Mocking the squeamishness and reserve of students who do not want to kill frogs can deeply affect a young student. How sacred is life? Apparently it is all right to kill a steer for hamburg and all wrong deliberately to run over a squirrel on the road. It is acceptable to kill an enemy soldier, but not a noncombatant enemy, unless by killing noncombatants one can save one's own people's lives. The verbal wrestlings over the morality of the Tokyo firebombing and the Hiroshima and Nagasaki nuclear attacks—they *may* have saved Allied lives, which Americans felt were "more valuable" than Japanese noncombatant lives—have real, if humble, echoes even in a high school biology class. Can I take this frog's life so that I can learn about reptilian innards? The adult who impatiently rejects the legitimacy of a student's confusion teaches a value. One cannot teach at arm's length: the world does not allow it. The issue of life is in the middle of every biology class, and most other classes too. To pretend it is not there is to say something about it; in that sense is the vacuum dangerous. Value issues infuse every classroom.

How are values taught? Teaching virtues like tolerance and generosity is neither easier nor more difficult than teaching any subtle art, such as literary grace or musical style. It is done, when at all, largely by example or, better put, by the "surround," by the insistent influence of the institution itself living out those values. This process is helped by explicitness; the ways of the school need to be explained, over and over again. Where these ways are uncertain—such as how the school should handle a particular problem among its students—the issue must be debated. Explaining must be incessant: This is how we at this school define tolerance. This is what decency means here. These are the kinds of attitudes we honor. These kinds of actions are intolerable. Of course, this explaining, together with the debate that accompanies it, is itself a fine form of questioning as well as of telling. It pushes students (and their teachers) back to the "whys" of their community, to the questions about decent living that apply in all situations.[36]

All this takes time, and few high schools allow much for it. Community "values" usually boil down to pep rallies. We're number one. Fight, fight, fight. Or that classic: Kill, kill, hate, hate; murder, murder, mutilate. Other issues of conduct (at their heart these are issues of value) are usually summarily handled by exhortation over the public address system ("today's cheers and jeers"). As is patently obvious, judgment in moral matters as well as any other realm is little developed by sermonizing, save to the congregation ready and willing to be saved. Faculties, with the exception of those in some private schools, rarely meet to discuss issues of the ethical tone of their schools. Indeed, many teachers and principals would be uncomfortable with these words "ethical tone," even though they may be quietly committed to the ideas behind them.

Some schools have tried to teach "moral reasoning" directly, either through exercises in "values clarification" or in more directive exercises in moral reasoning. The behavioral science evidence on the effectiveness of these approaches is both uncertain and controversial, but experienced teachers have found the approach useful, at the least to bring to the fore vital questions of ethics that surround any complicated issue of value. It is reasonable to assume that a person's heightened consciousness about a moral issue—say, a question of plagiarism or gross insensitivity or assault—should raise the chances of a decent reaction to it in the future. However, sufficient time for values clarification or other such exercises is rarely made available for teachers fully to test the approach. In effect, character education in schools infrequently goes beyond its own rhetoric, except for the periodic, well-intentioned exhortations by principals.

The "tone" of a school—the extent of its own inherent decency—

is the sum of its assembled humans' characters and not something that exists by fiat. A decent person has dignity; to order a person to be decent violates dignity. At best he can be persuaded, and the decency he ultimately exhibits will come from within, from his own convictions. The expression of decency and efforts to persuade younger folk to adopt the school's values involve judgment and are not matters that can be turned into readily disseminated "rules." The sought-for decency will emerge only when the students as well as the faculty want it, when its local definition is "theirs," when they have "ownership" of it. Because this is so, the authority and obligation for this aspect of schooling (as with so many others) should be vested in those working most closely with the adolescents, the teachers and administrators at each particular school.

This goal of decent character overlaps, clearly, with some definitions of "citizenship" and "religion," topics often stridently presented in discussions of school purpose. A significant part of citizenship, as promulgated in public schools, is often simple patriotism, usually expressed through rituals. For most high school students, these rituals, so often repeated, trivialize patriotism. Frequent, perfunctory, and unanalyzed pledges of allegiance and American flags in every classroom do not make citizens. At best they are ignored as part of the mindless routine of going to school; at worst they make students cynical.[37]

Patriotism for mature people arises from understanding, not from singsong rituals. Knowledge about the system of American government and social organization is necessary; critical appreciation of it is the mark of an effective citizen. That decency means fairness, generosity, and tolerance, and that these sturdy virtues are at the heart of the American system, are critical points for students to learn: by being decent one is acting American.

Such a limited view, however, satisfies few Fourth of July patriots, who would have us be more chauvinistic. It is, though, a view appropriate to schools, which are institutions where critical thinking and thoughtful behavior are stressed. Patriotism by propaganda can be presented to citizens elsewhere.

Religion is a more complicated issue, one as full of much sloppy thinking as of passionate bias.

At the end of a morning's visit to a strict Baptist school, I dropped in on the kitchen of its small, windowless cafeteria, at that noon hour full of talk and laughter. Students were allowed to bring their lunches or purchase items at the kitchen counter. Senior students were doing the cooking, and a lively girl, in her late teens, was serving nacho chips covered with a hot, heavy cheese sauce. I commented on them to her, and she said they were popular. As I left the kitchen, she followed me into the hallway, out of the hubbub of the cafeteria, to ask whether I would like to try the concoction. I demurred, but used this opportunity for a private talk with this veteran pupil to find out more about her and about her school. How long have you been here? Three years. What will you do next year? Go to college, in Lynchburg, Virginia. What will you study? Education . . . I want to be a teacher. How did you reach that decision at such a young age? Jesus told me to be a teacher.

She went on, describing her conversation with Jesus and how she had shared its contents with her parents. She was highly articulate and had a light, pleasant sense of humor. She seemed a clone of many of the able, attractive, but studiously secular older students whom I had taught in the Northeast, except for the literalness with which she characterized her religious life. I found this threatening, troubling to my academic ear. She said she had to return to the kitchen, and she wished me happy farewell.

My reaction to this exchange was dismay: that literalness must be brainwashing. *Of course* she hadn't talked with Jesus. My frost-belt Congregationalism had been assaulted. On reflection, though, I had to grant that all of us describe the decisions we make in a variety of ways, usually ones that mask the thought process behind them. Dad, I've decided to try to go to the Oberlin Conservatory and study the cello. Had I "talked" with someone in my mind's eye before reaching that decision? Could I articulate that "conversation," and would I dare tell anyone about it? Dad, my superego calls me to serve humankind as a musician. Such an assertion sounds absurd, and yet conscientious secularists ultimately act on such bases. Is an appeal to the specific Jesus so different? Why was it so threatening? Was it because this girl felt at ease in describing her personal "conversations"?

One might conclude that the girl was unsophisticated, that her family, community, and school had shielded her from much of the world. One might guess that, initially at least, she would be very troubled in a Socratic discussion, in any situation where she might be pressed toward relative rather than absolute values. However, one can say as much about many students in firmly secular public high schools.

Was a school climate that reinforced a literalistic stance on religious matters inconsistent with democratic education or with sound intellectual training? When should the community at large decide that a school's climate is intolerably inconsistent with the ends of good thinking and thoughtfulness? If the minimal competency tests are passed and students successfully complete a demanding academic regimen, is it any proper concern of the community whether a child's decency is expressed in biblically literalistic or in secular terms?

No, it is not. One has to conclude that the community should invade citizens' rights of choice of schools only at the great extremes—the Jonestowns, the diploma mills of Dickensian neglect, whether in the public or the private sector.

Resurgent fundamentalist Christianity serves to remind educators of how intrusive religious matter is in all schools, however pugnaciously secular they may proclaim themselves. The neat legalisms about Jefferson's putative wall between church and state find no place in reality, save at the extremes. Blatant sectarian preaching can be identified, but such preaching, while the stock-in-trade of an important minority among the American people, is not a major factor in most American schools. What is a factor is that the most acceptable American secular ethic is a direct extension of Judeo-Christian teaching and cannot be detached from it, however hard the constitutional lawyers may labor. Individualism, compassion, the sense of obligation for service to one's community, and a belief in literacy all have, surprising though it might seem to some, religious roots.

Few educators like to be reminded of this. The unconscious Protestant Christian bias of many public schools is often visible only to Jewish or Catholic families. Indeed, it was this bias which more than anything led to the establishment of a coherent system of Catholic schools in the late nineteenth century, and the current growth of Jewish day schools arises from an analogous sense of bias in the public sector.

The well-publicized current pressures from fundamentalist Christian leaders is but a chapter in a long book of religious influence on and in American schools. The argument about the existence of a "religion" called "secular humanism" is not a silly one. The belief in rational inquiry and the need to establish truth on the basis of fact rather than revelation has deep roots in the Protestant Reformation. Commitment to Calvinist Harvard's motto, Veritas— meaning for its seventeenth-century founders *divine* truth—has evolved over the centuries, and to argue that "unfettered" scientific or social scientific inquiry is unconnected with religion is plausible only if one gives a remarkably narrow definition to religion, essentially relegating it to the status of a mystery.

Where certain important curricular decisions are centralized, as in those states which have textbook-selection committees, political pressure is these days being applied to ban all but the most pallid or pro-fundamentalist material. A few highly publicized attempts to remove from school libraries books that are perceived to represent values at odds with those of fundamentalists rattle through the courts; the effect on school authorities is the exercise of harmful caution. The religious and, by extension, moral views of a well-organized minority (or majority) has substantial influence, as powerful in its indirect as in its direct result.

The message of this bit of current history is to remind educators of the religious element in all schooling. Accommodating it in a pluralistic but tolerant society requires compromise and patience, both anathema to zealots. By pretending there is a wall between religious issues and their schools, public school people remove themselves from the argument about the ways that religion must properly exist in their schools, and they leave the field open to unchallenged religious enthusiasts. Trying to settle these loaded issues at state or federal levels, far from the people being affected, lessens the chance for the local accommodations that are possible in small communities, where people, by having to work face to face, find compromise possible. Instead, it increases the need for legalistic precision in an area where deliberate ambiguity may be a virtue.

These confrontations over religion are ultimately about students' minds, their character and behavior. People struggle over them because they want to influence children. Perhaps the most absurd current hullaballo is over prayer in schools—as though a seriously religious child needed permission to pray under any circumstances. Advocates of "voluntary" prayer argue that the schools should encourage religious observances without requiring them. Opponents pointedly ask whose prayer will be used and assert that a student who opts out of prayer as a matter of conscience will be stigmatized. Voluntary prayer thus is not really voluntary. The church-state argument on this issue is again before the courts and Congress; either way it is decided will serve only to trivialize religion. Even in states that mandate a full minute of silence that can be used for prayer—"silent meditation"—the law can be readily sabotaged. Two teachers ostensibly affected by such a state law explained to me how they dealt with it. "I am sure that there are at least sixty seconds of silence when I am taking roll," and "I can sure add up sixty seconds of silence during my math class." Both did agree, however, that parents wanted them "to teach their kids what's right."

Clearly, schools are expected by most Americans to stand for certain values and to inculcate these in their students. Most of these values have religious roots, if not strict theological identification today. Educators who pretend that these are purely secular values are whistling in the dark.

Reasonable people can disagree about the implications of even such a moderate and limited concept as decency. Should a student on probation for drug-dealing be fully accepted back at school? Should demonstrations about some social or political issue—for example, nuclear disarmament—be allowed to take school time? How revealing should the cheerleaders' uniforms be?

The line between originality and incivility is a fuzzy one, as is that between freedom and vulgar intrusiveness. Inexperienced adolescents trying their wings—working up a new cheerleaders' routine or staging a play—will test that line. It is all right for John Updike to use the word "fuck" in a short story that is assigned in class, but not all right for the students to use it in their play. Most people enjoy surprising others, and adolescents are no exception. They often like to give a bit of a shock to old folk. Look at us. Listen to our freedom.

No one learns how to calibrate the limits of offensiveness without practice. Good character reflects skills at such calibrating. Allowing students opportunities to learn these skills requires patience and a toleration of more offensiveness than many adults can stomach, particularly those older people who have limited self-confidence (who have shaky calibration skills of their own) or who are being hammered by outside critics. Where to draw lines depends on values about which thoughtful people can seriously disagree.

Inevitably, some communities will be too split to accommodate their values in one school, to reconcile their differing specific definitions of decent conduct. However, there can be as much refreshing strength in the tension over values as there are seeds for discord. Many communities handle this tension by giving families choices, with a "traditional" program or an "alternative" (for which read "liberal") program within a public system or with private schools. Many of these options are formally identified primarily as academic alternatives, rather than ones of a value-laden ethos. My hunch, after seeing many, is that it is their tone—the people in them and the way that values affect their structure—that gives them their appeal. These are, in fact, options for different sorts of character education. Within legal and commonsensical limits, such options should be available to all families.

7

Principals' Questions

AS I TRAVELED among schools, their principals pressed me with questions, many of which were practical, specific.

What's your curriculum . . . What subjects should be offered? they asked.

I replied: Let's not start with subjects; that usually leads us into the swamp called "coverage." What counts are positive answers to three questions: Can graduates of this high school teach themselves? Are they decent people? Can they effectively use the principal ways of looking at the world, ways represented by the major and traditional academic disciplines?

What do you mean, "teach themselves"?

Learning how to observe and analyze a situation or problem and being able to make sense of it, use it, criticize it, reject or accept it. This is more than simple "problem-solving," since many of the enriching things in life are not, in fact, problems. "Teaching oneself" is nothing more than knowing how to inform and enrich oneself. Ideally a school would like not only to equip a student with those skills, but also to inspire him or her to use them.

How is this done?

By directly giving students the task of teaching themselves and helping them with it. It means providing fewer answers and insisting that students find the right (or at least defensible) answers themselves. It means that teachers must focus more on *how* kids think than on what they think.

This will take lots of time.

Yes, indeed. There will be far less opportunity for teachers to tell things, and, as a result, less coverage, of fewer subject areas. Of course, ultimately it means more coverage because the student is able to learn on his or her own.

Which fewer areas? Be specific.

I will, but with the clear understanding that there is no One Best Curriculum for all schools. While we all have to agree on some general outcomes that give meaning to the high school diploma, the means to these outcomes must be kept flexible. No two schools will or should have precisely the same characteristics; wise diversity is *essential* for quality. Furthermore, top-down edicts about "what" and "how" demonstrably do not work. Each school must find its own way, and in so doing gain the energy that such a search provides.

Let me give you the beginnings of one model. I would organize a high school into four areas or large departments:

1. Inquiry and Expression
2. Mathematics and Science
3. Literature and the Arts
4. Philosophy and History

You will immediately note that "English," that pivotally important but often misconstrued or even unconstrued "subject," would disappear. By "expression," I mean all kinds of communication, but above all writing, the litmus paper of thought. Some of "communication" is brute skill, such as the use of a keyboard (that sine qua non for the modern citizen) and clear, if rudimentary handwriting. Visual communication is included, as are gesture and physical nuance and tone, those tools used so powerfully by such masters as Winston Churchill and Ronald Reagan. A teacher cannot ascertain a student's thought processes unless they are expressed.

Mathematics is the language of science, the language of certainties. Science, of course, is full of uncertainty, as is much of higher mathematics, but for beginners it is the certainties that dominate. Number systems work in certain ways. Axioms hold. The pituitary gland secretes certain hormones; if it fails to do so, predictable consequences ensue. The world around us has its share of certainties, and we should learn about them, learn to be masters of them. Basic arithmetic, algebra, some geometry and statistics, physics and biology, are the keys. I would merge the traditional departments of mathematics and science, thus forcing coordination of the real and abstract worlds of certainty. The fresh, modern necessity for study in computer science can be the first bit of glue in this process of collaboration; that subject nicely straddles both areas.[38]

Human expression cuts across written and spoken languages, theater, song, and visual art. There is much common ground in these attempts of man and woman to explain their predicament, yet English, music, and art usually proceed in as much splendid isolation as do mathematics and science. This is wasteful, as aesthetic expression and learning from others' attempts to find meaning are of a piece. All need representation and benefit from an alliance.

History, if it is responsibly taught, is perhaps the most difficult subject for most high school students, because it involves the abstraction of time past. One often can engage it well first through autobiography and then through biography, proceeding finally to the "biographies" of communities, which make up most conventional history. Things were as they were for reasons, and from these incidents evolve concepts in geography, economics, and sociology. For most students at this stage, these disciplines should remain the handmaidens of history. The exception is philosophy, particularly moral and political philosophy. A political philosophy, essentially that associated with American constitutionalism, is the bedrock of enlightened democratic citizenship, and adolescence, more than any other stage of life, is filled with a search for values. The study of elementary ethics, for example, not only provides excellent opportunities for learning intellectual skills, but also powerfully engages students' interest.[39]

Why so few subjects?

There are several reasons. One is to lessen the splintered view of knowledge that usually confronts high school students. Their world rarely uses the fine distinctions between academic disciplines; insisting on them confuses young scholars. A second serves teachers:

strict specialization hobbles much skill training. Good coaching cuts across academic specializations. The current organization is very wasteful. A third reason: a few areas, taught in large time blocks, greatly reduce both the scheduling problems and the frenetic quality of the school day. Finally, more broadly and sensibly construed subject areas allow greater scope for teachers.

Won't students want electives?

Yes, in that they will want opportunities to study what interests them and what helps them. However, this personalization can be well accommodated *within* each broad area, rather than through a smorgasbord of unrelated courses.

This sounds deadly, very academic and removed from kids' lives.

It sounds deadly because it has often been taught in deadly ways. I am regularly assaulted for being an "elitist" for proposing this program, yet no critic will argue, when I press him, that any of the objectives I put forward is inappropriate for every adolescent. A teacher must start where the students are—and this may *not* be chapter one in the textbook. One works to engage each student, to get him or her to experience some aspect of an area, and to feel that experience to be successful. It takes time, ingenuity, patience. Most difficult to reach will be the demoralized youngsters, the ones who see school as a hostile place. Many of these students come from low-income families. They will need special attention and classes that use extensive coaching—not only to help them gain the skills they often lack but also to promote some fresh self-assurance in them. Vast classes heavy with lecturing must be avoided.

You've left out physical education and vocational education.

Let's start with physical education. Much of what happens in schools today under that rubric is neither education (or at best is disconnected applied biology) nor very physical (thirty minutes once a week playing volleyball does not mean much, except perhaps as a useful vent for built-up adolescent steam). Citizens should know about their bodies and be taught that the need for exercise is a good thing. These are worthy topics for a good science-mathematics area to present.

The same kind of argument can be made for vocational education.

Specific job training is a good thing, but not at the expense of a school's core. The best place to learn most jobs is on site. The common exception is business education, most prominently training for secretarial positions. The important points are ability to type and, beyond that, being well informed, literate, and able to handle numbers. If typing is a schoolwide requirement, and the other skills the inevitable consequence of the student's taking the core topics, the exception is moot.

Two more points about vocational education: tomorrow's economy will be volatile and dependent on flexible workers with a high level of intellectual skills. Thus, the best vocational education will be one in general education in the use of one's mind. Second, we must remember that most of today's high school students are or wish to be in the labor market. As the age cohort shrinks, the demand for its labor in most communities will grow. Educators are not going to reverse this trend; it will be better if they seize it, and adapt schools in demanding, sensible ways to the reality of adolescent employment. Working per se can be good for adolescents.

All that may be true in the abstract. But the fact remains that you'll lose a lot of kids if you cut out voc ed and athletics.

No, not necessarily. Remember that but a small minority of high school students are significantly involved in vocational education and interscholastic athletics. Furthermore, to the extent that these activities form a bridge to the central subjects, I'm for them. Unfortunately, today in many schools they have a life of their own, at the expense of an education in mind and character.

What of foreign language?

The cry for its requirement in schooling is abroad in the land as a cure for American isolation and chauvinism. For many adolescents, such study has merit; for others, little sense. If you cannot master your own language, it is inefficient to start another. If you have little immediate need to use a second language, the time spent in learning it is largely wasted—unless that "foreign" language is English. An absolute requirement for study of a foreign tongue can divert from other topics time that is crucial for a particularly needy student. The issue of ethnocentrism is more important than language study and must be addressed through the history courses.

What of bilingual education?

Ideally, all Americans should enjoy it—but the real problem is that of non–English speaking students. They should be immersed in English intensively. Their nonlinguistic studies should continue—for no longer than necessary—in their mother tongues. Their self-confidence, often associated with their facility in language, should be reinforced. Empathy and patience are crucial here; rigid formulae passed down from central authorities *guarantee* inefficiency and frustration. The goal is confident youngsters, adept and effectively fluent in two languages.

I'm still skeptical about your overall plan. You can pull this off only if you had none but highly motivated students in your school. What of tracking and the turned-off student?

Just as now, some kids won't hook in; I know that. If they've shown themselves competent in the minima of literacy, numeracy, and civic understanding, let them leave high school—with the promise that they can come back in the future. The community college system in many regions makes this an easy alternative.

In addition, there are the troublemakers, the kids who don't want necessarily to leave school, but want just to stay there because it's fun, where their friends are. Of course, good teachers can work with them to try to change their attitudes. However, if they disrupt, they should be expelled, with the same opportunities to return later as all dropouts have. As long as they have met the state's requirements, no one should force them into school. Ideally, too, they should have a variety of programs from which to choose. Highly personalized alternative programs have frequently worked for this sort of student.

As to tracking: there would be none and there would be a great deal. Every student would be enrolled in each subject area all the time. There would therefore be none of the current tracks, usually called honors, college preparatory, general, technical, and so forth. But within each subject area, the students would progress at their own pace. This would create multiple tracks, ones that are flexible and that put no child in any dead end.[40]

That will be very messy.

Yes, it will. Learning is messy. It can be handled if the units (separate high schools, or "houses" within high schools) are kept small enough to allow a particular group of teachers to know particular students well and develop a track for each. Class patterns will vary by need, some larger for telling, some smaller for coaching and questioning. Students will be working much more on their own than they do now; there will be no strict age grading. One learns how to learn by experience, not by being told things.

Won't this add financial cost?

Some, perhaps. It need not, as long as schools retreat from the objective of "comprehensiveness" and concentrate on classroom teaching. There are models of "zero-based budgets" which demonstrate that schools, if simply organized, can have well-paid faculty and fewer than eighty students per teacher, without increasing current per-pupil expenditure.[41]

You haven't mentioned guidance counselors.

Counselors today act either as administrators, arranging schedules and job and college interviews and the like, or as teachers, coaching and questioning young people about their personal concerns. Good teachers *are* good counselors, in that second sense; students turn to them for help, whether or not their titles identify them as "guidance" people. Most high school guidance departments are overloaded with obligations, many of which are contradictory—for example, serving both as a place where students can obtain confidential personal counsel and as a disciplinary arm of the school (perhaps running the "in-school suspension" program for students who have repeatedly broken rules).

A decentralized school with small academic units has less need for specialized counseling offices; improved faculty-student ratios make this possible. The administrative obligations now traditionally handled by such offices can be placed directly under the principal. Staff members who are well trained in counseling and testing skills can support the teachers in each small academic unit.

We are being asked often these days about "computer literacy" and the needs of a "new technological society." How does your plan address these areas?

Computers, like calculators, books, and other familiar products of technology, should be welcomed by schools. Well used, they might significantly extend teachers' coaching efforts as well as help students learn. While we should learn to employ the products of the new technologies, we should keep in mind two critical points: it is up to us to select the data to be put into them, and we must choose with care the uses we put them to.

Should public schools formally provide time for voluntary prayer?

No. There is ample time and opportunity outside school for religious observances. Furthermore, the fact that public schools would not set time aside for prayer does not imply rejection of its importance. Schools should *not* claim to be comprehensive, arrogating to their routines every consequential aspect of an adolescent's life. High schools are limited to helping adolescents use their minds well—and this includes becoming thoughtful and decent people.

What of standards?

The existence of final "exhibitions" by students as a condition to receiving their diplomas will give teachers a much greater control of standards than they currently have. These standards, combined with a variety of external examinations, such as the Advanced Placement Examinations of the College Board, Regents' Examinations in some states, and, it is hoped, a growing list of other instruments that a school or an individual student could adopt or take voluntarily, would give outside authorities, like regional accrediting agencies, a good sense of the quality of work being done.

A lot turns on those teachers. Are they good enough?

They've got to be.

Remedies like all these are neat, but abstractions, castles in the air. Seeing adolescents in classrooms reminds one that, in substantial measure, school is *their* castle, that they have to want to build it.

I arrived by car at the school at 7:15 A.M., thirty minutes before the first bell. It was a cool day, and the first arrivals to the large high school I was visiting were gathered in clots in the sun outside, around the low, meandering structures that housed their classrooms. Parking lots and hard-used lawns encircled the buildings. There were no sidewalks in this neighborhood, even though it was quite built up; the school property was ringed by small houses and business establishments. Everyone came to school by bus or by private car.

I turned into one of the driveways leading toward what appeared to be the school's central building and was immediately bounced out of the seat of my rented Datsun by the first of a series of asphalt bumps in the road. These barriers, it was painfully obvious, were there to slow down the dozens of vehicles that used the drive-way and were already lined up in the lots next to the school, row on row of loyal steel beasts tethered by this pedagogical water hole. I found a place and parked.

It was immediately clear from the stares I received from nearby students that I had picked a student lot, not one for staff or for visitors. Since it seemed to me large enough to accommodate one more little car, I left the Datsun where it was. It was ridiculously out of place, surrounded by pickup trucks, high on their springs and mud spattered, and by jalopies, late sixties' Chevrolets, old Ford Mustangs, Plymouth Satellites, each cumbrously settled upon great oversize rear tires. While all appeared poised, snouts down, to roar purposefully off to God knows where, for the moment they simply cowered here, submissive. Their masters and mistresses leaned against them or sat on them, chatting. Many drank coffee out of paper cups. Some smoked furtively as I drew near; though unfamiliar to them, I was wearing the drab coat-tie-slacks uniform of the school administrator who might admonish them.

My first instinct was to snicker at the parking lot scene. It was an eighties' version of an *American Graffiti* strip, indeed an over-drawn one, because the dusty trucks and drag-equipped cars were grotesquely numerous. My condescension disappeared, however, when I paid more attention to the students gathered around these vehicles, kids observing the visitor who had taken a space on their turf. Their attitude was in no way menacing, but it was freighted with an absence of interest. I was an object to be observed and, if they were smoking, to be mildly reacted to. Beyond that, I might have been a bird in the vast aviary of a boring zoo; I was a piece of the scenery, glimpsed as part of hanging out before school. None of these kids was playing principal's pet by coming up and asking me whether I needed help or directions to the office, but no one hassled me, either. The human confrontation was neutral, nearly nonexistent.

These were older students, drivers. In their easy chatting among themselves, in their self-absorption and nonchalance, they showed self-assurance bordering on truculence. They had their own world.

My reaction was nervousness. I tried to smile a sorry-fellas-but-I-didn't-know-where-the-visitors'-parking-lot-was message, but it did not come off. I felt the awkward outsider, at distance from these composed young people. Even as I knew that at the bell they would enter the buildings and engage in the rituals of dutiful school-going and that they would get more boisterous and engaging as the early morning mist over their spirits parted, I also knew that these were considerable people, ones who would play the game adult educators asked them to play only when and how they wanted to. The fact that many of them, for a host of reasons, chose to go along with the structures of the school did not lessen the force of the observation: they possessed the autonomous power not to.

In this sense, kids run schools. Their apparent acquiescence to what their elders want them to do is always provisional. Their ability to undermine even the illusions of certain adult authority and of an expectation of deference was admirably if benignly displayed by the students on that parking lot. A less benign challenge can be made by students in any classroom when, for whatever reason, they collectively, quietly, but assuredly decide to say no. The fact that most go along with the system masks the nascent power that students hold. Few adults outside the teaching profession understand this.

The evening before, I had met the superintendent of this school district. He was a man of great force and national reputation. His administration ran the district with efficiency and closely centralized authority. In talking of his work, we had both used the ready metaphors of schoolkeeping, most turning around an image of old folk (the teachers) passing something of self-evident importance to young folk (the students). This morning all of these metaphors seemed naïve. All assumed the young student to be a passive receptacle or, at the least, a supplicant for knowledge. The adolescents in that parking lot were neither passive nor suppliant. However much we adults may want them to be eagerly receptive and respectful of our agenda for their schooling, the choice to be that or something else—neutral, hostile, inattentive—was unequivocally theirs. If we want our well-intentioned plans to succeed, we'll have to *inspire* the adolescents to join in them—inspire even the sullen, uninterested kids one sees in parking lots at the start of a school day.

The vision of school as an uncomplicated place where teachers pass along the torch of knowledge to eager students is sadly innocent.

III The Teachers

1

Three Teachers

THE SENIOR English class included fourteen students and the seventy-two-year-old teacher, Sister Michael, a Catholic nun with over fifty years' experience, much of it at this school. The modern, second-story classroom was sunny, sparsely furnished, but there were hundreds of books in shelves along the walls. The students' desks were formed in a neat semicircle, the teacher's desk in front of them, before the chalk board. Sister Michael stood behind her desk or paced slowly back and forth, chalk always in hand. She was a square, kindly woman who, in her habit of black and cream, met the specifications of everyone's stereotypical teacher-nun.

The assignment had been to read Graham Greene's "The Destructors," a short, depressing story about a gang of adolescent toughs, who, for kicks, elect to demolish an old man's house. The central figure is a remote boy called Trevor, a typically English somebody who combines malevolence with a hint of gentle manners, a well-bred hoodlum. Sister Michael started off the class by asking why Greene used the word "destructors," rather than the more expectable "destroyers." The students were at first surprised by this, but in due course began to offer answers. Sister Michael received each with a nod, commented on none, but used several as the springboard for other questions. Her tactic in this class was Socratic: she was trying to help the students learn to ask original questions about a

143

work of art (or any situation, for that matter), to see new sides to otherwise ordinary things. A string of questions tends to tease out ideas that have been locked up or to force into the open relationships that, to the student reader's eyes, had not been there. "Destructor" *says* something different from "destroyer," yes. Its very irregularity puts one on notice. It is as irregular as a well-bred hoodlum or the name "Trevor" for a gang member. Sister Michael kept prodding the students to see and then to examine these incongruities and to ascertain what Greene may have had in mind when he used them.

Although the teacher kept pushing forward questions about the language and plot of the story, she readily digressed when a student answered a question with what (for Sister Michael) was a useful word. One youngster said that a character—Ken Thomas, the elderly owner of the house—was "idealistic"; Sister Michael jumped on it. What did the student mean by it? Why was "idea" as well as "ideal" at its center? What several meanings of the word might there be? The students got two indelible messages from such a digressive foray: that words have precise meanings, all of them important, and that the words a student used in this classroom were important. There was no sloppy language in Sister Michael's domain.

The class went back to the story. They talked of the gang. Sister Michael maneuvered the discussion, still through questions, to a particular phrase in the text, "pure devotion to the gang." Pure? she asked. As with "destructors," the students seemed startled, quiet. Why *pure?* Silence. Sister Michael let it sit there; she looked across the dozen faces around her, without impatience or challenge, merely with anticipation. Someone would have to stick her neck out, and someone ultimately did. Sister Michael did not pounce on this solitary expression, because it was made so tentatively. She received it warmly, asked others if they agreed, and then went on with a new set of questions.

Greene's story ends with a truck driver, having freed Mr. Thomas from the privy behind his house, where the gang had incarcerated him, becoming "convulsed" with laughter as he saw the total rubble before the two of them. The house had been elegantly toppled when a rope, surreptitiously tied to the driver's truck, pulled away a prop as the driver unwittingly started off in his vehicle. To the appalled old man, the driver says, "I'm sorry. I can't help it, Mr. Thomas. There's nothing personal, but you got to admit it's funny." Sister Michael landed on "funny." When does it mean "laughable"? Could it mean "unexpected"? The students gave examples; she wrote them on the board.

The class now was drawing to a close, and Sister Michael, in order to make one point or another, returned several times to comments made earlier by students. No remark in Sister Michael's class seemed to get lost, to be unremarkable. Needless to say, the students paid attention and were rewarded, even when their responses were prosaic or simply wrong, by Sister Michael's subtle signal that it is all right to err if it is in the cause of ultimately getting something correct.

In the midst of the class, Sister Michael had provoked the students to consider Greene's phrase "a sense of kindness." She had elicited examples of it from the students' own experience, but one could sense that the sister herself personified a style of kindness that was married to rigor and demand. Her judgment, timing, and sense of direction were clear but not obtrusive. This class was a model of the craftsman at work, a craftsman of sensitivity and judgment. It was an experience not reducible to a lesson plan for a substitute to use or a curriculum guide.

A bare three minutes before the class's end, Sister Michael left the text and asked, Should this story be in a textbook for students? Immediately the response, Why not? Sister pressed: Does it give the wrong message to growing people? Is art for entertainment, or preachment, or is it simply a neutral description of reality? The students left the class off balance, pondering.

A classroom like that of Sister Michael's works well when students want to be there and are at least reasonably ready to engage in discussion and attend to the use of their minds. The typical classroom is not designed for rambunctiousness, for noise, for confrontation. Most high school classrooms are designed to hold upward of forty people, a good crowd for such a small working space. To have much of orderly consequence go on, these up-to-forty souls have to agree that they want to work together, as did those in the class discussing "The Destructors."

Unhappily, by the time they reach high school, many adolescents find the word-and-number-filled life of school irrelevant and the classrooms often hostile, places of humiliation. Such students are hard to reach with Graham Greene's abstractions. Most go through the motions, painfully unresponsive to Socratic challenges about a short story. Others simply do not show up at school. A few rebel, destructors inside school and without.

A curriculum guide which said that all twelfth-graders were to read Graham Greene short stories would be totally unsuitable for such youngsters, and a teacher with an ounce of judgment would ignore it. But the pedagogical ends of Sister Michael's class are still apt. Precision—in this case with language, one's own and others', the perception of the unexpected among the familiar, and the questioning about the purposes and function of things, including short stories and much more—is an intellectual attribute appropriate for all kinds of young citizens, those turned off from the rituals of school classrooms as well as those comfortable with them.

A teacher with judgment, while keeping the end in view, varies the means. Charles Gross is an example of such an instructor. Gross, a teacher of electricity in a large vocational-technical high school, looked to be in his forties and was the owner and principal figure in a small electrical-contracting business. The school on this December day had an enrollment list of 1396, virtually all from minority groups and without exception from low-income families. Some 75 percent were in attendance. The school had started the academic year with 1507 students; the drop of over a hundred enrollees was somewhat smaller than in previous years. The attendance rate for those on the list was on the rise: three years earlier it averaged 55 percent per day. The major fall-off in enrollment took place during the tenth-grade year; only 40 percent of those who started in ninth grade made it into the eleventh. The principal had put it simply: "If I could get them into the eleventh year, the battle could be won"—the battle being for the provision of solid basic skills of literacy and numeracy, a salable trade, and a sense, for these desperately poor and usually very neglected and demoralized youngsters, that they can make it.

Gross each year "held" (into eleventh grade) a significant number of his students. When they were ninth-graders, all in the school took an "orientation" class in each of the trades, including electricity. Those of the young people who elected the electrical trade made that choice as tenth-graders, and some started then with Mr. Gross's course, along with the required study of mathematics, English, social studies, and health. The key elements in Gross's approach were his demeanor, which was friendly, no-nonsense, and optimistic, and the opportunity he provided for work experience. The student who successfully completed the tenth grade with Mr. Gross then became part of a team, led by him, that rewired burned-out residential properties being renovated. A church in this slum district, through a special nonprofit corporation created for the purpose, bought up these derelict properties and, with substantial government aid, rehabilitated them. They hired Gross's company to do the electrical work—and Gross's company was, in this instance, Gross and his high school kids. Did the building inspectors mind? I asked the principal. No, Gross is a properly licensed electrician, and he signs off on all the work. Do the unions accept this? A chuckle. Union electricians don't come up to this part of town.

One easily spotted Gross's advanced students. He made them all wear thick-soled boots and plastic helmets, and the latter stayed in place even while the students were in school. Each student had a leather holster of tools, and again, even though this clumsy, heavy bit of regalia was not much used there, it was worn in the school building. Gross did not insist on this at all; it simply was the uniform, and it was worn with pride.

Gross's classroom had too few desks for the thirty ninth-grade orientation students whom I witnessed in session there. The young people, virtually all male, black or Hispanic, were copying material from the blackboard. Some were perched on the radiators, others on tables at the room's side. The room was as dark and cluttered as Sister Michael's had been sunny and sparse, yet the attention paid by the students to their teacher was comparable.

Electricity is a subject demanding great accuracy: a mistake can mean a fire or a painful injury. Precision in planning, in following a wiring system logically and sequentially, and in understanding its operating realities (if not all the underlying physics), is as essential as is precision in language. Gross pressed both electricity and language: the students had to show and tell him what they were doing and why. As a result, his classes were both "vocational" and "academic": each student had to explain his own reasons for wiring or switching a situation in a particular way. Precision, logic, hypothetical thinking, clarity of expression—all were staples of Gross's classroom. Embodied as they were in a subject of demonstrable practicality for students who thought they had time and energy only for immediately practical things, these intellectual ends of education were powerfully joined to well-chosen means, ones that captured the commitment of these particular students.

Even with existing racial discrimination in the community, minority people can make a fair career in electrical contracting in the large city for which Mr. Gross worked, most usually in nonunion, "mom-and-pop" businesses. The students saw that. They also saw that the work of Mr. Gross's course had applications within a world they knew, their own neighborhood, applications requiring skills that their neighbors respected and sometimes even saw as magical. They also knew that Gross's contract with the church group would provide wages for them during their eleventh- and twelfth-grade years. Thus, the incentives for these students were there and implied a real demand for work at high standard. Staying in Mr. Gross's group meant staying successfully in the other required courses, as well. Mr. Gross made his young people deliver on their own, and he gave those who made it not only the pride of knowing that they were competent but also the insignia of that pride while in school. Sister Michael made sure that each of her students knew that whatever was said in class was important, and Mr. Gross, in his strikingly different milieu, did likewise.

Most classes have more than fourteen students in them, as had Sister Michael's, and most exist in schools and neighborhoods less desperate than those where Mr. Gross's electricians worked. Fred Curtis' ninth-grade mathematics class in the suburb of a big city was set in a pleasant, sunny room opening on a handsome courtyard. There were twenty-four students, fourteen girls and ten boys, and as in many groups of fourteen-year-olds, all shapes and sizes were represented. One boy looked barely four feet tall. The tablet-arm desks were loosely arranged facing the front of the room, but students clustered these as they came in, clots of girls here and knots of boys there.

Curtis had been out in the hallway, and the youngsters chattered on when he came in. He barely looked at them, but wrote on the blackboard, "Write a program which generates all the prime numbers from one to A." The students quieted down, watching. They had previously worked on another simple program for the computer, one that was to ascertain whether any inserted number was or was not prime. Some of the students had drafted it successfully, others had not.

Curtis turned now to the class. "Those of you who got yesterday's problem correct are to start on this one," gesturing toward the board behind him. "Those who didn't get yesterday's should try again. I'll help you." There was acquiescence to these instructions and a bit of chair-moving. Some of those who were to work on the new problem created new clusters, and some of the strugglers did likewise. There was a bit of chatter over this, and most students moved their chairs simply by using their feet as oars, clumsily duck-waddling themselves to or fro. Curtis paid no attention to this bit of comedy and plunged right in with the nearest clutch of youngsters who had failed the previous problem. The room quieted, though whispering continued. As far as I could tell from the back of the room, most of the talk was on the problems.

One girl sat alone, fiddling. She had failed the first problem. She gazed off, then made a face. Curtis moved around the room. When she thought he was watching her, she sighed, audibly and petulantly. He seemed to ignore her and continued talking with others. She fiddled some more and finally said firmly, as he passed in front of her, "Mr. Curtis, I'm waiting for you to help me." Curtis turned briefly: "Don't wait." She pouted. "But I need help." Curtis, now with a smile: "Do some thinking for yourself." He moved on to another student. With a touch of resignation and more audible sighs, bordering on truculence, she got down to work. Curtis, while consulting with others, kept an eye on her, stealing looks at her paper. In due course, he spotted something she'd done correctly. He swept over, pointing, and said for all to hear, "That's great! That's great!" Everyone looked up, noticing. The fiddler flushed. Curtis abruptly moved on. The girl continued to work. There was no more sighing. He soon returned, asking quietly, "Are you any better off than five minutes ago?" The girl nodded, asking questions. Curtis now consulted with her on her solution. It looked as though it might work. Curtis suggested that she go now to the computer room, along with some of the others, to try it out. She left the classroom purposefully.

I observed this class late in the year; Curtis had had a good many weeks to establish its routine. The students worked on their own; the work was to be theirs, much as it had been in Mr. Gross's electricity class. The program that the frustrated, fiddling girl eventually wrote, which she would immediately and privately be able to test on a computer, would be hers. Because of her ownership of the exercise, she would far more likely remember it than if she had been merely walked through a predigested program.

Curtis designed his class to allow students to work at different rates, with two exercises going on concurrently, a new one for the quick and a repeat for the not-so-quick. Apparently he shuffled the class enough so that if there was a stigma to being in the second group on this occasion, it was invisible to a visitor. By his actions, Curtis told the frustrated girl that she could do it, on her own, without his help (or, as it turned out, with a bit of his help). He focused as much or more on her need for self-confidence as he did on her solution to the particular problem in mathematics.

Curtis, Gross, and Sister Michael are all successful teachers. What makes them especially so is their judgment, their ability to find the appropriate recipe for engaging the attention and ultimately the minds and energies of their particular students. Adaptability is at the core of their judgment. Their work suggests no Pill for Good Pedagogical Judgment that can be packaged and distributed by school authorities. Their judgment was an extension of their personalities, their solid confidence in themselves and their subjects, and their ability to move flexibly to achieve their ends. They exemplify the subtlety and complexity of getting things right so that students can learn, and the importance of adult judgment and style throughout.

Learning is a complex, effortful, and often painful process. It can be exasperating too and also full of the wonder of new ideas and new skills. It can be painful to open one's mind, to change one's views, to try the unfamiliar. Doing such things is often threatening, even as they may be exciting.

We learn all the time, of course. As Robert Frost once said, "Education is . . . hanging around until you've caught on." Fail to put the yeast in the dough, and you learn that bread is not the result. Add incorrectly, and your bank starts bouncing your checks. Visit a new city and see new ways of solving old problems, trolleys instead of subways, solar heat instead of oil furnaces. Such learning, though, while incessant, is happenchance and depends entirely on where one is and what one does. It is totally culture bound.

Learning can be focused and made efficient. That is the function of schools. Schools can also present ideas that people would be unlikely to stumble over, ideas that extend beyond a person's particular surroundings. The possibility and potential of the unfamiliar is far greater in a good school than on the typical street.

The key worker in a school is the student. The only important product is his or her learning. All else is a matter of means—lively or dull classes, big or little libraries, happy or fearful buildings. As on the street, much that is incidental is learned in school. But school goes beyond this incidental world with its formal program, cast usually as the agenda put by adults before the students. Whether or not this agenda is adopted depends largely on the disposition, energy, and skill of those adolescents.

Teachers help, of course. The only function of the teacher is to assist the student to learn. Any other kind of teacher performance is irrelevant. Did you teach a good class today? is a miscast question, because it emphasizes the teacher. One rarely asks how your Toyota worked today; the critical issue is whether you got where you wanted to go. Did your students learn what was expected of them and by them today? That is the more apt question, though it is rarely asked. The difference between it and the first one is more than semantic, since it forces into relief an emphasis on the student, which is essential.

Nearly all formal learning in schools involves the interactions of three actors: the student, the teacher, and the subject of their mutual attention. The character of this triangle is subject to change, varying from pupil to pupil, teacher to teacher, subject to subject, day to day, even minute to minute. Change any one of the triangle's members, and the others have to shift, to accommodate, or even to break apart. The mathematics teacher acts in a particular way when he is answering in class a question whose answer he is certain of. The next moment there may be a question whose answer he is uncertain of. He will deal with that situation differently, with a different impact on the students and on the subject, especially if he gives a wrong or misleading answer. A student with a stomachache faces his teacher and subject with a different attitude from one without a stomachache. In most American classrooms, a discussion of the rights, wrongs, perils, and opportunities of revolution is different if the case under study is not that of America in 1775 but that of Cuba in 1960.

As long as schools are for learning, no relationship within them is more important than this triangle. That these triangles vary for different people, subjects, and times makes the task of providing constructive schooling an extraordinarily complex and subtle business.

At any given moment during a class, an alert teacher and an alert student plausibly may be asking themselves dozens of useful and critical questions about their work together—a list as long as it is obvious. For the teacher: Are the kids paying attention? Do they understand what I am saying? Do they see the connection between what I'm saying, the problem on the board, last night's homework, and last week's movie on our topic? Some of the kids aren't watching me; are they hearing me, though? Or are they in some fantasy world? If they *are* in a fantasy world, how can I get them back here?

A teacher looks at individuals as well as the group: I'm trying to give the class an overview. Will literal-minded, orderly thinking Scott over there get it? Roger's vocabulary is awful. Can he understand what I'm saying and the words in the homework that I'm going to assign? Will Celeste, who failed this course last term, try to get the point I'm stressing? Can I make her more self-confident? How can I get the kids to take this line of logic on their own, rather than merely following me? How can I find out whether the kids are getting this material? Can I do it with a written test, or do I need some other way? As any class proceeds, these and dozens of related questions may reasonably pass, however fleetingly, through a sensitive teacher's mind. (Insensitive teachers do not ask such questions; that is why they are insensitive.) Many teachers make the mistake of thinking that the students inevitably will—or should—be interested in just what interests teachers. It takes effort and experience both to empathize accurately with one's adolescent students and to know what to do with that empathy.

Teaching is, of course, a form of theater. While the point is to have the students learn, the teacher has to explain, provoke, cajole, inspire, criticize, demand, love. He or she often has to be a ham and to love being one. Sister Michael and Messrs. Gross and Curtis were all hams in their way, comfortable in and enjoying their limelight. Like acting, teaching demands much of personality. There may be one Falstaff on Shakespeare's pages, but there are as many Falstaffs as there are actors. One cannot clone a Mr. Gross or a Sister Michael. The human dimension of the craft of teaching, that aspect of personality which both employs judgment in seeking a student's position and elicits the best from him is not bottleable, for sale.

The student has his or her questions, too. What's the point of this? Where does it lead me? What does the teacher want me to do? Students are no less self-conscious than are teachers. Do my friends like me? How should I behave in class? What are those two girls over there whispering about? Will I make the team? The list is endless. The trick of the teacher and student is to get sustained attention on those questions which are of greatest common importance.

One visits classes and sometimes sees experts, each with her or his own special style. One reflects on how different the students are, from each other and indeed from themselves, hour by hour. One easily becomes paralyzed by the diversity and complexity. Is there *anything* in learning and teaching that allows generalization? Of course there is. We do not simply have to hire Rembrandts and Mozarts, Sister Michaels and Fred Curtises, and leave them to it. There are patterns that the teacher/scientist/artist can fruitfully use. Most of these patterns are commonsensical, and most, happily, are supported not only by the opinions of experienced school people, but also by the findings of behavioral science.[1]

2

Agreement

A SUCCESSFUL CLASS is one in which students and teacher agree on what they are about and on the rules of their academic game. As with other platitudes, however, troublesome issues lie below the surface of this one. How can students agree to an end before they have learned anything? How can they accept an end whose nature is unfamiliar? And just because the students and teacher agree does not mean that their particular agreement is worthy. In fact, it may be a conspiracy of convenience, a way to fill time with neither strain nor untoward effect. In a school system that has as its principal value the time spent, rather than the demonstrated achievement, the dangers of such a conspiracy are palpable.

This was exemplified at a well-regarded high school in an Eastern city, one with a new and well-publicized reputation for being "orderly" and "effective." In a city public school system that was overwhelmingly black, this school, set in a white upper-middle-income enclave, had a student population of twelve hundred, 50 percent white, 50 percent minority. Most of the students were bused in; the few adolescents living in the grand houses nearby chiefly attended private schools. The high school's hallways were friendly, and though discipline was visibly strict, the students appeared happy and contented. The blunt young principal put me for the day with a man whom he described as his ablest social studies teacher, Steve Brody.

Brody taught only honors sections of tenth- and eleventh-graders. His classroom was windowless but air-conditioned; desks were arranged in rows facing the teacher's desk and blackboard. The students entered boisterously and flopped into their seats, books piled in front of them, boys slouched with feet splayed and extended, girls cross-legged, twisting around, leaning on their desks. There was friendly chatter, much of it with Brody, who was a basketball aficionado and full of the previous night's game. The bell rang, but the chatter continued, quietly but aimlessly, for almost five minutes. Brody finally called for and immediately got general attention and began a string of announcements, mostly about extracurricular matters, laced with jokes and witticisms. The students loved it, and Brody loved their loving it. The classroom filled with warmth.

Over ten minutes into the period, Brody finally turned to history and announced that the purpose of this class was "to cover chapter six." The students, slouched or leaning, just looked at him. No one (save me) picked up the heavy textbook. I discovered that chapter six covered some aspects of the American westward movement. Brody moved through the text, slowly asking a question of no one in particular and then slowly answering it himself. The students quietly watched this performance.

The door to the classroom was open, and three times student messengers from the office came in and consulted with Brody. While he talked with these emissaries, the class remained quiet; there was only some low whispering. After each interruption, Brody continued. Several students had their notebooks open, but neither they nor anyone else took any notes. Brody meandered through chapter six, all in the ask-the-question-answer-it-himself mode. He unwittingly kept calling the U.S. Cavalry the U.S. Calvary, a point that provoked no visible or audible response. He inserted jokes along the way, and the class eventually petered out to quiet, genial chatter between Brody and the students. Brody ended the session with the announcement that a test would be given later in the week and that "you should know what will be on it." That much was clear: the questions that Brody had been himself asking were copies (it soon became clear to me) of those at the chapter's end in the text. These were what was expected. Memorize those, and you're home.

Brody's other classes were the same—genial, orderly, limited, vacuous. He signaled to the students what the minima, the few questions for a test, were; all tenth- and eleventh-graders could master these with absurdly little difficulty. The youngsters picked up the signal and kept their part of the bargain by being friendly and orderly. They did not push Brody, and he did not push them. The classroom was tranquil and bland. By my watch, over a third of the time in each class was spent on matters other than history, and the two thirds of the classes ostensibly devoted to the subject were undemanding. Brody's room was quiet, and his students liked him. No wonder he had the esteem of a principal who valued orderliness and good rapport between students and staff. Brody and his class had agreement, all right, agreement that reduced the efforts of both students and teacher to an irreducible and pathetic minimum.

It would be nice to report that Brody's class is an exception. It is not. The agreement between teacher and students to exhibit a façade of orderly purposefulness is a Conspiracy for the Least, the least hassle for anyone. Such a conspiracy is necessary in many schools and for many classes, because it is impossible for teachers or students to sustain rigorous, adventurous activity over a full six hours. Brody saw some 150 different students each day. He was on his feet in front of his classes four and a half hours every day, a performance that would exhaust the hardiest actor. The students sat in classrooms (except for the twice-a-week physical education meetings) almost six hours per day, an arduous bit of immobility indeed, rugged on the rump. The requirements of the school were to be in attendance, to be quiet, orderly, and predictable, and to pass tests of multiple-choice questions of easily divined nature. So why not agree to minima, genially applied? To do otherwise was to upset the principal's public relations applecart. This was a happy school. Attendance was up. Fights were down. Scores were up (from abysmal to merely embarrassing). In all, that school was a place of friendly, orderly, uncontentious, wasteful triviality.

Classrooms without much agreement of any kind at all are no prettier. At the extreme, of course, there are those wholly out of control, bits of chaos. However, most agreementless places are merely grotesque and exist in what can often be otherwise easily functioning schools.

A biology class of tenth-graders, eighteen youngsters in all, in a school situated in a pleasant area of a small city, was a sad example. The students were seated on high stools, two at a demonstration table; the tables were bolted down in rows facing the teacher. The room was long. The students at the back were at a considerable distance from the teacher, who nevertheless stayed rooted behind her desk.

I entered the room after the start of the class and was introduced to the teacher, Martha Shiffe, by the assistant principal. Though Shiffe had been warned that I was coming, she blanched on seeing me. She asked me whether I wanted to teach the class, and I demurred embarrassedly, apologizing for my tardiness. I took a chair against the back wall. The students, a nice variety of children in this settled, provincial city, checked me out good-humoredly. Girls and boys were sitting on opposite sides of the room, an arrangement, Ms. Shiffe said, that "just happened."

Shiffe restarted her teaching, working through lists on the blackboard. Phylum chordata . . . Subphylum gnathostomata . . . Superclass pisces . . . Superclass tetrapoda . . . She went from one to the next, pointing out various examples from handsome charts displayed on racks at the front of the room. The students paid her little attention. Some had swiveled themselves around on their stools and kept watching me, the odd visitor. Others talked among themselves quietly. One girl took out her compact, popped the mirror open, and went over her face in detail, squinting at each incipient blemish, poking here and rubbing there. She was oblivious of all around her, and her facial twistings and scrunchings were droll. The students around her watched this narcissistic performance.

Even while the names of living things poured out of Shiffe's lecture, no one was taking any notes. She wanted the students to know these names. They did not want to know them and were not going to learn them. Apparently no kind of outside threat— flunking, for example—affected the students. Shiffe did her thing, the students chattered on, even in the presence of a visitor.

Shiffe moved to class Reptilia, and handed out some samples, mounted in little boxes or floating in formaldehyde. The students passed these along, sometimes looking at one or another intently. Out of nowhere a student asked a question: How does a sidewinder move? A gush of giggles erupted. Sideways! The girl who asked the question, which had been as sincere as her query was totally unconnected with the particular samples of reptiles being distributed, blushed. Shiffe replied, "You almost have to see it to know how it works." The consternation quickly blew over, but the cheeks of the humiliated girl remained red.

Shiffe moved to class Aves, and the giggling and talking increased. In response, she raised her voice and the speed of her lecture. It was a sort of monologue, with no one listening. On she went: A bird is a glorified small dinosaur . . . see the archaeopteryx. Then on to endotherms to "class Mamalia" (sic), as she wrote on the blackboard. She started talking about bats, and the class almost magically quieted down. Bats had been found under the eaves of the high school's bus garage, and the task of evicting them had been a source of much interest. Shiffe picked up this interest, but the public address system interrupted with news about the class elections. Modest chaos resulted and persisted for several minutes to the end of the period. The noise level, however, never rose to a point where someone walking in the corridor—such as an assistant principal—could be troubled by it. Shiffe kept her door closed. At the stroke of the bell, the kids tumbled off their stools and out of the classroom. Shiffe gave me a resigned, mournful look.

Here was a class that was full of disembodied names in which the students had no interest at all. Indeed, they were in total agreement to ignore the substance of the class. Their common front of uninterest probably made examinations moot. Shiffe could not flunk them all, and if their performance was uniformly shoddy, she would have to pass them all. Her desperation was as obvious as the students' cruelty toward her.

Mr. Gross's electricity class had had agreement. The students knew what was expected and why, what the standards were and why, and just how to behave, both in school and on their job.

Mr. Curtis' ninth-graders did not know enough mathematics to know what lay ahead (Mr. Gross's electricity, its presence and its absence, is a more visible, practical part of our everyday experience than are prime numbers), but they trusted the teacher because of his enthusiastic command of what he was doing. He made them feel good for going along. While his school and Ms. Shiffe's were comparable in the level of helpful support from the administration and from fellow teachers, these two classrooms were dramatically different. In his there were shared expectations and energies. In hers, there were no such things.

Sister Michael had established a climate in her classroom that allowed for persistent questioning. Students had to expose their ideas, and they had, certainly by the time I observed their class, agreed to accept this threatening practice. In a sense, their class was less orderly than that taught by Martha Shiffe; Shiffe had a full, sequential outline, full of data. Sister Michael had but a few ideas, kept in her head, with no written outline, and she spun these prominently into a rich cloth as the variety of answers to her question gave her opportunities.

If effective learning is to take place, student and teacher must agree on the objective and on the means to reach it. For the student this often requires trusting the teacher, as the objective and the ways to it are obscured by the student's inexperience. This is demonstrably so for elementary school children, but becomes less so as people grow up. Adolescents have minds of their own. Explicit reasons, however abstract, often engage them. Any person who sees, at least to some extent, why he or she is asked to do something is ahead of the individual who is merely absorbed into some inexplicable but compulsory activity. And if those reasons are persuasive, the energy and effort that are provoked will help the individual learn.

Some subjects are more difficult to explicate than others: Sister Michael had a more strenuous selling job than did Mr. Gross. As a result, some teachers have to carry their students largely on the basis of trust. It is not an easy task, but it has to be done. Teachers who do not try, who merely say, Learn it because that's what we learn, elicit from their students predictably superficial work.

There is hurt in learning, and it is difficult to persuade someone to hurt himself. It is the castor oil problem: Take this and you'll feel better some time in the future. Expose your errors so that I, the teacher, can catalogue them for you, thus helping you to make fewer in the future. Working hard with a teacher, or any mentor, is masochistic. It is especially so for adolescents, whose vulnerability and inexperience are attenuated. Getting agreement with them to pursue this often lacerating process of exposing that inexperience, and the errors it reaps, is a subtle, delicate business.

Explaining ends and means is also simple courtesy. People deserve to know the "whys" for things they are forced to do or into which they enter for some long-range reason. Some of us adults become so sodden with the regulations of schoolkeeping that we forget to tell students why it is all taking place. We are too busy to explain or too bored to be willing to explain it over and over again, each year with each new wave of students. The trusting people in our classrooms deserve better, and their own reactions to, and suggested emendations of, these whys and wherefores deserve attention and, where sensible, adoption.

As the major goal of schooling is developing the intellect, the very exercise of explaining ends and means and gaining agreement is itself educational. The essential word throughout is *why,* which is the central interrogative of all learning. Agreements in classrooms are never quite alike. They are negotiated by each teacher and each class, with the concessions on each part being over the distance between the students' pleasure and level of awareness of a subject and the teacher's sense of their need and the imperatives of that subject. For example, an agreement on why and how a U.S. history course is usefully to proceed will be different for a group of adolescents recently arrived from abroad from what it will be for a group of Americans who have gone to schools together all their lives. Finding common ground in an English class with ninth-graders who have consistently failed that subject in elementary or middle school is different from finding such a consensus for ninth-graders who have consistently received honors.

Some impatient folk will argue that an English class is an English class, that a teacher is a teacher, that standards are standards— so just stick it to the students. Such an attitude, which is lamentably widespread, ignores realities and results in terrible inefficiencies. Martha Shiffe's well-meaning effort fitted the curriculum guide, but it ignored the agreements necessary in the classroom to allow the substance of the curriculum to proceed. If she had spent fifty imaginative minutes on bats, she would have helped the students learn a good deal of science. Getting agreement takes persuasiveness, flexibility, trust, and time. Failing to get agreement, and agreement on ends and means that forward serious intellectual activity, however painful, results in an empty school.

3

Motivation

HER NAME was Melissa. She entered the classroom alone, yet still seemed easily a part of the mob of kids arriving for the English class. This was a college-track group of seniors in a large Midwestern city high school, one enrolling students from a wide mix of lower-income, working-, and middle-class families. The teacher, Ellen Romagna, was a feisty young woman who had placed a lectern almost in the middle of the classroom, with the thirty-five individual tablet-arm desks in semicircular rows around her. The room was a happy shambles of books, posters, papers, dictionaries piled on the window-sills, chalk and blackboard erasers on the floor as well as in their intended receptacles.

Looking at no one in particular, Melissa headed toward a desk to the teacher's left, against a wall. She toted a large pile of text- and notebooks in front of her, slung between outstretched arms. She backed into the chair and, swiveling, deposited the books on the tablet arm. She said nothing to her neighbors, but she seemed at ease with them and they with her. She looked about her, neither pleasantly nor unpleasantly, with no particular recognition, enthusiasm, curiosity, or hostility.

The chatter, mostly focused on the teacher, who clearly was a favorite, ceased, and the class—on the poetry of John Donne—started with a brief, lively lecture, spiced with anecdotes. The students listened. A few took notes. They chuckled at the account of Donne's travails, conversions, reconversions, and love affair. Romagna soon switched to a poem by Donne that had been read in class the day before. What did it mean? She pushed questions out into the students.

Melissa watched all this without animation. Her face was not blank, quite; there was ennui, acceptance, a trace of wariness. A question was directed to her. She looked at the teacher with little change in expression. A pause. I don't understand. Romagna repeated the question, kindly, without reproach. Another pause. I don't know. Maybe Donne means . . . Melissa, speaking slowly, quietly, said something, a phrase using words earlier spoken during the teacher's lecture. It was enough to end the exchange, but not enough to provoke a counterquestion or a follow-up by the teacher. The next question went elsewhere. Melissa kept watching, deadpan, still wary.

The class ambled on, the lack of connection between the recitation of Donne's biography and the poems discussed unnoted. The room was genial, to a fault. There was meat there for students to chew on, but only if they wanted to. Ms. Romagna asked good questions, and these were answered by those students who either were interested in them or eager to connect with this cherished instructor.

Melissa's cautious impassivity was unremitting. It wasn't bovine, a blank stare of ignorance, nor was it the apathy of despair. The detachment was indeed very shrewd. Melissa, however unwittingly, was a master at nonengagement. She sat at the side. She didn't move much, thus drawing little attention to herself. She did not offer ideas to the class, but when questioned, parried to buy time and then answered with something just plausible and relevant enough to avoid being chided for inattention or remarked on for perceptiveness or judged for error. She did well enough on tests to be in this college-track group—actually, a class in the middle of the school's ability groupings, with the honors sections above her and the general sections below. She was an educational artful dodger of considerable skill.

I could imagine Melissa moving through her entire school day in the fashion she exhibited in Ms. Romagna's class. Probably most of her classes had fifteen or more students in them, groups large enough to give cover. Her contacts with teachers could be kept to simple sentences, single exchanges. Probing could be parried. Once she got the hang of dodging, school could be quite effortless. She did enough to pass; her attendance was satisfactory; she would surely get a diploma. However, she would not be inspired—she fended off that prospect—and what she gained about the stuff of academic life and about disciplined intellectual inquiry would be largely by chance. My hunch is that if I were to ask her whether she was wasting her time, she'd demur, saying that she is reasonably happy and that she *will* graduate. The diploma is her goal, and she will do the minimum of whatever is expected of her to achieve it.

Every high school teacher knows Melissa; her tribe is a large one. These are the youngsters who blend deliberately with those pastel colors sensed in Janet and Will's high school, with the friendliness and the absence of productive tension that marks all too many classrooms. Good teachers know that Melissa can be constructively provoked, if there is time and if the class is not too large. They know too that she is not stupid and that she has hopes for her future, however well she succeeds at masking them in school. Unless these hopes are understood and turned into responsible incentives that will spur energetic learning, Melissa's drifting will persist.

Melissa dodges engagement with school for at least four reasons. First, she is not *required* to be engaged. Ms. Romagna doesn't press her, doesn't insist, even in a kindly way, that Melissa's train of thought can benefit from exposure. Melissa's hiding is tolerated. Second, there seems little connection between her world and Donne's, at least as presented in this class. As a result, she feels no intrinsic pressure to become engaged. Third, Melissa may be scared. Risking failure in front of her peers and teacher can be painful. If you don't engage, she may well reason, you don't get hurt. And, finally, Melissa knows that her primary goal is the diploma and that the easiest way to get it is to show up at school regularly and to do the exercises set her. Only minimal engagement is required (for example, she has to listen in class most of the time), and taking risks is certainly not required. Given her goal, Melissa's strategy is reasonable.

How to stimulate engagement is the first question every good teacher asks. The answers? Get the incentives right, for this particular student or these students. Let them succeed at legitimate things; success breeds success. Attract their ideas; everybody learns best from what he values as his own. Get the level right: don't ask too much or too little of the students. Gain the students' respect so that they will want to learn in order to please you. Threaten and punish sparingly.

Virtually all of learning comes down to incentives. I learn what I want to learn. I want to learn what I value or am convinced by people whom I trust that I will eventually value. I want to learn what is fun, what is interesting, what respected elders tell me is important, what gives me a kick, what I am good at. These verities are true for sixty-year-olds as well as sixteen-year-olds.

If one wants to get someone else to learn something, to provoke a Melissa, the first step is to figure out what that other person's motivations are and what strategy of incentives will hook that person's commitment. Some of these incentives may be intrinsic, some extrinsic. The legitimately intrinsic make life easy for the high school teacher, as the student carries them into class. Usually these incentives have grown because of earlier successes. It is fun to succeed, to receive kudos, to feel good about oneself. So why not get some more success? Being good at something is its own reward.

Being intrinsically interested in some subject and being interested in success are two different things, of course, though they greatly overlap. A teacher has difficulty knowing which is which. I knew a fine cross-country runner who trained faithfully and joyfully during her high school years, sweeping meet after meet. She entered college, discovered she was only one of a number of fine runners and certainly not the best, and immediately gave up running.

But competence does not always create its own fuel. Kudos for doing some one thing palls for some people; they reject continuing it, wanting some new thrill or anonymity. Sometimes one wants *not* to be on the honor roll, perhaps, to stop Mom from bragging about her "successful" offspring to her friends.

The most powerful and attractive intrinsic motivation is learning something merely for itself, pushing for something new simply because it is there, with or without kudos or Mom's bragging. That aggressively inquiring posture is neither more nor less rare among adolescents than among the rest of the population. That is, it is exceptional. However, self-induced incentives—self-motivation—can be encouraged by schools.

This "success" cannot be spurious, faked honor rolls or tests on which getting 100 percent is absurdly easy. Adolescents can spot the spurious as easily as they identify the adult hypocrite, the one who says, "You played a great game," to the halfback who gained a total of eight yards on fifteen carries and fumbled four times. Few take much satisfaction from excelling at an easy test, particularly if they know that they ultimately face examinations set by more demanding authorities, such as state regents or the College Board.

Jerome Bruner put it simply: "We get interested in what we get good at."[2] One hopes students get good at things worthy of their interest. A wise teacher starts where he or she can with each pupil. Success at something is better than no success at all. A typical principal's aphorism at an opening-of-the-year faculty meeting is: Make sure that every student succeeds at *something* by Thanksgiving. From something one can move to the important things. Success is the fuel for such movement. It can readily energize Melissas, whose disengagement may be due to intense fear of failure.

If success is part of motivation, ownership is its companion. People remember those things which they claim as their own, things in which they feel they have some stake. Over twenty years ago, James Coleman concluded:

> Modern adolescents are not content with a passive role. They exhibit this discontent by their involvement in positive activities, activities which they can call their *own:* athletics, school newspapers, drama clubs, social affairs, and dates. But classroom activities are hardly of this sort. They are prescribed "exercises," "assignments," "tests," to be done and handed in at a teacher's command. They require not creativity but conformity, not originality and devotion, but attention and obedience. Because they are exercises prescribed for all, they do not allow the opportunity for passionate devotion, such as some teenagers show to popular music, causes, or athletics.[3]

Coleman later softened this assertion, agreeing that some sorts of assigned drill are often useful, but the thrust of his conclusion is accurate. Furthermore, there *is* opportunity for student ownership in every class in every subject—if the teachers value it. Melissa felt no connection with her English class, no proprietorship of any of its ideas and routines. Ms. Romagna would have had to lure her into it.

We all like our own ideas. Most of us want these to be admired by others, too; we then know that our ideas and products may have autonomous merit. There is little joy in accurate regurgitation. Sister Michael signaled that with her skillful use of students' comments, some of which had been made many minutes earlier. By this use she implied that every statement by a student was important, something that could be used again. One often sees the opposite, the teacher who asks a question and then either does not listen to or seems to forget the answer. This signals to the student that the teacher feels that what he thinks and says is not worth much. The result is a stifling of motivation, a validation of disengagement.

Traditionalist critics often carp at apostles of student interest, assuming, in a patronizing way, that adolescents will be interested only in trivia. But people, young and old, are attracted to competence, or at least to the esteem they receive if competence is displayed. A teacher who has his students' respect and who clearly rewards useful and rigorous work is likely to have his students choose useful and rigorous challenges. There will be cop-outs; there always are. But the alternative of having the teacher decide everything is predictably inefficient for everyone.

Finding the students' level of potential accomplishment is important. Even the most committed and clever student will be stymied by a problem or concept that is far beyond his comprehension and thus will not succeed. For example, one simple concept that is both mundane and a problem for some students is, as Joseph Adelson put it, "the concept of mutability." Little children think in alwayses and nevers, eithers and ors, is's and isn'ts. "One of the unrecognized achievements of the adolescent period is the acquisition of the concept of amendment, which is itself part of a larger movement of the mind away from static, either/or conceptions."[4] Permanent tentativeness is a complex notion, especially for a literal, childish mind. That something or some idea may be always in motion, constantly changing its shape, presents major conceptual problems for some students. Moving to it too early leaves the younger minds behind.

I had this problem with my own students when, as I earlier described, I introduced the concept of social class in a history lesson. It is one thing to "see" a person, with all his or her personal, idiosyncratic attributes. It is another, more abstract, thing to see— to conceptualize—groups of people who have certain attributes in common. Little children first face this distinction when sorting out the difference between any older person and an older person who is sister, brother, parent, or other relative. One does not come suddenly to an ability to deal with abstraction or to conceptualize. One is faced early in arithmetic with the number zero; knowing what nothingness means beyond that symbol, however, in mathematics and elsewhere, requires a very mature mind. If a student is asked to deal with concepts beyond his level of abstraction, he fumbles or gets frustrated or fakes it. One sees the last reaction at its most grotesque in social studies classes—for example, where students who do not have the remotest idea of the political concept of sovereignty bombastically debate the rights of Arabs, Jews, and Christians to Jerusalem and the West Bank of the Jordan. Such superficial "debate" carries with it no sense of competence (though some of the more articulate "debaters" may like the praise they receive for play-acting an ambassador). The exercise is spurious.

Jerome Bruner's oft-quoted and liberating assertion that "any subject can be taught effectively in some intellectually honest form to any child at any stage of development" carries with it the obligation for the teacher to ascertain at what level of intellectual abstraction a student is and how to move him forward.[5] "What is most important for teaching basic concepts is that the child be helped to pass progressively from concrete thinking to the utilization of more conceptually adequate modes of thought. But it is futile to attempt this by presenting formal explanations based on a logic that is distant from the child's manner of thinking and sterile in its implications for him."[6] One cannot succeed at something totally beyond one's experience, beyond one's grasp. One is interested in that at which one succeeds. Thus, a clever teacher sets a student's work, and the expectations for it, at a level where some modicum of legitimate success is possible. However, because "experience has shown that it is worth the effort to provide the growing child with problems that tempt him into next stages of development," an effective teacher keeps the subject of study at an arm's length from the student, but no further.[7] The joy of success comes especially sweet when that which was mastered had earlier seemed unachievable.

Most people like to please others, particularly those whom they love. Young adults want to please their parents, want their admiration. If a teacher is respected, his or her admiration is sought. Students will put it, "You have to work hard for Mr. Browne." Really they are saying, "We want Mr. Browne's respect." Peers are sources of admiration too, sometimes as competitors. I do well in order to beat out Mike.

The sword can cut the other way. If Mom and Dad and Teacher don't care, why should I? If parents speak of their disrespect and lack of trust in teachers, the children are likely to disrespect and distrust the teachers.

Inside schools, the most common motivating devices are lures and threats, sugar lumps and sticks. The stick is firmly in place in American schools. It will surprise many to find that stick actually, as well as metaphorically, in use there, in public as well as in private high schools. One public senior high school I visited had a line of students, male and female, one weeping, sitting outside the assistant principals' offices, waiting for a hearing and the likely "popping" that would follow after it. In this school, the male assistant principals would pop the boys; the female assistant principal, the girls. These three administrators reported to me that each carried out such punishments about six times per day; there were twenty-two hundred students in their school. They used wooden or fiber-glass paddles. They felt that the system worked and that simple popping made a useful point and then cleared the air in a way that so-called counseling, which they felt was a form of never-completed humiliation, did not. A nearby church-related school pursued the same policy, and the reasoning behind it, but preceded and followed each punishment session with prayers by and for the wayward student and his chastener.

The majority of punishments are less physical. Most common are forms of censuring (being sent to "the office"—usually of an assistant principal—and being chewed out), of humiliation (calls made home, letting it be known within the student body that some particular student has broken some rule), of extra duties (a required study hall, sometimes on a Saturday morning; at some private schools, physical labor; at a naval JROTC magnet academy in a city public school system, marching for a period of hours on a parade ground), or of suspension or total expulsion from school. Teachers use humiliation most often. Test papers are handed back in order of grade received, the highest first, a form of torture in anticipation as well as result. Grades are posted. In one small school I visited, each student's averaged score appeared, labeled by name, as a point on a chart that graced the school's front hall. Ridicule or sarcasm is found in classrooms. One more dumb remark out of you, John . . . Now, let's see whether Mary can get at least *this* one . . . Oh, God, you again, Keith . . . Another device is putting a student in limbo, simply ignoring him or her.

Being the bad guy can often make a student a hero, of course, and sometimes the application of humiliation has precisely the opposite effect of that intended. Clever students will manipulate insensitive teachers to achieve such ends, sometimes with exquisite cruelty. A school that relies on threat for its motivation eventually provokes unrelenting, hostile reactions by students.

Threat as a motivating device is as ineffective as it is superficially efficient. No one learns much while being threatened. A humiliated worker performs poorly; so does a humiliated student. "Aversive" behavior, B. F. Skinner has amply demonstrated, may have short-range benefits (the class may become quiet), but is likely to leave long-term scars (the seething resentment in the class distracts everyone from learning the subject under study).[8]

The threat seems to appeal to many adults as a symbol of their authority. Children are at school to learn what we adults expect them to learn, and they should understand that we're the boss. That power relationship may in fact be accurate, but if it is not softened with humane respect, with understanding of the adolescent's inexperience and need to test things and with an effort to encourage the student to take some independent responsibility for his own education, the results at school will be thin. Schools in which students feel themselves partners, or at least respected constituents, where they are held accountable for some of their own education, something that they can take pride in for themselves, are effective places. The stick is an inefficient motivating device for high schools.

Anyone who, like me, has been a school principal lives with the contradiction that aversive measures stunt learning and that punishment is a part of a school's necessary discipline, whatever philosophy and psychology may recommend. One may try to understand and work with violent adolescents, but violent people have to be removed from school. Cheaters must be unequivocally dealt with. No student should ever be made an example of—a head on a spike for the populace to see—but everyone in a school needs to know specifically what goes and what does not go and the penalties for the latter. As a disciplinarian, I always tried to do "what was right for the student," hoping that would be the most effective educational signal. It did not always work, of course; to protect students' privacy, one often could not explain all the reasons for an action taken. One suffered in silence, feeling others' resentment and wallowing in it oneself.

Some schools shift the focus of their threats by involving students in the punishment process. A small high school in a rural area had a seemingly intractable problem of speeding and joyriding in the student parking lot during the lunch break. In exasperation, the principal "solved" the problem by shortening the length of this lunch break: there would not be time to go to the cafeteria (a popular place) and also to horse around in one's car. However, many students felt that this was unfair. All were punished for the clearly dangerous antics of a few. With the encouragement of a respected social studies teacher, a group of students proposed an alternative solution. If the principal would restore the full lunch hour, these students, with the advice of the teacher, would see that a committee—in fact, a student court—would be created to police the lot and mete out punishment, in the form of cash fines, to the offenders. The principal agreed. The system had been in effect for over six months at the time of my visit, and the results seemed to be happy ones. The resentment of the joyriders was limited, students told me, because the arguments for safety (that is, slow driving) in the parking lot were self-evident. The involvement of the students as judges gave them useful experience and a proper sense of their own responsibility, their "ownership" of their school. The principal gained allies among the students, where before he had had hostility.

Not all issues are as easily solved as that one, but the message it gives is useful. Hostility gets in the way of learning. Involvement—a sense of ownership—assists it.

How does one motivate Melissa? In her particular case, Ms. Romagna should prevent her from hiding in class, by pressing her with questions and insisting that she answer clearly. This will likely frighten Melissa, and she almost surely will disengage further. Romagna will then have to arrange an individual meeting after class. Melissa's withdrawal and the reasons for Romagna's pursuit of her should be clearly outlined and explained. With luck, the conversation between Melissa and Ellen Romagna in time will shift to why Melissa is not at all engaged in school. The answers may give Romagna a clue toward how to pull Melissa into the work of the English class, productively and without crippling threat.

No two Melissas are precisely alike, making Ellen Romagna's task slow and often frustrating. However, until such students are engaged, the hours they spend in class are an almost total loss.

4

Conditions

MOST AMERICAN FAMILIES grapple in March and April with income tax returns. Most of those family members who assemble the materials and do the calculations need quiet, enough space to spread out the papers, sufficient hassle-free time to get the job done correctly, good enough light to read the fine print, and sympathetic husbands, wives, or children, who say, "You poor, poor thing for having to do that terrible job," and periodically bring coffee and brownies. Of course, not all tax-return assemblers are alike: some work well with a jumble of papers around, others need neat piles; some want total quiet, others want a "white sound"—Muzak— behind them; some prefer bourbon to coffee. In fact, no two of us efficiently complete this annual democratic chore in precisely the same way.

It is so with learners in schools. The environment is important. If it jangles the mind, or interrupts or demeans or frightens, there cannot be the kind of focused, sustained intellectual activity that is required to write a clear and graceful paragraph or accurately complete a Form 1040. One's flanks need be secure so that one can focus on some central object. Covered flanks require trust (I know I won't be interrupted by these people, because they understand my need to concentrate), predictability (I know I can count on the next thirty minutes for this), and adequate resources (I know I have the tools to do this job).

It does not take much to ruin a class, to break the thread of thought. So it was in a social studies lesson in a small-town public high school. The classroom contained thirteen seniors. They chatted amiably among themselves and with Jim Gerry, the teacher, for a few minutes after the bell, an obviously necessary exercise, as five more students came in late, one by one, each in turn whispering to Gerry and handing him an excuse slip. He nodded pleasantly to each, and the student then found a chair, unloaded an armful of books in a tumble on the floor, and, once seated, stretched and looked expectantly at the movie projector that was set up at the center of the room.

This was a seniors' social studies elective, called sociology. Gerry told the students that he was going to open the class with a movie on the 1960s. He reminded them that they had seen it before, in tenth grade, but he said that it made sense to screen it again, because it was a fine film and was closely related to the current course's topic of "cultural change." Several of the students mentioned remembering it.

Gerry turned off the lights, asked several students on his right to pull down the shades, and started the film. It was a collage of newsreel and film clips taken during the sixties, with a sound track of speeches, Vietnam, the crowds outside the Chicago Democratic Party convention, the Beatles, Dr. King, the Kennedys, Bull Connor, the Newark riots, and more. It was an excellent production, as Gerry had promised, gripping the students, who had been born in the middle of the decade, almost as much as it did Gerry and his visitor, who as adults had lived through it. The piece opened with President Kennedy's inaugural speech and returned to it periodically, sometimes in irony, sometimes in pathos. At one of the ironic moments, well into the film, the public address system rasped on. Gerry cut the film. Four announcements were made, on a wrestling camp, on freshman summer programs, on a meeting of the National Honor Society, and on tryouts for the swing choir. The blare extinguished itself as abruptly as it had erupted. Gerry turned on the film again, the sound track swooping back into audibility. Kennedy, before a living figure, was now papier-mâché.

Public address systems are the most malevolent intruder into the thinking taking place in public school classrooms since the invention of the flickering fluorescent light. In the name of efficient management, they regularly eviscerate good teaching. They are a symbol of misplaced priorities, of schools that fail to value conditions for serious intellectual activity. Their cousins—the intruding messenger from the office and the extracurricular or public relations exercise on behalf of the school system that pre-empts class time—are no better. They all signal the low priority that routine teaching may hold, and they certainly puzzle students who on one occasion observe the school casually canceling some classes to make time for a Mr. and Miss Junior America Assembly and on another severely admonishing individuals not to miss any classes at all.

A good school should be a place of unanxious expectation.[9] Although some expectations certainly are *angst*-producing, a good school's standards are challenging, not threatening, energy-producing rather than defense-producing. Neither a casual school, where no one does anything except that which seems to titillate him at a given moment, nor a tyrannical school, where cruel jockeying for position, involving both students and teachers, is the answer. Casual schools practice the Conspiracy—I'll not hassle you, Mr. Teacher, if you don't push me, the Student. Tyrannical schools simply scare people, whether by shakedowns in the lavatories, humiliation in classrooms, or the psychological warfare that some bigger, older, rougher, whiter, or blacker people impose by treating others as dirt, nonpeople, or worse.

Learning involves exposure—the exhibition of things not known, skills poorly developed, ideas ill formed. One learns to get things right by revealing where one is wrong. Such a display of incompetence, however well intentioned, makes one vulnerable, easily marked. Good schools promote displays of incompetence (strange though that may sound) in order to help students find their way to competence. A test that one fails may be a far more helpful test from which to learn than one on which one gets a perfect score. In a word, good schools make it O.K. to exhibit one's lack of learning and make it safe to do so—safe in the sense that ridicule will have no part in the process, even as correction does.

At the same time, a good school has standards, expectations about what students (and teachers—all the adults working there) can and should do. There is a difference between good effort and good performance, and evidence of the first, while it should be recognized and encouraged, should play no part in the fair assessment of the second. An adverb is an adverb, however nice, well-meaning, and hard-working the student is who insists that it is an adjective. Good teachers and wise students know how to separate performance (you flunked) from person (you're O.K.). Making a child feel stupid is itself stupid and cruel, but pretending that $2 + 2 = 5$ in order to massage the student's ego is cruel, and dishonest in addition.

Unanxious expectation applies as well to less subtle things. If anyone—student or teacher—is anxious about actual physical violence, little useful learning can take place in the school. Safe schools are essential, but in some strained communities may be difficult to attain. Expensive retinues of security guards, police, and aides, in school merely to protect students from each other and from hostile parties from the outside, are unfortunate but necessary. That they are visible and active, with their walkie-talkies blaring, is no cause for embarrassment. It is simply an unequivocal statement that this place will be *safe*. No other priority can or should precede that. Nearly all students and teachers value it.

A good school is a stable school. One does not learn well in snippets, a bit snatched here and a morsel nibbled there. The processes of trial and error, of practice, of building up a repertoire of skills and a body of knowledge, take time. Rapid changes in routines, groups, settings, and expectations are confusing, and cause the very students who most need help to make fewer commitments. Why should I listen carefully to this teacher if he may not be here in four weeks? Why struggle with this material if I don't know whether anyone is going to be sympathetic and helpful next term? It is the same issue for the teachers: Why put hours into this demoralized child if he is absent half the time and will be transferred to another school in two months?

Governing authorities persistently underrate the importance of stability.[10] For dozens of other pressing reasons, student school assignments are shuffled, often late in the summer. Teachers will be assigned abruptly, and reassigned during the year. Principals scream at "downtown": You can't do this! The program will be gutted! The answer is always: We know, but these other issues are paramount. Keeping a school together, keeping it stable, is clearly a low priority compared with other issues.

Part of stability is predictability: one is *sure* of certain things— times, policies, attitudes. A fetish can be made of this, of course. Some of the schoolkeepers' passion for punctuality, for example, is anal tidiness. No, Sally, you can't do that, because it says right here that you can't. The trick, of course, is to temper orderliness with flexibility, never an easy task.

Other qualities of good schools are as obvious as they are often difficult to practice. Good schools are clear on their mission (which is unsurprising: we tend to show up at places when we know the way to them). They are fair. Very simply, they are decent places, deserving loyalty. They are demanding, but not threatening, places of unanxious expectation.

Human factors rather than physical ones most shape the climate of a school. As one thorough research study reported, the "differences in outcome between schools were *not* due to such physical factors as the size of the school, the age of the buildings or the space available; nor were they due to broad differences in administrative status or organization. It was entirely possible for schools to obtain good outcomes in spite of initially rather unpromising and unprepossessing school premises."[11] In a memorandum, prepared for our study, on the influence of physical environment on student achievement, Betsy Parsons, a secondary school teacher from Portland, Maine, pointed out the well-known fact that "we all know stories of brilliant teaching under the most adverse conditions." She went on, "Among my favorites are the tales of an Irish friend of mine, a high school literature teacher and incidentally a nun, who did her most inspired teaching and witnessed her students' most inspired learning in a cold, windy, yawning airplane hangar with the dust blowing on the class in biting sheets."

Be this as it may, physical conditions can yet have substantial effect. I visited a social studies class in a suburban high school built within the last twenty years. It was a large school—some twenty-two hundred students—and classes were held in a cluster of large steel-and-cinderblock prefabricated buildings. These had been intended for "open plan" teaching; the social studies block I visited had three classes going on simultaneously, separated by acoustical curtains. Two of these three classes were to be joined on the day of my visit, so the curtains between them were drawn back. The sounds of the lecture in the curtained-off third class were fully audible, however.

One class of thirty-five students, crowded together in tablet-arm desks, faced east. At their northeastern front, which was one corner of the building, there was an overhead projector and screen. One of the two teachers manned this station. The other class of thirty-five students faced north, toward a blackboard, desk, and lectern where the second teacher held forth. These students could swivel in their seats, or lean, to see the screen, and their colleagues in the first group could swivel to see the blackboard.

The class started with one teacher asking for votes for the basketball homecoming king and queen. This provoked giggling and gossiping. One of the teachers efficiently orchestrated the collection of votes himself. The other turned the process over to a student, who, confused, took far longer to complete the poll. Low-order chaos resulted, especially in the first group, which had completed its balloting.

The class continued with an assigned exercise, the preparation of a job application for a famous figure. Copies of such an application for Harry S Truman were distributed, a clever piece of brief biography. Each student was to select his or her own "important figure" and prepare a similar sketch, and the teachers passed out an "Application for Employment" to assist them in the exercise.

When this brief written exercise was completed, the teacher next to the overhead projector started the formal lesson, a study of the American West—"number nine on your vocabulary sheet." This sheet, which some but not all of the almost seventy students present now rustled up, was a study guide, "what you'll be held accountable for." The lecturer continued, with attention now on "the American Indian and . . . the conflict between them [sic] and us." After a review of some of the points that were outlined in the study guide, the task of teaching swung to the second instructor, who picked up the lecture. The students swiveled to watch him. He told the story of Sutter's Mill. Then the thread went back to teacher number one. Students swiveled. Then back, to talk of "Pikers' [sic] Peak."

We learned that the reason that Chinese were brought to the United States in the mid-nineteenth century was that it was cheaper to bring them here than to keep sending dirty laundry all the way across the Pacific. Back to teacher number one . . . The performance was like Ping-Pong (played occasionally with a very faulty ball), the students twisting back and forth, moderately entertained but as confused as I. No notes were taken, no additions made to the orderly study guide the teachers had prepared. The students near the third classroom were privy to the conversation in that class as well. For most of the students, the fifty minutes spent in that overcrowded, bewildering, acoustically calamitous place were not valuable, in any important educational sense. (The school's principal, attending the session with me, must have sensed my dismay; leaning over, he said that the students did not find this arrangement as bad as I obviously did.)

This is, perhaps, an extreme example. For some purposes—for example, a large lecture for all three social studies sections or for some kinds of classroom group work—the space so disastrously used on the day I visited could be functional. Lectures are well served by orderly rows of chairs for the listeners, each with a good view of the teacher. A seminar needs a smaller space. As argument among the participants requires excellent communication, students and teachers ideally should be seated at a round or oval table. (Since people like the psychological protection of an object between them and others, as well as a place to park their books, a table is preferable to an open circle, where "exposure" is total.) Recitation may suffer in the round; recitation is dialogue between the teacher and one particular student, with the other students to be kept as much as possible at a psychological, if not a physical, distance. Recitations are best served by small rooms with chairs in rows. There can be other configurations, varying with the teachers' tactics of instruction, the needs of the subjects, and the characteristics of the students. Form follows function, and different functions require different spaces, levels of quiet, and equipment.[12]

Space teaches. A trenchant example was found in a Southern high school, one that had been founded over thirty years ago for an all-white student body. Today, it is an all-black school. It was shabbily maintained. Responsibility for upkeep lay "downtown."

The principal could only send in requisitions to the central office and plead, curse, and pray. He could not get any of the work, even obviously needed simple painting, done on his own—even by himself—because that would breach contracts with the system's unionized and overscheduled painters. (His own ruse, a clever one, was to have hallway walls covered with murals by art classes—that was "education" rather than "maintenance," and he controlled the former.)

The students and staff got the message, as did the principal: no one really cared whether the school was a dump, and that showed that no one really cared about them as people. Most telling were the photographs on a long, third-story corridor. Starting in the 1940s, each graduating class had had a framed plaque hung on the walls, one that included the graduation photograph of each student, along with a group picture. These large photographic collages still hung on their wires, covered with grime, some dangling awry, with rows of white smiling faces. A close look found two or three black faces in the mid-1960s, more by the late sixties—and then no more plaques. Ghosts and questions hovered around those dusty frames. Every student must have noticed them.

Most middle- and upper-income Americans would be both shocked by and afraid of some of the places where the young citizens of the poor are now at school. They would be indignant about the Byzantine politics that entangle most understaffed and underfinanced maintenance operations. I have seen a sad poster on the walls of many tattered schools, one that is a poor substitute for the simple courtesies of decently maintained places for learning. It says, simply: "I *am* somebody because God don't make no junk."

Good schools expect no child to be junk. That expectation includes a commitment to provide each child with an education in a place that is attractive and free of fear. It is a pity that some schools, especially those serving the poor, fall so far short.

5

Teachers

THE VISITOR to schools repeatedly looks for signs of good quality and patterns that promise success. Inescapably they point to the teachers. Who Horace Smith and Sister Michael and Martha Shiffe and Fred Curtis are is the crucial element. An imaginative, appropriate curriculum placed in an attractive setting can be unwittingly smothered by journeymen instructors. It will be eviscerated by incompetents. On the other hand, good teachers can inspire powerful learning in adolescents, even under the most difficult circumstances, as Charles Gross bears witness. Improving American secondary education absolutely depends on improving the conditions of work and the respect for teachers. No new technology, training scheme, licensure revision, or new curriculum will suffice.

Today as one listens to teachers talk about their station in life, one hears a flood of idealism, complaint, self-doubt, exhilaration, anger, commitment, and resentment.[13] Teachers, never held in high esteem by American society, are a stubborn lot. They have to be to take both the slights to which the culture subjects them and the overload of obligations that greets them every day at school. Teaching has its share of malingerers and incompetents, teachers who happily contract into a Conspiracy of the Least or who are barely literate. However, if one were to select a profession in which malingering was easy, one would not pick teaching. While the classroom is a very private place as far as other adults are concerned—most teachers labor unobserved by their colleagues over 95 percent of the time—it is very much a public activity for the students. It takes energy and skill to strike and sustain a bargain with your classes. It is easier to be a goldbricker in most business offices or on shop floors than in classrooms. Teachers are too much on show to hide easily.

The litany of commitment and demoralization is paradoxical. The typical teacher to whom we listened is an idealist who genuinely wants students to succeed, who wishes them well. Most teachers accept unquestioningly the American conviction about the worth of schooling. They want schools to prosper and believe they can.

Yet teachers are dismayed. We heard this especially from public school folk and particularly in states hard hit by economic woes, such as Michigan, or in the throes of taxpayers' revolts, such as Massachusetts and California. In the former, there is despair; in the latter, incredulity. Do the people really know what they are doing to their schools? Do they really *care?*

One hears less disillusion from private school teachers, even though in a relative sense most are less well off financially and less protected by tenure than their public school colleagues. One speculates that private school teachers have made their peace with their chancy poverty and, more important, that they feel more in control of their schools. Many of the financial decisions that are crucial to public school teachers take place in arenas far from them—in school board–union negotiations, state legislative actions, and federal grant policies. Tuition-dependent private schools see their income, or lack thereof, at excruciatingly but comprehendably close range.

A good teacher is self-confident. Teaching is being on show. It is challenging a student's ideas, an arrogant art if you are not well informed. It is being the oracle, passing along truths to less knowledgeable folk who depend on their teacher's accuracy. It is playing God, because a teacher's attitudes and expectations can profoundly affect young people, particularly the most vulnerable among them. Legitimate self-confidence arises from objective feedback. You are reassured when your students do well on other people's tests or when they use in their further education the skills you taught them and recount to you how effective your classes were. You are reassured when students seek your advice, or when colleagues watch your students and your classes and respect what is happening.

Confidence ebbs if you do not have the tools to do the job. If there are no maps for a geography class, too few instruments for a physics laboratory exercise, inadequate books in the library for a social studies assignment, teachers can feel vulnerable—and it will visibly affect and weaken their teaching.

If students are truant or casually late or threatening beyond that with which an individual instructor can cope—in other words, if the community, the school administration, and fellow teachers do not support minimal conditions for good instructors to ply their trade—teachers feel their flanks uncovered, vulnerable. The consequences will show up in their classes.

If students are readily excused from class, for example for choral or athletic trips or for tutoring, if lectures and discussions are abruptly interrupted by announcements on the public address system or emissaries from the office—if, in sum, teachers cannot be sure of the time at their disposal with the students for whom they have responsibility—they lose certainty that what they have planned can be accomplished. Their dismay will show.

Students like confident teachers, and it takes time for an instructor to prove himself or herself. Mr. Curtis, Mr. Gross, and Sister Michael are all confident people, and their students have been with them long enough to know the expectations that confidence exhibits. Sister Michael can ask a question and wait out an answer, leaving the query hanging in charged silence, rarely losing a student's focus on the issue presented. Silence is always threatening. Creating a climate in a classroom that not only tolerates but uses silence requires a confident teacher and students who respect that confidence. Sister Michael wants the students to know that she will get an answer from them, that they *can* answer, and that whatever they say will be used. Less-confident teachers do not know whether anyone will respond, and as a result many American classrooms are led by adults who ask questions and then promptly answer them themselves.

Good teachers are patient, and patience flows out of the confidence that quiet "thinking time" can be well spent. One can visualize

Mr. Gross waiting out an all-thumbs student struggling with a wiring problem at the practice wall, or, even more poignantly, waiting out the stumbling oral explanation of the solution to that problem which the student struggles to give. Gross has to know that the student can do it, and by his patience signal that assurance to the youngster. Confident teachers create confidence in their students. Likewise, a teacher who exhibits spurious confidence—trying, say, to convince students that they can do something that is beyond their reach—is the architect of the students' disillusionment.

A good teacher tells students the truth about themselves. How the truth is articulated is, of course, a matter of sophisticated judgment. But this good teacher has to know confidently what the truth is, what a fair critique of Greene's "The Destructors" may be, what piece of complex circuitry will work and why, what computer program will dependably answer an important question. The teacher's confidence is not only in his subject; it also reflects the conviction that the school expects its teachers to tell the truth and will back them in that often painfully confrontational undertaking.

Our culture signals respect in at least three ways. We give people autonomy: we say, We trust you enough to solve this problem not only for yourself, but for us all. In the world of work, we dub this autonomy "professionalism." The lawyer writes the brief for us. The doctor makes his diagnosis. The roofer decides how to sheathe the faulty gutters.

Second, we signal respect with money. We pay people what we think they deserve. Salary policies are more complicated than this, of course, but money clearly is an expression of our priorities.

Finally, we signal respect by expressing it: we bestow a Nobel Prize, a Rhodes Scholarship, a Pulitzer.

In one sense, high school teachers should feel that they are greatly respected, since they are allowed to teach in remarkable privacy. Few teachers watch each other teach. However, this privacy may be less the result of social respect than of indifference. One can read some parents' minds: Our kids'll learn that history stuff on their own, and it really doesn't matter if they don't learn it all, because they'll never actually use it much. But be nice to our kids. Give them good grades. Many teachers hear this quiet signal, with or without cynicism. Undoubtedly it is there. Thus, the privacy of the classroom is not always the honored badge of the professional but an indication that what happens there is thought to be of relatively little consequence.

Few find much mystery in teaching. The technical expertise is not arcane and it has a familiar vocabulary, the monstrously pretentious language of some educationists notwithstanding. The distance between professional and client that often exists in medicine and law and the autonomy created by many business people does not exist for teachers. The qualities that make for good teaching are generally available qualities—knowledgeability, energy, clarity, empathy. Given this fact, the teacher lacks the respect-laden autonomy enjoyed by other professionals. The individual instructor or groups of instructors rarely decide what the basic outlines of their curriculum will be. That is handed down, either by administratively senior colleagues or by lay boards, often with elaborate teaching guides. (Teachers can sabotage or ignore these, of course, and few people will find out.)

Teachers are told the amount of time they are to spend with each class—say, fifty-five minutes five times a week. Even though they are expected to be competent scholars, they are rarely trusted with the selection of the texts and teaching materials they are to use, a particularly galling insult. Teachers are rarely consulted, much less given significant authority, over the rules and regulations governing the life of their school; these usually come from "downtown." Rarely do they have any influence over who their immediate colleagues will be; again, "downtown" decides. One wonders how good a law firm would be if it were given manuals on how to apply the law, were told precisely how much time to spend on each case, were directed how to govern its internal affairs, and had no say whatever in who the partners were. Teaching often lacks a sense of ownership, a sense among the teachers working together that the school is theirs, and that its future and their reputation are indistinguishable. Hired hands own nothing, are told what to do, and have little stake in their enterprises. Teachers are often treated like hired hands. Not surprisingly, they often act like hired hands.[14]

According to one's point of view, teachers' salaries are reasonable or too high or too low. They are reasonable today in a market sense. With the growing exception of mathematics and science teachers and specialists in various aspects of special education, there are today more job seekers than jobs. (But by the late 1980s, this may no longer be so.) One can conclude that teaching positions are not undercompensated, as few remain vacant very long.

Some 75 to 85 percent of most school budgets are for salaries. At a time of economic retrenchment, existing compensation may be higher than many communities are able (or, more accurately, are willing) to pay. Therefore, salaries come down, most commonly by the school board's holding increases under the inflation rate. That is, a teacher today can buy less with his or her salary than he or she could yesterday. One estimate revealed a 13 percent drop in public school teachers' real salaries from 1970 to 1980, and a 16 percent real reduction in the compensation for independent school teachers.[15]

Teachers' salaries seem especially low if one takes into account the seriousness of the obligations that teachers are asked to fulfill. The 1982–1983 salary schedule used by a large Western public school system is illustrative.[16] Consider the case of a twenty-two-year-old man with a bachelor's degree and no experience who is employed by this school system. He is paid $14,228 per year, a sum only $50 lower than the average annual wage earned by all eighteen-to-twenty-four-year-old American males with four years of college who are employed full time.[17] In contrast, entry-level industrial chemists with bachelor's degrees and no experience average $19,640 per year, and their counterparts in engineering average $23,622.[18] Our novice's teaching colleagues in this system who have bachelor's degrees and ten years' experience earn $20,251. Colleagues with advanced degrees (or "90 credits beyond the B.A.") who have taught for thirty years and are nearing retirement earn $30,000—almost 20 percent less than the average yearly earnings of their fifty-five-to-sixty-four-year-old counterparts working full time in other occupations.[19] Teachers do have summer "vacation" times, so they can supplement their salaries somewhat then. Often, however, the months of July and August are needed for study; almost always, some portion is needed for rest. "Summers off" sounds nice, but in practice the time does not provide likely employment that can add appreciably to a teacher's salary.

The typical salary schedule takes account of years of experience (a crude but reasonable distinction) and of credits of postbaccalaureate study completed (an unreasonable practice). Teachers, like most people, learn from experience, and on that hope one can rationalize part of a salary schedule. The connection between teaching competence and graduate credits earned, particularly if the field in which they are earned is unspecified, is remote. Certainly people who know well what they are teaching and how to assist students to learn are likely to serve children better than those who do not, but the correlation between course credits and pedagogical effectiveness, at least as one observes it in practice, is tenuous.

Few salary schedules take significant account of teaching ability. Some systems include "merit" increments, but these tend to be marginal. The political difficulties of making judgments about teaching effectiveness are paralyzing.[20] These judgments, like the most important judgments teachers make about their pupils, are necessarily subjective, and the creation of a fair process to reach such evaluations usually seems politically impossible. Thus, schools retain "objective" criteria—years of teaching, credits earned—even if they are only marginally relevant and consequently capricious. The message to the teacher is shimmeringly clear: How good or bad I am as teacher plays virtually no part in the assignment of my salary. My employers lack the political courage to reward any exceptionally good work that I may do. Obviously, they don't value the quality that is the source of my self-esteem—my effectiveness in helping young people to learn.

Other occupations reward exceptional competence by promotions. Virtually the only promotion for a teacher is to get out of teaching and perhaps enter administration. To be sure, there are hierarchies of sorts among teachers—some are department chairmen, some are not—but these tend most commonly to follow seniority. While school boards periodically make noises about rewarding demonstrably effective teachers with endowed "chairs," like university professors, the reality is that a teacher has the same "rank" in his or her last year as in the first.[21] This classlessness has a certain ideological glamour, but it flies in the face of most humans' need for personal incentives.

When people succeed, they want both increased challenges and the opportunity to assist others to master their craft. There is little scope for these natural desires in school work. How many people, save those of great self-possession, feel good about doing almost the same task at the day of retirement as they did on the first day of work? One can take enormous pleasure both at the mastery one may have developed and particularly at the students' lives one has touched, but the sameness of professional life for teachers gives little incentive for recognized excellence and influence, those powerful fuels for useful self-esteem.

A final blow to teachers' self-esteem is, ironically, the well-intentioned but patronizing efforts of some to recognize it. There are the Teacher of the Year awards—as though there was in fact a reputable way of assessing who might be the most deserving. There is not, of course, and as a result the politicized nature of these awards makes them hollow. There are articles in magazines by celebrities, praising dear old Miss Jones or eccentric old Mr. Brown, who "taught me all I know." One searches in vain for articles on "my favorite lawyer," "my favorite surgeon," or "my favorite banker," based on the same method of selection. The saccharine quality of these exercises cloys, however gracious the thoughts that lie behind them, and makes serious teachers wince. Few awards are consequential, in financial terms or in the sense that the competition for them consisted of widely respected criteria.

In my first year of teaching, I, a college English major, was given, in addition to English classes, two sections of mathematics—thirty-five eighth-graders in Algebra I and thirty ninth-graders in Algebra II. My own formal education in the subject had ceased with eleventh-grade plane geometry, seven years earlier. To put it charitably, my scholarly achievements in the field were modest. However, as an artillery officer for two years prior to my entry in the profession of schoolteaching I had had to use some mathematics, in surveying and in fire direction, and that gave me some confidence. I felt I was at least semicompetent. I needed the job, and I thought I could get through it with the bravado of a recently retired army first lieutenant and with the help of a wife who was good at algebra. My judgment was correct: I *did* get through the year without being summarily fired.

The salvation was the textbooks, the answer books, and my wife. I knew which chapters I had to cover and laid out my program accordingly. I found a good "problems book" (also complete with answers), from which I could lift questions for tests. Each day I would assign homework, and each night my wife would help me do the problems. We would ascertain which were likely to be the toughest ones, and I would work up a presentation of the solution of each. I would start each class with a one- or two-problem quiz, which I would grade on the spot. Each class was, then, precisely the same: collection of homework, quiz, review of quiz, presentation of the solution of one or two of the harder problems from the homework, and assignment of homework, accompanied by a highly circumscribed lecture on what was in the new material, this in fact being a paraphrase of the text.

The students did learn what was in the text, and the text, fortunately, was for its time an excellent one. The students on the whole were modestly respectful, and I could, with old army scare tactics, muzzle the few protesters and wake up the almost irretrievably bored. My cover came close to being blown only once. A problem emerged late in the Algebra II course for which even my competent wife could not get an answer similar to that printed in the teachers' guide. We stayed up until 2:00 A.M., struggling. Was the flaw in her mathematics or in the answer book? Even after we had turned out the light and tried to sleep, one or the other of us would periodically leap up: "I think I've got it . . ." We never did, and the following morning I had to ask a colleague how to do the problem. The answer book had been correct; the solution actually was very obvious; I was mortified; my colleague was surprised and amused.

The students in my classes learned mathematical operations pretty well. They learned virtually nothing about mathematical inquiry or mathematical thinking, because I knew virtually nothing about these things. Certainly, my pupils were not inspired by the subject. In a word, they became competent algebraic drones. However, if I had not had good texts, an ability to keep discipline with a tough administration behind me, and a supportive spouse, the year would have been a total disaster. Competent drones were the best I could hope for. Fortunately for high school youths, I have not taught mathematics since. My experience would be irrelevant, except that it represents a sadly common situation. Many high school teachers do not know their subjects. They teach, as I did, from day to day, and the textbook is the source of everything.

Some teachers of cripplingly limited scholarship believe they are scholars and that they do know their subjects. They may have been the victims of standardless college courses and were given A's and B's for work of dismal quality. As a result, they believe that they are competent, when in fact they are not. There is very little quality control in higher education, and it is difficult for many college students to know just how well they stack up as scholars in their fields. Institutions of higher education are as victimized by credit-counting as are the high schools. One can "earn" a B.A. in English at many colleges, for example, merely by accumulating so-and-so many credit hours in English, with no regard for which English courses these may be. Few colleges give cumulative general examinations, the only means the institutions have for ultimately ascertaining the breadth and depth of a student's knowledge.

The problem of scholarly competence takes on an even more difficult form after people have been teaching for some years. These individuals may have put on a show similar to mine in my algebra classes for so long that they have memorized the textbooks and convinced themselves that they know their disciplines. However, no foray outside the confines of that particular book becomes possible. Teachers like these make curricular improvement monumentally difficult.

Yet others may be graduates of good programs and may be teaching in what are apparently their areas of specialization, but in fact have little knowledge of the key material taught in high schools. Mathematics majors may have had no exposure to traditional or modern geometry. History majors may have studied almost no modern history or European history or non-Western history, or they may have had no serious exposure to the social sciences other than history, disciplines that figure large in so-called social studies classes. English majors may be exhaustively prepared as literary critics, but know nothing of the systematic craft of writing or linguistics or the study of language. In a word, a seemingly "solid" college major is not necessarily enough. One may hope that a well-trained graduate is able to fill in the gaps, as when the competent Americanist "gets up" Asian history. This is surely possible and often the case, but rarely do schools give a teacher time to do this. Few school systems have any kind of paid sabbatical or other kinds of leave. Extending one's education must be done on one's own time.

Few undergraduate programs, even at highly regarded colleges, include scholarly experience in bringing together areas of knowledge. Many colleges have "distribution" requirements—the history major may have to take a science course—but few ask a young scholar to use various disciplines *in combination,* the history and the science used together in a valuable way. Departmental divisions are deep, and this is transmitted to the ethos of the high school. Students rarely see high school teachers exhibiting their *general* education; they witness a display of their mentors' specialist education and, if anything, pick up signals of boredom or even sarcasm about subjects other than the one taught by each teacher. The mathematics teacher will be condescending about the theater teacher. The English teacher may show horror when asked a question rooted in science. Don't ask me, I'm no science teacher. The result of excessive specialist training is to freeze high school organization into specialist molds. But most high school students are not going to become specialists, and they, in their often wise naïveté, frequently refuse to see the world through discipline-approved spectacles. For them, philosophy seeps into physics, statistics into history, geometry into art, and art into geometry. Teachers lose opportunities to help students when, because of the narrowness of their training, they shy away from these promising real views of the world.

Compounding this dismal picture is the fact that, apart from their rhetoric, governing authorities pay little attention to the scholarship of their teaching staffs. Little money is allocated for fresh study of the disciplines. Teaching certificates are vaguely construed, usually solely in terms of credit hours. Little effort is made by public authorities at any level to gauge the depth and breadth of prospective or veteran teachers' grasp of subjects (although efforts are underway in several states to mandate competency tests for teachers). Nothing is more illuminating than the easy willingness of school authorities (and federal and state courts) to reassign teachers at the last minute. In one extreme example in an Eastern city under a court order, a veteran kindergarten teacher was targeted to become a senior high physics teacher because her old "general" teaching certificate showed some credits taken in physics years before. Because of her seniority in the school system, the computer-driven teacher-assignment program sent her to teach at the city's most prestigious academic high school.[22] The assumption that anyone can teach anything within his or her "certificated" field on a few days' notice makes a mockery of teaching and of students' learning.

When I questioned these sorts of policies, administrators explained: It's out of our hands. The enrollments changed. The courts demand it. Other pressing priorities intervened. All those explanations are, at best, limp. Teaching by the seat of one's pants or skirt is no way to help students learn. However, capricious teacher assignment is the first compromise usually tolerated when a difficult situation arises. The hunch "downtown" is that the teachers will manage, somehow. They do, at a real if often immediately invisible cost to the students and the professional standards of the teachers.

If the subtle quality of judgment is the key to effective teaching, how is it learned? Some will say one is born with it or that one's personal radar sets are installed at Mother's knee, and to a degree these hunches appear correct. Teachers are born, not made, the truism goes. Likewise, great writers are born, not made, yet rigorous training at the craft of writing is part of their make-up. Few great writers spring as youths, fully shaped, to the American Book Award. While rigorous preparation does not make a great writer, few great writers have not had such preparation. So it is with teachers.

Writing and teaching have much in common. Both are means to ends, not ends in themselves. The goal in both cases is the new insights of the reader and student. That reader and student have to make their contribution too. The book as written and the class as presented are just part of the process.

Like writing, teaching is science, art, and craft. There are certain rules and conventions, so many and of such complexity that their orchestration becomes a matter less of science than of craft. Good teachers sense when progress is being made, not so much by objective tests as by impression born of a wide variety of signals from the students. The intuitive, the serendipitous, the mysterious ordering of things that suddenly makes a learner say, I see! To the extent that others evoke them, these visions are evoked by artists, artist-teachers. The tight, apt prose of an Updike is kin to the sparse, apt questions and creatively tense silences of a Sister Michael's classroom.

One is helped to be a good teacher much as one is helped to be a good writer, by *coaching*. Lectures on style and on pedagogical technique, on the structure of language and on learning theory, on literary and educational criticism, are nice and often useful, but they are only a prologue. One writes and has that writing criticized. One writes again, for more criticism. One teaches and is criticized. The process is incessant.

At a special summer high school for teacher training, thirty noisy ninth-graders filled the sunny, rectangular classroom, two to a desk. Two tasks had been identified by the intern teacher, to introduce the topic of a new unit—Australia—and to assess and review these particular students' awareness and understanding of the interplay of ocean, land forms, winds, and rain-bearing air masses. The latter would be important for an appreciation of the former: climate explains Australia. The intern, however, figured that neither topic would have intrinsic interest for these easygoing kids, who were not quite sure whether this summer experience was a camp or a classroom.

The intern had decided to borrow an idea from Jerome Bruner's *Process of Education* to present a set of geographic facts about a region to the students and to ask them to reason out where people would live. He worked up an approach and presented the plan to a master teacher and some fellow interns. He would not tell the students what the unit topics were, he explained in his plan, but would abruptly start the class by drawing a map of the eastern half of Australia and asking the students to copy it. He'd tell them of winds, currents, coastlines, mountain ranges, major rivers, and more. He assumed the students would docilely go along, and when, with a flourish, he asked them to "draw in the people," they would be hooked on the problem. He'd thus find out whether they could master such an exercise (these students presumably had had geography in grade school), and at the end of the class he would fill in the rest of the map and thus announce Australia as the unit's topic.

The master teacher and other interns discussed the proposal, pressing hard on the kinds of evidence that might satisfactorily prove the students' competence in geography.

The intern had some hours to sharpen his plan, and then conducted the class, with the master teacher and other interns observing in the back. The kids weren't docile at all, and he had trouble getting them to copy his map. They did not see the point of it and resented the labor. He had to raise his voice often, and his voice was shrill and harsh. Some students clearly were offended by it. His popping of the where-are-the-people question did not hit like the intended thunderclap: intense, forced silence followed. The kids worked quietly, and the intern stood behind his desk, watching them, his confidence visibly returning. With a minute to go, he called the class's attention to the blackboard, roughly closed in Australia's coastline, announced that country as the unit topic, and dismissed the class. The youngsters left more quietly than they had come in, even quizzically.

An analysis followed. The intern had the first shot at himself. He felt that he had underestimated the boisterousness and thought he should have given more specific directions for copying the map. He believed that the later minutes of the course had been very effective, and that the students now had some interest in Australia and geography.

Another intern then followed with questions and observations; the master teacher, a veteran instructor, spoke last. Why was it necessary for the students to copy the map at all? Wasn't that a distracting diversion? Might they have concentrated better if they had been made to watch the blackboard exclusively, and not their pads of paper as well? How could the intern have kept to his plan of "suspense" but held the kids' interest better? Could he have been more aggressive or funny? Which students had not been interested? Was he "seeing" the differences among students in the classroom? (His counterquery: How do you do this? One answer: Slow down.)

Was he sure the students got the point of the exercise? Why didn't he move around the room, peering over students' shoulders? He could quickly have got a sense of things then and shifted his plan if necessary (for example, if he found that most of the students were uselessly floundering). Again, why did he have them make their own maps? Couldn't the entire exercise have been done by him at the board, with greater focus and efficiency? What were the students to do with their laboriously completed maps? Did the intern think them important? If so, why didn't he collect and correct them? If not, why assign them?

Why did he wait for the last sixty seconds to fill out the map? Why did he tell them it was Australia? Would anything have been gained by letting them guess at it? What real evidence did he have that the students knew what the unit topic was?

Had he observed the note passing in the back row? Had he noticed the teasing of one of the kids before class? He had. Was the teased student upset or hurt by it? No. On what did the intern base this conclusion?

The questions went on—and they illumine the main point for all teacher training, which is that after teacher candidates have gained a solid mastery of their subjects, *their training must be almost wholly school-based.* One learns to teach by coaching; one needs to be teaching in order to be coached. The best coaches are usually fine teachers themselves. The analogy to writing deserves endless emphasis.

Teaching is a complex craft, one class never being quite the same as another. Treating teaching as a mere technology either reduces its goals to brute training of the children in rote skills or permits great inefficiency. Standardized high school teaching is wasteful. That students differ may be inconvenient, but it is inescapable. Adapting to that diversity is the inevitable price of productivity, high standards, and fairness to the students.

6

Trust

IT WILL REQUIRE an unprecedented leap of faith for Americans to trust their teachers. They never have, not very much. Furthermore, the current public mood is punitive, albeit with some justification. Much teaching in high schools is abysmal. While some of this clearly is due to teachers' incompetence, insensitivity, and carelessness, some also flows from the conditions of work—giving rise to Horace's compromise—and the demeaning attitudes, and the policies that flow from them, with which the public treats the profession. America and its teachers are in a cul-de-sac of attitudes and practice. Reversing direction will therefore be difficult. As effective teaching absolutely requires substantial autonomy, *the decentralizing of substantial authority to the persons close to the students is essential.* "Downtown" continues to set goals, but decisions over how teacher and student time is organized, the materials and the approaches used, and the way staff are deployed must be at school level, or, in large schools, at house (or other subschool) levels.[23]

I have listened to many concerned school board members and central office administrators agree with this recommendation in theory, but emphatically not in practice. They argue that many teachers are not competent enough to take responsibility and that some principals are unable or unwilling to lead an autonomous school. I

195

have seen enough inept teaching and mindless leadership in American high schools to understand their concern.[24]

But we are caught in a vicious circle. Constant control from "downtown" undermines the ablest teachers and administrators, the very people whose number should be expanding. These top professionals are discouraged and frustrated, often to the point of cruel cynicism. With few exceptions we observed this sad fact in all sorts of schools in all parts of the country. The system is organized with an eye on the incompetent rather than the competent. All are shackled, to "protect" students from the bad teachers. Many of these ablest folk will leave or have left teaching—or will never enter the profession in the first place.

Excellent schooling requires excellent teachers and principals. Excellent people have self-confidence and self-esteem, and expect reasonable autonomy. Therefore, if we want excellent schools, we must give more power to the teachers and principals.

But what of standards? The answer has to be found in the public graduation exhibitions and in accreditation. Schools with demonstrably able faculties should be given much autonomy; those with weak or green faculties, less. How to decide which is which? Perhaps this can be done through inspection by neutral professionals and lay people who can both examine the objective record of student progress and the probably more important subjective record of how the school functions. There are precedents for this type of "visit," in the regional accreditation organizations. At worst, such an inspection exercise is dominated either by long lists of "protocols" that produce piles of paper and little else, or by cozy approbation of whatever is going on. At best, the visit inspires useful self-consciousness within a school's faculty and a fair assessment of overall quality and of the direction in which the school is heading.[25]

One can visualize a state, city, or county system of secondary education, with each school in one of three categories. An *A* school would be given wide latitude, with central authorities represented only at student graduation exhibitions and in visits on a seven-year cycle. Schools ranked *B* would be more regularly checked. *C* schools would be administered centrally. Distinctions like these are familiar in other kinds of enterprises, including general public administration.

196

Visits for purposes of inspection are expensive and time-consuming, and their findings are based on people's judgments. Yet just as with the motivation and assessment of students, they cannot be avoided. They exist de facto in the private school sector, with the parents serving as outside assessors. If they don't like the school, or find it unresponsive or incompetent, they withdraw their children and tuition, and the school closes. Given the fickleness of the marketplace, however, that system is often little better than the monopolistic system in the American public sector. Some middle ground for inspection can both protect standards and offer the energy-producing autonomy to able professionals that is a precondition to excellent schools.

As is obvious to even the most casual visitor to high schools, the conditions of work for teachers and principals need to be sharply changed. Horace Smith should not have to compromise; he should be responsible for only 80 students at a time, not 120 or 150 or 175, as is common today in many public and parochial schools. How can this be done? With more money for salaries, obviously. With a redefinition of adult roles within a school system. For example, in a typical Eastern city there was one adult employed by the school system for every eight pupils; in a nearby suburb, the ratio was about one to fifteen.[26] Yet in each case high school teachers had daily contact with and substantial responsibility for well over a hundred pupils. A fresh, undefensive look at school budgets is suggested by these findings, and new kinds of compromises to be considered.

Other steps, equally unfamiliar and threatening, will be necessary to get the teacher-student ratios down. For example, students for their own good will need to be told less and asked to teach themselves more; much of current class time is wasted and could be better used. Or the narrow disciplinary specializations of teachers can be broken down; perhaps it would be better if Horace taught English *and* social studies to 60 students than just English to 120 different young people. There is a trade-off here, obviously; but in many situations it is worth making.

The list of proposals can go on. It will never apply equally to all districts, owing to varying circumstances. Nonetheless, ways must be found to give high school teachers a load that allows them to personalize their work, and thus to help pupils and avoid the stunning waste of everyone's time that now characterizes so many schools. Changing teacher-student ratios and organizing a school on student mastery rather than on age-organized attendance will inevitably upset other traditions of schoolkeeping. Class organization, how time is spent, the purposes of homework, the way space is allocated—all will be up for grabs. However, the surely turbulent reappraisals of these "regularities" (as Seymour Sarason has termed them), if well led, can be liberating.[27]

Most difficult of all to accomplish will be a change in attitude toward and of teachers and principals. The professionals cannot see themselves or be seen as interchangeable "service delivery systems." The leaders among them, at the least, must be creative, flexible people, much as are the leaders of the other scholarly and academic professions. One sees groups of these people in some schools (too few) now, usually academically oriented "magnet" schools in the public sector or some independent schools. One finds extraordinary individuals everywhere, the Curtises, Sister Michaels, Grosses, Smiths.

The best will have to be paid better; a more steeply scaled salary schedule is essential. There will have to be more variety within the schoolteacher's career; traditional teaching must be mixed with periods of work as supervisor, counselor, developer of curricular materials, and administrator. Such arrangements can be accomplished without extravagant new infusions of money—*if* there is professional and political will to make the changes.

What of the school principal? He or she is the *principal teacher.* Schools need business management, and there should be executives for this. (Australian schools sometimes call them bursars and treat them with awe.) But the *principal* is the lead teacher and needs to be among colleagues and students, as that is where the most vital judgments in the life of a school must be made. The "mood" of a school, the drift of a trend (such as the workings of a group of troublemaking students or the excessive sarcasm of a group of aggrieved teachers), the assessment of what is possible at a given moment and what is not: these are the principal's tasks. He or she is the school's primary "visitor," not in a destructive inspectorial sense, but in a collegial yet candid one.

What of teacher unions? Conventional wisdom assumes that they are big barriers to change. I'm not convinced, though no two union groups at the local level are alike. Many states suffering from precisely the same ills that we identified in unionized areas have never had unions. And where there are strong unions, a glance at the history of their foundation indicates such political abuse of teachers that organization was inevitable. For good or ill, unions are the result of bad conditions, not the cause. These bad conditions, and an ethic about schools that perceived them as factories—service delivery systems, with inputs and outputs—combined to create a union-management system that is industrial at its heart, not professional.[28]

Many of the ablest teachers I met are also active unionists (as are their covert counterparts in states where collective bargaining is illegal). They can lead toward a better system, because they are teachers first and power-brokers second. My critics call attention to the national political activities of the central secretariats of the unions. My response is that national leadership is, in education, probably less important than state and local leadership. These local folk are the people to persuade, and they may be no more difficult to persuade than their "management" counterparts.

I leave Jefferson High School at 2:30, ending my visit there. I drop in the teachers' room to thank the social studies department chairperson for his courtesy, but find he's left for the day. The big TV set in the corner is still on, though, tuned to a soap. As I had discovered that morning, its sound system mercifully is broken. The loves and hates of some shiny triangle of earnest thirty-two-year-olds on the tube are reduced to pantomime, which is quite enough. A few teachers still watch.

I push out through the student throngs waiting for buses. The mating game is going on, knowingly by some, unintentionally by others. Look at me. Don't look at me. Who am I to look at? It is raucous, uncouth, colorful with its mindless self-centeredness.

I walk across the street to the central administration building to meet the superintendent. His office is large, its anteroom dominated by cases full of trophies and walls covered by plaques, each citing his service. The ex-army officer in me feels right at home.

The superintendent is quick, able, political. He talks about "raising" mathematics and science requirements. Business wants it, he tells me. Attendance is up. Vandalism is down. Management systems are now fully computerized; Horace's compromise (I think) is embedded on a floppy disk. He's impressive and is looking for a city superintendency, a job demanding more of his undoubted bureaucratic skills. His system is effective, "efficient."

Perhaps it is such schools that America wants, predictable conduits for a smattering of information and vehicles for the rituals of the society. My wanderings among schools convince me that such is now what most people want. They don't want to examine the wisdom of their schoolkeeping habits: they like the way they are. The national media may rant about a "crisis" in high schools, but one senses little of this strident energy in many schools. Some improvement, yes. Fundamental reassessment, even honest reflection on the structure of school? No.

Is it realistic to expect a significant change in the structure? The conventional wisdom is that change in schools is always incremental. Reform of several aspects of school at once is impossible, I am told. One must go slowly. Don't be "radical." And yet, I wonder, who is the *true* realist? The schools' current design is clearly unproductive. To avoid facing this fact, I think, is the ultimate unrealism.

The present structure is so wasteful, I know. The countless hours of detachment, of Melissa-like dodging, of Will- and Janet-like playacting is time—their time—that is lost. It costs billions of dollars, wasted too. What troubles me is that few Americans seem really to care very much. So Will is naïve and Pamela stereotyped and Brody's classes cheated. So what? There is little American outrage here; indeed, there rarely has been. Americans have been generous with their schools but have asked little of them.

This frustrates me, makes me angry. I spend the next day in the city where Horace lives and meet him that evening for dinner. He is bemused by my anger. What did you expect? He tells me that *of course* the Outside Influentials will decide that the "solution" to their sense of the Current High School Crisis is to change the curricular labels once again, to urge more in mathematics and science, and to puff up the autocratic tendencies in each school principal ("instructional manager"). They will find another panacea this time, probably the computer. And *of course,* he assures me, it won't make much difference.

The empowerment of Horace could make a difference. Underneath his defensiveness, he knows that. For some reason, we start morbidly comparing the U.S. Army's top-down activities in Vietnam to the Viet Cong peasant army. Could Horace be a peasant soldier? We slide off the analogy: it isn't right. But he persists in this direction. If I had my way . . . he goes on. It all rings right, because Horace knows how he could find a way to improve each student's self-esteem, how standards could be raised, how the sloppy routines could be shaped up. I leave our dinner, knowing that Horace is the key.

IV The Structure

1

Hierarchical Bureaucracy

LEARNING is a human activity, and depends absolutely (if often annoyingly) on human idiosyncrasy. We can arrange for schools, classes, and curricula, but the game is won or lost for reasons beyond these arrangements. The readiness of the students, the power of the incentives they feel for learning, and the potency of teachers' inspiration count more than does any structure of any school. Run a school like a factory, and you will get uneven goods.

This is not to say that there is no order to learning, that some framework is not useful. There is. People do learn in patterns, even as these patterns at times twist and shift, person by person and time to time. A good school judiciously balances the order these represent with the flexibility needed to give room to constructive human idiosyncrasy. Too much order stultifies; too much flexibility confuses. It is Horace—each teacher and principal—who can best adjust and continually readjust the balance between them.

Unfortunately, Horace has limited opportunity to do so, because twentieth-century Americans' breathless belief in *systems* to run their lives tilts the scale markedly toward predictable order. Disorder terrified the late-nineteenth-century middle-class American, who thought he saw his stable life ruptured by newly populated cities, industrialization, and hordes of immigrants. In response, and in a quest for social order, progressive reformers placed great faith in "scientific management." Rational, politics-free system, driven by dispassionate professionals, was their cure for the country's ills of chaos.[1]

Not surprisingly, this model of reform profoundly affected education and resulted in systems of schools, in both public and Catholic sectors, organizations arranged in pyramidal tiers, with governing boards and administrators at the peaks and classrooms at the base. Directions—"governance"—flowed from top to bottom, in the fashion of all hierarchical bureaucracies.

These pyramids stolidly survive. Indeed, they have become so familiar that any other form of providing for the schooling of young Americans seems unimaginable. While there are obvious advantages to hierarchical bureaucracy, it has its costs, and these are today paralyzing American education. The structure is getting in the way of children's learning.

Top-down bureaucracies depend on orderly predictability. What is desired at the peak must find its way to the base. Since the top managers are held accountable for the efficient functioning of the system, they have to know what is going on. Information, standardized in order to be comprehensible, must flow up from the classrooms at the base, again in a predictable, timely fashion. Inevitably, the result is a monolithic system.

The progressives would be amazed at the scale of these modern hierarchies. For example, New York City's school system, the largest in the country, today enrolls as many children as there were people of all ages in the Commonwealth of Massachusetts in Horace Mann's time and as many as there were in all the nation's secondary schools in 1911.

The trend today is toward greater centralization and thus ever larger scale. As state governments become more involved in the regulation of the schools (the inevitable result of their increased assumption of educational costs), the distance between the directors and the directed has become greater, and standardization more pervasive. We hear now of schooling reduced by state edict to minimum "minutes per year." Most educational commentators are so numbed by the tradition of such authoritative top-down direction that they fail even to see the humor in such outlandish orders, much less the waste that will result from them. Minutes per year is hierarchical bureaucracy finally run totally amok.[2]

There are at least six defects in this system of pyramidal governance. First, it forces us in large measure to overlook special local conditions, particularly school-by-school differences. Students differ, teachers differ, administrators differ, and the chemistry between them in one setting at one time is not quite like any other. Communities vary in what they want and need. While central authorities almost always try to provide local options and "consultation," the *framework* of school remains permanently fixed. This framework includes the organization of schools by the students' ages (ninth, tenth, eleventh, twelfth grade), by similar subject departments (English, mathematics . . .), by time blocks (hours per week, minutes per year . . .), by specialized job descriptions (teacher, counselor, principal, librarian, custodian . . .), by calendar (180 days, commencing near Labor Day . . .), and, in many states, by precise forms of staff contracts and licenses. Differences among schools are usually seen as weaknesses; that there may be educational efficiency in allowing, or even ordering, schools to adapt to their immediate situations is rarely recognized, at least to any significant degree.

Second, bureaucracy depends on the specific, the measurable. Large, complex units need simple ways of describing themselves, so those aspects of schoolkeeping which can be readily quantified often become the only forms of representation. The endless and exclusive talk of attendance rates, dropout rates, test scores, suspension rates, teachers' rank in class in their colleges, reminds one of Vietnam War body counts.

When school data are collected sensibly, the results may be helpful. When the data are collected in silly ways to convenience the researcher (for example, treating every course labeled English as of equal value), the result is distortion. When some correlations are ignored (such as those between socioeconomic status and certain test scores), the results can be serious misrepresentations. Meanwhile, the problem of how to describe the unquantifiable—the inspiring qualities or energy of some teachers, the courage of some students, the commitment of some communities and parents—remains unaddressed and invisible. None of us would want our marriages judged solely by a squabbles-per-year factor. If families were run by large bureaucracies, they probably would be.

Third, large administrative units depend on norms, the bases of predictability. Inevitably, a central tendency becomes the rigid expectation. In September, a sixteen-year-old *will* be an eleventh-grader, and eleventh-graders *will* score in certain ways on certain tests. The fact that a group of sixteen-year-olds, all of whom can ultimately master the material on those tests, shows a wide spread in scores of achievement and aptitude on any given day is usually overlooked. All are schooled alike, and rewards and penalties are assigned. The "low" scorers "fail"; the high scorers receive honor; the school with higher scorers is a "better" school than one with lower scorers.

There are other examples of central tendencies becoming universal mandates. *Many* students learn a language well by an audiolingual approach; therefore *all* will. *Many* Hispanic parents want a fully bilingual program for their children; therefore *all* will get it. *Many* classes are fruitfully taught in groups of twenty to twenty-five students; therefore *all* classes will be of these numbers. *Many* subjects appear well learned in fifty-minute, once-a-day, five-times-a-week blocks; therefore *all* classes will so be offered. But in learning, the margins are wide and the exceptions numerous. Insisting on strict norms—which hierarchical bureaucracies require in order to function—is wasteful and in some cases unfair.

Fourth, centralized planning requires a high level of specificity. In a people-intensive industry (which education quintessentially is), a certain objective is likely to be carried out if it is assigned to particular professionals who are held specifically accountable for its execution. Bureaucracies depend on elaborate job descriptions; they cannot function without them. Unions pick these up. Colleges offer training programs along the lines of these descriptions. Special professional associations spring up. State governments give the ultimate blessing with restrictive licensure: only those people trained in a certain skill can exercise it in school. The result is high schools run by specialists, each of whom is expected to "deliver" a specific "service" to each student. A pupil thus "gets" English from one teacher, history from another, "guidance" from another, and a stiff lecture about his deportment from yet another. Even if he has an adviser or homeroom teacher, he rarely has time to talk one on one with that adult. Most high school students have several teachers who know a bit about them, but no teacher who sees them whole.

Unless they are in some limited enclave—such as those made up of special education students, star athletes, students in a highly visible honors track, or habitual troublemakers—they are, for all intents and purposes, anonymous.[3] This ill serves the students, obviously. It also frustrates good teachers. The villain is the specialist system.

Bureaucracies lumber. Once regulations, collective bargaining agreements, and licensure get installed, change comes hard. Every regulation, agreement, and license spawns a lobby dedicated to keeping it in place. The larger and more complex the hierarchy, the more powerful the lobby becomes, ever more remote from frustrated classroom teachers, poorly served students, and angry parents.

Finally, hierarchical bureaucracy stifles initiative at its base; and given the idiosyncracies of adolescents, the fragility of their motivation, and the need for their teachers and principals to be strong, inspiring, and flexible people, this aspect of the system can be devastating. One sees it in the demoralization of many teachers and in the explanations able college students give for not taking up high school teaching as a career. One jokes about it with adroit principals who have made a fine art of circumventing bureaucratic ukases. At the same time, one relaxes a bit about it when one sees how ineffective most school bureaucracies are in supervising their outlying provinces. No one visits class, and reports can be fudged.

It is astonishing that so few critics challenge the system. In an absolute sense, the learning exhibited by even a "successful" student after over twelve thousand hours in classrooms is strikingly limited. When one considers the energy, commitment, and quality of so many of the people working in the schools, one must place the blame elsewhere. The people are better than the structure. Therefore the structure must be at fault.

Why does hierarchical bureaucracy persist?

Going to school is an important democratic ritual, and graduation is a sort of secular bar mitzvah. All societies, even the most "modern," need their folkways, social signposts to mark citizens' progress through life. Entering high school is one of these; leaving is an even more important one. Not getting a diploma is a catastrophe. The ceremony attending its bestowal is usually choreographed with the exquisiteness of a religious rite. No one messes lightly with such rituals. For example, a proposal for awarding a diploma to anyone who earns it, rather than to the roughly eighteen-year-old age group, will cause serious social problems. For example, getting a diploma tacitly means in many communities that it's now all right to get married. Once in place, standardized structures serve many functions, many of them having nothing to do with learning.

Most people dislike change. Predictability eases minds, and in times of turmoil one especially values the familiar. The status quo thus has special momentum.

The existing hierarchies are comfortable for the people at the top of school bureaucracy and for their influential colleagues in the universities with whom they are interlocked in a variety of training-to-license programs. There is money in the hierarchy. Furthermore, in professions such as education, where success is difficult to measure, status turns on abstractions—on college degrees, on position, on specialties. One tampers with these abstractions at great peril, because careers depend on their stability.

Ironically, some of hierarchical bureaucracy's persistence is due to its very ineffectiveness. As long as the folk at the top accept the notion that high school should be "comprehensive," then anything someone at the base wants to add is almost surely acceptable, as long as money is available and the norms of operation are observed. Those at the top can see only the vague outlines of the structure—attendance reports, grade levels, test scores, age-grading, days per year in class—so those at the base can do what they want around that structure. This is useful as long as the structure doesn't seriously restrict teachers and others at the local level. In most contemporary situations, unfortunately, it does.

Another reason that the structure remains in place is that reformers are impatient. They wisely realize that redesigning the system will take time and much political effort. They want quick results, so they accept the constraints and try to work within them.[4] This accommodation is often accompanied with soothing statements, like those of James Bryant Conant ("I believe no radical alteration in the basic pattern of American education is necessary in order to improve our public high schools"), even when reformers have serious, though private, misgivings.[5] Many who try to improve the schools assume that educators cannot take too much negative criticism of their system. After listening to hundreds of able educators who work at the base of the school system pyramid, I am sure this restraint is as misplaced as it is patronizing.

The internal structure of most high schools is complicated. To be orderly, routines must be finely tuned. In a typical school of fifteen hundred pupils and ninety-five teachers, the orchestration of the adults with their teaching or counseling or administrative specialties and the students with their five or six course or "activity" options is a complicated process. Trying to change one piece affects every other, causing all sorts of political flak. Accordingly, things remain the same because it is very difficult to change very much without changing most of everything. The result is sustained paralysis.

Finally, the students accept the system. As long as school is fun some of the time and rarely humiliating, they go along. They strike their bargains with teachers, and they value the rituals of going to school. For them, school is a rite of passage, and they accept it, even though they may be bored by much of it. The American adolescent is a remarkably tolerant animal.

If truly "scientific" managers were today given the task of freshly designing ways and means for adolescents to become educated, they would doubtless create mechanisms very different from those we have inherited from the progressives. If effectiveness, productivity, and the avoidance of waste are important ends, an analysis of our practices would start at the base of the existing hierarchy, at the triangle of student, teacher, and the subject they confront together. The primary question would be, How can adolescents be assisted in learning most efficiently?

Examination of the triangle would disclose its inevitable and often constructive variability. What is effective at one point may be ineffective at another. Only the people at the level of the basic triangle will know which is which. Accordingly, they need a large measure of autonomy in making the necessary adaptations.

Further scientific examination would uncover students' differing learning styles and teachers' differing teaching styles. Again, local adaptations would be required. As all these adaptations would take

211

varied forms, the basic structure of a school's schedule and program would have to be simple, with a minimum number of requirements and subjects of study. The focus would be on the major intellectual skills, because they are the necessary prerequisites for all useful involvement in society.

Since the energy and morale of the teachers are crucial influences on the success of students, every effort would be made to free instructors from distracting or demeaning duties and to reinforce their sense of control (and the self-respect that flows from it) over their work. If effective schools are, very simply, "orderly environments where there are adults who care,"[6] a scientific manager would be sure that a school was clear on its purposes and staffed by people who are moved by and who can move adolescents—however difficult it may be to train teachers to develop these characteristics and politically tricky to evaluate them. Furthermore, to move people, one needs to know them. A high school teacher should have direct responsibility for fewer than a hundred students, preferably fewer than eighty.

A scientific examination of the fundamental triangle will quickly expose both the fragility and the power of adolescents. Efficient schoolkeeping calls for patience with students who are struggling with new things, trying on new masks. Allowing time for this process is not only an act of courtesy, or even of sentimentality, but also of cold efficiency. A student preoccupied with a personal problem is an inefficient learner of algebra and history. Yet, though inexperienced, adolescents have the ability to teach themselves and to take responsibility. The earlier and better they do these things, the more productively they will learn. A scientifically managed school would place emphasis on these skills and the self-esteem they engender, recognizing that we all learn at different rates at different times.

Examination of several student-teacher-subject triangles will quickly show that some teachers are abler than others, some more and some less experienced. As a practical matter, the abler and more experienced need to be given more authority than the less able and the inexperienced. This may, paradoxically, create mini-hierarchies, contrary to the claims for autonomy. However, they are necessary, and they are tolerable as long as they are kept close to the pupils being served. Furthermore, hierarchies within teaching provide the variety of experience and responsibility that most career professionals want.

Above all, examination of the basic triangle will demonstrate the importance of incentives—the fuel that drives students and teachers. If the goals for students are clear ("These are the areas you need to master for your diploma") and relevant ("Succeeding at your graduation exhibition will honestly demonstrate that you can use your mind and knowledge rigorously and imaginatively"), student energy, much more often than not, will be productively focused. If teachers are given autonomy and held ultimately accountable for the work of their students—in itself a gratifying compliment—they will perform to the best of their imaginative ability. Equally important, the career of teacher will become more attractive than it is now. Talented people seek jobs that entrust them with important things.

Good schools, scientifically managed, are as simple and as complicated as that.

2

Better Schools

THERE ARE five imperatives for better schools:

1. Give room to teachers and students to work and learn in their own, appropriate ways.
2. Insist that students clearly exhibit mastery of their school work.
3. Get the incentives right, for students and for teachers.
4. Focus the students' work on the use of their minds.
5. Keep the structure simple and thus flexible.

Giving teachers and students room to take full advantage of the variety among them implies that there must be substantial authority in each school. For most public and diocesan Catholic school systems, this means the decentralization of power from central headquarters to individual schools. For state authorities, it demands the forswearing of detailed regulations for how schools should be operated. It calls for the authorities to trust teachers and principals—and believe that the more trust one places in them, the more their response will justify that trust. This trust can be tempered by judicious accreditation systems, as long as these do not reinfect the schools with the blight of standardized required practice.

The purpose of decentralized authority is to allow teachers and principals to adapt their schools to the needs, learning styles, and learning rates of their particular students. The temptation in every school will be to move toward orderly standardization: such is the instinct, it seems, of Americans, so used as we are to depending on structure. Good schools will have to resist this appeal of standardization: the particular needs of each student should be the only measure of how a school gets on with its business. Greater authority is an incentive for teachers, one that will attract and hold the kind of adults which high schools absolutely need on their staffs.

The requirement for *exhibitions of mastery* forces both students and teachers to focus on the substance of schooling. It gives the state, the parents, prospective employers, and the adolescents themselves a real reading of what a student can do. It is the only sensible basis for accountability.

Effective exhibitions will be complicated to construct and time-consuming to administer. To be fair, they need to be flexible: not all students show themselves off well in the same way. They cannot, then, merely be standardized, machine-graded, paper-and-pencil tests.

The process of constructing and overseeing these exhibitions can be threatening, because it will force teachers to see and to deal with the gaps and redundancies that arise from the traditional curriculum. Teachers find it safe to work in the privacy of their classrooms, delivering the credits their courses bestow on each student. A commonly constructed exhibition invades this privacy—a step that is as necessary as it may be intimidating.[7]

The existence of specific exhibitions is itself a strong *incentive* for both students and teachers. Exhibitions clarify ends. The student knows what she or he has to do in order to progress and graduate. If pursuit of that high school graduation diploma is voluntary, the adolescent is left on his or her own; the games attendant on compulsory attendance can no longer be used as excuses. To the young person who has met the minimal competencies in literary, numeracy, and civic understanding, the high school says, Here is what our diploma means; join us and we'll help you master the knowledge it represents, but the work is basically yours to do. The challenge of such an arrangement is powerful. There is self-esteem to be gained from being the key worker, and if wise teachers appropriately adjust the study to the pace of each student, success will breed success.

The personalization inherent in such adjusted pacing is also rewarding; it signals to the student that he or she is important as an individual.

Not all adolescents will find any one school setting congenial. Some students respond well to judicious prodding. Others wilt under it, but flourish in gentler places. The claim for personalization extends to a variety of school settings (separate schools or schools-within-schools), and the opportunity for choice among them itself is a spur to energy. Loyalty roots only with difficulty, if at all, in places forced on us; commitment readily follows from free choice.

The focus of high school should be on *the use of the mind.* Although young citizens need to learn about and be exposed to many sides of life, the mind is central, and the school is the principal institution that society has for assisting adolescents in its use. High schools cannot be comprehensive and should not try to be comprehensive; there are some aspects of an adolescent's life in which a school has no right to intrude, and helping students to use their minds well is a large enough assignment, in any case.

The only way to learn to think well and usefully is by practice. The way a teacher assists this learning is by coaching. What a student chooses or is asked to think about is important, obviously, but secondary to the skills of observing and imaginatively using knowledge. A self-propelled learner is the goal of a school, and teachers should insist that students habitually learn on their own. Teacher-delivered knowledge that is never used is temporary.

Issues concerning values inevitably arise in every school, and learning to use one's mind involves making decisions of conduct and belief. How one uses one's mind, and how one accordingly behaves, raise questions about character: Is this fair? Is it thoughtful? Is it generous? Is it *decent?* Schools should not teach merely pure thinking; they must also promote thoughtfulness, at core the qualities of decency. Schools should accept that obligation, not only because it is important, but because it is inescapable. A school *will* affect its students' character, willy-nilly. It should do so carefully, in a principled way.

Personalization of learning and instruction requires a flexible school structure. A flexible structure implies *a simple structure.* A school day segmented into seven or eight time units, each with

216

its own set of imperatives, is almost impossible to bend. A curriculum represented by six or seven autonomous subjects quickly freezes hard: if each gets what its teacher feels is its due, all lose substantial freedom. Furthermore, such a fractionated and specialized set of subjects distorts knowledge for young minds; a simpler, more cogent organization of subject matter is wise.

Any effort to simplify the curriculum will be as threatening to teachers as will be the creation of general graduation exhibitions. We have been trained in our specializations, and we step outside them with trepidation. Our university mentors may often mock these forays, too; for many of them "specialization" and "standards" are synonymous—a false equation, but one that they will nonetheless scathingly defend. Reconstituting the shape of the curriculum—strengthening it by simplifying it and making it cogent to adolescents—will be a lonely, politically rocky effort.

Fortunately, each of these five imperatives governs the work of one or another existing school. There is no novelty here. However, pressing them ahead *together* would be novel, a school reconstruction effort of considerable scope and risk.

We hope that many schools will find one or more of these imperatives persuasive enough to push them vigorously. We also hope that some will have the courage to embrace them all, simultaneously. We need new model schools, ones resting on imperatives, like these five, that appear to serve well modern conditions and adolescents. The imperatives interlock, and as they are engineered into practical forms, their interconnection will become a source of strength—and of efficiency. The financial costs of better schools can be justified if the pretentious practices of comprehensiveness are stalwartly eliminated.

Better schools will come when better structures are built. Those structures have no inherent merit, however: their sole function will be to provide apt and nurturing conditions that will attract students and teachers and make their work together worthwhile and efficient.

3

A Paralysis of Imagination

HACKLES RISE when recipes for changing school system structures are offered. From the Ocean Hill–Brownsville controversy in New York City to proposals for tuition vouchers, controversy seems inevitable. The issues instantly become ideological, it seems, paralyzing our imaginations.

Educators, so often criticized, are defensive. That most self-styled school reformers are not nor have ever been practicing high school teachers or administrators adds insult to injury. Educators may well ask, How would lawyers react if the rest of us handed them prescriptions for legal reform? It is no surprise that school people are instinctively resistant to change. Like a large flywheel spinning at great speed, the traditional hierarchical bureaucracy has a headlong momentum. Suggestions for changes in the process—such as holding serious faculty meetings and empowering teachers to adapt their schools to the local circumstances they collectively identify—undermine the predictable sureties that systems require. It is easier for central authority to mandate fifty-four thousand minutes per year than to give discretion to local groups. The specificities of schooling and the seemingly endless requirements of standardized practice strangle not only learning, but also the imaginations of educators and politicians.

Behind top-down regulation lies a distrust of American teachers.

The argument is simple: the fate of an adolescent cannot be left in the hands of a semicompetent adult, however well-meaning. So supervise and carefully control that teacher and, by necessary bureaucratic extension, *all* teachers. However, proud people rarely join professions that heavily monitor them. Being trusted is the elixir of commitment. Unless we trust some teachers (and are prepared to live with the political cat fights that will ensue from making what are ultimately subjective judgments as to who those "some teachers" are), we will only get more semicompetent people in the profession. Eventually, hierarchical bureaucracy will be totally self-validating: virtually all teachers will be semicompetent, and thus nothing but top-down control will be tolerable. America is now well on the way to this state of affairs.

Today, there is a sizable core of fine teachers and administrators in our schools. They are often demoralized, but they could, if empowered, lead a renaissance of American high schools: their numbers are large enough. But they need the trust of those in political power. Unfortunately, they have difficulty even getting these people's attention.

One hears much skepticism about reform by means of models like those I favor. The approach has not worked in the past, it has been said with some justification. It could work, though, if money were redirected to back it up, as has been shown by social revolutions from Medicare to higher education after the passage of the G.I. Bill of Rights to schooling for the handicapped. The pressures of successful models can be powerful, even if slow in their effect.[8]

The public's most troubling skepticism is about adolescents. Teenagers are a throwaway generation, and they resent it. It is not for nothing that no age group has a higher crime rate. What Vera Randall has called that "terrible, mocking smile of adulthood"[9] is not lost on young people; inexperienced, they choose to act as though they deserved the mockery. Their awkwardness, particularly their sexual fumbling, is exploited with old folk's sweaty-palmed glee, and the young people flock to *Porky* and then *Porky II* to find out what show biz thinks growing up is all about. When there is a reaction to all this, it is a patronizing one. Let our children be children, it says. They want structure, it argues. They want us to direct them. In practice, these somewhat sensible notions get exaggerated; they become overkill.

We stereotype adolescents in other ways. In spite of the rhetoric to the contrary, they are largely tracked by social class and gender. Too few adults really believe that poor kids or minority kids can make it. Don't educate them to use their minds, the conventional wisdom goes, because they aren't interested, and anyway, we do them a big service by preparing them for (semiskilled) jobs. The possibility that turned-off kids can be turned around, that young women can see a world beyond the pep squad, that poor kids, imaginatively taught, will respond to academic abstractions, remains vividly alive only to that band of teachers and principals in the schools which is making those things happen. America writ large does not believe it possible.

Horace Smith and his ablest colleagues may be the key to better high schools, but it is respected adolescents who will shape them. America must take its young more seriously, not out of some resurgence of 1960s' chic, where the Word from the Kids was considered the Real Truth, but out of simple human courtesy and recognition that adolescents do have power, power that can be influenced to serve decent and constructive ends. This power can only grow person by person—each tender life sustaining the assaults of the universe, to paraphrase James Agee again.[10] High schools must not be party to those assaults.

James Bryant Conant once said that for any recommendation to be taken seriously, it had to have a number attached.[11] He was a master at this process, arguing in *The American High School Today* that no English teacher should have more than a hundred students or guidance counselor more than three hundred clients or senior high school fewer than a hundred seniors. I hope he was wrong, because the problems of contemporary American high schools and the opportunities within the schools' grasp often do not lend themselves easily to quantification. The hours per week of homework and credits per year of courses are important, but nonetheless secondary to issues of attitude, to the subtle, confusing, controversial humanness that infuses every school. Give me, a student, a teacher who inspires me to learn on my own, and the bric-a-brac of schoolkeeping—the course labels, the regulations, the regularities, the rituals—will cease to have much importance. And give me, a teacher, hungry pupils, and I'll teach them in a tumbledown warehouse, and they will learn.

Inspiration, hunger: these are the qualities that drive good schools. The best we educational planners can do is to create the most likely conditions for them to flourish, and then get out of their way.

Afterword
An Experiment for Horace

WITH LUCK, a book is an important fragment in a continuing thoughtful conversation. A volume on secondary education like *Horace's Compromise* is an organized argument made at a particular moment. Publication spawns reaction to that argument; and time passes, altering (though often subtly) the context in which high schools, and the arguments for their improvement, reside. This paperback edition is a reprint of my first statement on Horace's compromises, but it is also, through this Afterword, part of a continuing conversation about high schools, about adolescents and their learning.

Horace's Compromise was part of a blizzard of reports and manifestos on education that swirled through America from April 1983 through the end of 1984. If there was a common theme among them, it was concern over the uneven quality of secondary education afforded young citizens. The remedies suggested were largely systemic, calling for an increase in regulation from central authorities, but some observers, such as John Goodlad, Ernest Boyer, Joe Nathan, Mortimer Adler, Seymour Sarason, and those of us in A Study of High Schools, puzzled over the obvious inefficiencies of the basic structure of schools. Merely greasing the existing gears might not accomplish very much, some of us wrote. For example, would insisting that a teacher like Horace assign more writing to his pupils help much, when he is responsible for 120 to 180 students at once? Hardly, our Study concluded, as the mere arithmetic of the minutes required for him to read, comment upon, and "correct" these papers bluntly testifies. Would adding time to the school day and school year help? Perhaps. But unless the genial incoherence of so much of Mark's day is lessened, little will show for this new investment. The weaknesses of the high school lie deeper, in how it is organized and in the attitudes of those who work there. As long as Melissa dodges and Steve Brody fakes it, the stubborn hold of mediocrity will persist, whatever the regulators impose.

Accordingly, we called attention to the structure of schools and urged a fresh challenge to the assumptions that shape it. The "time" spent in school ("four years of English") should not be the system's coinage, its unit of measurement, we argued. People learn at different rates, and substantive accomplishment should be the only product on which the school places importance. Age-grading, while bureaucratically neat, hurts children, we insisted, as some youngsters develop more rapidly than others. Take young people where they are, we counseled, and move them forward as efficiently as possible. How they compare with age-mates is a matter of secondary importance.

Simplify the school day, we said, if for no other reason than to lessen the frantic, colorful, wasteful rush over "knowledge" that a seven- or eight-period day requires. A curriculum of many courses, taken in rapid succession, has only the political virtue of accommodating numerous subjects that compete for students' time; as an educating system it creates incoherence and promotes superficiality. When challenged at this, we pointed out that no other serious educating institutions—those in business or the military, for example—have ever copied the frenetic eclecticism of the high school day, for the obvious reason that it is inefficient.

Less is more, we said. Thoroughness counts more than coverage. Make the routines simpler so that the inevitable complexity caused by the differences among individual students can be addressed. Above all, get the teacher's load down to a tolerable level. Don't force Horace to make compromises that cripple his students' opportunity to learn.

The readers of *Horace* who agreed, more or less, with its central theme almost always pressed a particular question, cast in a number of ways, usually in accusing or skeptical language. So the existing structure is ill designed, they would say; but how can it be improved, practically? Does anyone really want it changed? What are *you* going to do about it? In a word, as a practical and political matter, *can* Horace be uncompromised?

The answer is yes, very likely so. We must experiment with changes in the ways high schools keep. We must try to change the compromises, in actual schools. Let us see if the "five imperatives for better schools" can find real form, see if the nitty-gritty details of daily schoolkeeping can be shaped by principles more sensible and sensitive than those often now in practice.

Of course we must be humble and patient in attempting this. Schools are complicated and traditional institutions, and they easily resist all sorts of well-intentioned efforts at reform. Furthermore, many Americans may not want change, for to accept the need for it is an admission of error, however unintended. Such an admission is painful, and, accordingly, many find persisting with a status quo that they privately know is flawed to be the better part of valor. A public relations campaign is easier to stage than a serious attempt to reform schools—and, alas, the education establishment today is full of hype on behalf of things as they are. Challenge, in the eyes of some, is traitorous. In spite of this doleful reality, an attempt at restructuring is still worth making. Indeed, not to try would be truly traitorous, a failure to act to improve the education of children when we know that improvement is urgently needed.

For us, the key general questions are obvious. Can a new design for schools improve their quality—the standard of students' learning, the decency of students' life at school, the effectiveness and joy for teachers and principals and other schoolpeople? Can such a design, which will necessarily be comprehensive, be installed, as a *practical* matter? Can it be adopted, even in experimental form, as a *political* matter? That is, will enough people, somewhere, want it enough to risk it, nurture it, be honest with it, give it time? Is there money available to buy the teachers' and principals' after-school hours to plan and test and replan? Can designs be both true to some common standards and at the same time respectful of local traditions and of each faculty's need for a deep sense of ownership of its own school?

In response to these questions a number of schoolpeople have joined us, agreeing to band together their schools, which corporately share some principles and appear to have the political, practical, and financial support to play these principles out, however substantial the required restructuring might be. These institutions, together with Brown University and with the continuing sponsorship of the National Association of Secondary School Principals and the National Association of Independent Schools, have created the Coalition of Essential Schools, which will experiment with ways to reduce the compromises schoolpeople and students must now make. The Coalition of Essential Schools is based at Brown University (Box 1938, Brown University, Providence, Rhode Island 02912) and has initial generous support from the Carnegie Corporation of New York, the Danforth Foundation, the Charles E. Culpeper Foundation, the Exxon Education Foundation, and the Edward John Noble Foundation.

The Coalition has no model to "plug in," no program to "install." Models and programs, to have sustenance and integrity, must arise independently out of their communities and schools. What the Coalition has in common is a set of nine principles, as insistent as they are largely general:

1. *Focus.* The school should focus on helping adolescents learn to use their minds well. Schools should not attempt to be "comprehensive" if such a claim is made at the expense of the school's central intellectual purpose. That is, Essential Schools should not attempt to provide an unrealistically wide range of academic, vocational, extracurricular, and social services for adolescents.

2. *Simple goals.* The school's goals should be simple: that each student master a limited number of centrally important skills and areas of knowledge. While these skills and areas will, to varying degrees, reflect the traditional academic disciplines, the program's design should be shaped by the intellectual and imaginative powers and competencies that students need, rather than by "subjects" as conventionally defined.

225

That is, students' school experience should not be molded by the existing complex and often dysfunctional system of isolated departments, "credit hours" delivered in packages called English, social studies, science, and the rest. Less is more. Curricular decisions should be guided by the aim of student mastery and achievement rather than by an effort to "cover content."

3. *Universal goals.* The school's goals should be universal, while the means to these goals will vary as the students themselves vary. School practice should be tailor-made to meet the needs of every group or class of adolescents.

4. *Personalization.* Teaching and learning should be personalized to the maximum feasible extent. Efforts should be directed toward a goal that no teacher have direct responsibility for more than eighty students. To allow for personalization, decisions about the details of the course of study, the use of students' and teachers' time, and the choice of teaching materials and specific pedagogies must be unreservedly placed in the hands of the principal and staff.

5. *Student-as-worker.* The governing practical metaphor of the school should be student-as-worker, rather than the more familiar teacher-as-deliverer-of-instructional-services. Accordingly, a prominent pedagogy will be coaching, to provoke students to learn how to learn, and thus to teach themselves.

6. *Diploma by exhibition.* Students entering secondary school studies are those who are committed to the school's purposes and who can show competence in language, elementary mathematics, and basic civics. Students of traditional high school age who are not yet at appropriate levels of competence to enter secondary school studies will be provided intensive remedial work to assist them quickly to meet these standards. The diploma should be awarded upon a successful final demonstration of mastery for graduation—an "exhibition." This exhibition by the student of his or her grasp of the central skills and knowledge of the school's program should be jointly administered by the faculty and by higher authorities: the exhibition represents the latter's primary and proper influence over the school's program. As the diploma is awarded when earned, the school's program proceeds with

no strict age-grading and with no system of "credits earned" by "time spent" in class. The emphasis is shifted to the students' demonstration that they can do important things.

7. *Attitude.* The tone of the school should explicitly and self-consciously stress values of unanxious expectation ("I won't threaten you but I expect much of you"), of trust (until abused), and of decency (the values of fairness, generosity, and tolerance). Incentives appropriate to the school's particular students and teachers should be emphasized, and parents should be treated as essential collaborators.

8. *Staff.* The principal and teachers should perceive themselves as generalists first (teachers and scholars in general education) and specialists second (experts in only one particular discipline). Staff should expect multiple obligations (teacher-counselor-manager) and feel a sense of commitment to the entire school.

9. *Budget.* Ultimate administrative and budget targets should include, in addition to total student loads per teacher of eighty or fewer pupils, substantial time for collective planning by teachers, competitive salaries for staff, and an ultimate per pupil cost not to exceed that at traditional schools by more than 10 percent. To accomplish this, administrative plans will inevitably have to show the phased reduction or elimination of some services now provided to students in many traditional comprehensive secondary schools.

These principles, and *Horace's Compromise,* have provoked many good questions, mostly from schoolpeople.

What's new here? What you're suggesting here is as old as McGuffey. Why, in my school . . .

Yes, nothing we're suggesting here in these principles is new. All nine find successful expression somewhere. What *is* a bit new, however, is putting them all together. Piecemeal reform is no reform.

Don't these principles smack of the 1960s, with all their preaching about treating kids "individually"? We tried all that and it didn't work.

Yes, some of these ideas are reminiscent of the 1960s—and of the 1780s, too, when "exhibitions" for graduation were routinely expected. We hope to take the best from several eras, including the recent past: from the sixties, the special concern for individual differences and the special needs of the poor, and from the late seventies and early eighties, the concern for quality, for demonstrable achievement, for standards. We believe the priorities of the late 1970s cannot, in fact, find fruition without adopting some of those of the 1960s, and vice versa. Personalization of schooling and common standards go hand-in-glove; one without the other won't make it, as we have discovered.

Will anyone take seriously these radical ideas of yours? You want to tip the cart over.

My critique and the plans of the Coalition are the result of common sense and experience. What *is* truly radical, however, is the idea that serious intellectual activity can go on in rushed fifty-five minute snippets, seven in a row. It *is* radical to think that even an able, devoted teacher can help the intellectual development of more than one hundred youngsters simultaneously. It *is* radical to think that a large corps of devoted, full-time teachers will evolve just because we say it must, when we both pay teachers a fraction of what they are worth and patronize them with regulation from on high. It *is* radical to think that time spent (thirty-six thousand minutes per year) is the most important variable in learning. If you want truly radical ideas—radical in the sense of extreme— there they are, *deep in current practice.* On the other hand, if you use "radical" in its less familiar sense of going back to first principles, then we happily embrace the label.

What of standards? The Coalition's nine principles, and Horace's Compromise, *are awfully vague on them.*

We accept that criticism, but beg for patience. True standards of intellect—even those of a restless, noisy adolescent—do not lend themselves wholly to quickly collected, precise, standard measurement. We need to devise clusters of instruments (to use a bloodless but apt word) to probe our students' ability to think resourcefully about important things. Indeed, we need time to reflect deeply on what we mean by "think resourcefully" and what we feel are the most "important things." The Coalition will get more specific as our work unfolds. Design of "exhibitions"—the culminating exercise in high school—is a first priority.

That's a waffle. We already have tests. Let's use them.

Yes, let's use them. Carefully. And honestly accept the fact that some well-regarded tests, such as the Scholastic Aptitude Tests of the College Board (SATs), have severe limitations, ones well understood by their designers but ill recognized by the public at large. Furthermore, mastery—a word often used in *Horace's Compromise*—can be reduced by some to narrow, easily quantified scores. Adolescents, whose education should involve the claims of intuition, imagination, and subtlety, are not well served by such reductive measures of learning.

Yes, we know that it is no better to end with that assertion than it is to wind up with standards defined merely as rank in high school class, SAT scores, or class attendance. It sounds evasive. However, we will work to get beyond what you see as a waffle. Just give us time, and sympathy.

If the "exhibition" is what gets a student a diploma, what happens if he or she can "pass" it without having attended school?

Exhibitions—"performance" diplomas—open a Pandora's Box, I know. But open it we should; school *attendance* isn't what education is all about, *learning* is. If exhibitions weaken the argument for compulsory schooling, so be it—as long as a student's ultimate performance is of high standard.

That teacher-pupil ratio—one to eighty. It's impractical without greatly increased expenditures. Get realistic!

The work load of high school teachers will not decline without new compromises—ones such as teaching two subjects to 80 students rather than one to 160. Or narrowing the curriculum. Or expecting a larger percentage of the adults in a school building to teach students, and to teach them well, than is now often the case. Yes, the load *can* be brought down, if people are willing to reconsider some of our cherished assumptions about the structures of secondary schooling.

As I said, be realistic!

The status quo—the sum of Horace's compromises—is demonstrably unrealistic. The existing school structure clearly serves many students poorly. However, I know that the realism to which you are referring is found in certification laws, union contracts, and tradition. But realism is also found in students who are drifting anonymously through a friendly but soft school program. That's *our* realism. Yes, changing rules and attitudes and doing things differently will be difficult—but these factors *are* susceptible to change. The learning of a largely neglected student (however much that student enjoys that neglect) is not going to change unless we do; that fact is the ultimate realism. Some school authorities accept this, painful though the implications are. We'll work with them and hope that their honesty and courage are contagious.

What of the course of study? You are as vague about the curriculum as you are about standards.

As the Coalition schools converge upon the substance of the final "exhibition" for graduation, this will become clearer. A careful survey of the four areas outlined in *Horace's Compromise*—Inquiry and Expression, Mathematics and Science, Literature and the Arts, and History and Philosophy—will soon be under way. But care should be taken to remember both that the details of any curriculum must reflect the community and the students served and that any "course of study" represents only one point on the triangle of student, teacher, and subject. Alter any one and the others shift—or the triangle breaks.

Give me an example.

Let me give you an extreme one, one represented by the Charles Gross of whom I wrote in *Horace's Compromise*. In the vocational school class I described, his ultimate goals were the general intellectual training of his students and their ability to express themselves. The way he got their attention was through his course on electricity; without this, most of the students would be truant. But the details of electrical work—procedures with devices and materials that would soon be obsolete in a rapidly changing industry—were secondary. What was foremost was Gross's effort to get his students to be constructively thoughtful about their work and able to verbalize that thought. "What would happen, Billy, if you switched that circuit in (some different way)?" he'd ask. The young man would point, and Gross would assert, "Billy, I'm blind. You have to tell me." So Billy would work at telling Mr. Gross clearly the results of his (to put it pompously but accurately) hypothetico-deductive reasoning. Only with such prowess, Gross knew, could Billy and the other low-income minority kids make it in society. Mr. Gross was, very simply, teaching "Inquiry and Expression" in a powerful way *in the form and setting required by his pupils.* Other teachers would head toward the same goal over very different paths. (It should also be noted that Gross's total student load was 50, the maximum allowed for vocational-technical schools receiving federal funds in his community. If Charles Gross were expected to teach 175 students, the load of his colleagues teaching in the "academic" areas, he'd quit.)

But I thought you were opposed to vocational education!

I'm opposed to schooling that focuses narrowly on particular job training. I'm for general education, but arranged so as to attract and to hold pupils. If hands-on skill experience is a route to general intellectual prowess, that's fine with me. There is no One Best Curriculum, and there can never be, if school is to be effective. Students— inconveniently, perhaps—differ. So, then, must the ways to help them learn differ, even if there are common standards for the learning that is ultimately exhibited. Common ends, then, and diverse means.

So couldn't foreign languages be taught in school? You seem to be opposed to them, too.

I'm all for the study of a foreign tongue in American schools, most especially if that tongue is English. My point is not to *mandate* foreign language instruction. For example, a fifteen-year-old Anglo youngster who can barely read or write English should not be asked now to learn French too. Concentrate on English.

This is not at all to denigrate the importance of a second language. Indeed, an *ideal* school would be wholly bilingual: all ultimately can deeply benefit from a multilingual experience. My view here, however, merely states a priority today forced on schools where conditions are not ideal.

And physical education?

I'm all for physical education, but not for Physical Education as it is currently pursued in many schools, as I argued in *Horace's Compromise.* I'm also for competitive sports—which are different in important respects from Physical Education. Many schools "hold" their pupils because of sports; but all too many of those pupils play Melissa as well as basketball. That is, they cop out of their academic education.

"School spirit" driven by athletics is educationally meaningless unless that spirit is somehow ultimately directed to the principal purposes of the school. That can be done, and sometimes is. However, the sports tail often wags the academic dog.

Isn't your program, so focused on the "intellect," very elitist, and dull in addition?

It is elitist only if one thinks that using one's mind resourcefully is the preserve of some special minority group. Our view is that it is the right of every citizen and the ultimate bulwark of democracy. A populace that is difficult to con is a people who will prosper in decent ways—such is the democratic faith. Learning to use one's mind well need not be a dusty academic exercise, devoid of connection to one's world and not fun at all. Learning is both joyless and useless when it is prescribed in mindless ways; but in the hands of a Sister Michael or a Charles Gross or a Fred Curtis it is not. The trick (again) is to respect the triangle—the chemistry of a *particular* teacher with *particular* students engaged on a *particular* subject. The first two shape the third, and vice versa.

That's romantic nonsense. The Fred Curtises of the world are rare. And many kids really want a practical education, to go to work and not to college.

Fred Curtis is rare, but not so rare as conventional wisdom implies. Get teaching conditions right, and Americans will discover thousands of Curtises it never knew it had. Organize sensible in-service programs, get the incentives right for teachers to engage in them, and even more will emerge. The people are already there, in most schools.

As for those students who "want a practical education": There is a self-fulfilling prophecy here. The kids who fail at school say they want something different, so we accommodate them. Our response, then, isn't more vigorous or more imaginative teaching for these students in the subjects they are failing: we sidestep that difficult prospect by rationalizing that these students have "different needs" from youngsters who are learning to read Hemingway and do algebra. So, we conclude, make them hewers of wood and drawers of water.

The fact remains that these students are the very ones who need *more* "academic" education, not less. And they need legitimate success at it. If they don't get it, or are denied it, they will not be able to function with even a modicum of freedom in modern society.

The fact that most of the students who are presumed to want something else are from lower-income groups adds to the outrage. There is blatant class discrimination in how schools "meet individual needs." An intellectual education is every citizen's right and need, and schools must learn to provide it. Giving up on a child's mind is simply unacceptable.

O.K. But what do you do with the ninth-grader who can't read?

You invest heavily—almost exclusively—in teaching how to read. Get her or him (Dennis, for instance) to have some success. If this implies one-on-one tutoring, as many literacy programs have shown, ways must be found. If a school is not saddled with strict "class" structure (ninth grade, tenth grade, and so on), one can bring this youngster along with his age-mates some of the time; that is, the pre–high school study that Dennis needs may take place in the high school building, where social mates readily mingle. But he must be helped on his basic studies—and he must not be handed a monster textbook that he cannot read and for which he is somehow held accountable. When he has met the three pre-conditions for entering high school–level studies—literacy, numeracy, and civic understanding, as outlined in *Horace's Compromise*—he can be brought along, accelerated if possible. Above all, he must be both nurtured (we'll help you) and told the truth (you cannot read). This takes time and resources—the essential place for "compensatory" funding from state and federal sources. And it takes great sensitivity on the part of teachers to help Dennis keep his self-respect.

What of the student who is so adept a scholar that he or she passes the high school exhibition at age fourteen?

If such a student passes the exhibition but needs to stay in school with his or her age-mates, a broadened program is possible—a third language, a second science, and so forth. Part-time attendance at a local college is a possibility. Most schools that we've visited handle this problem well, usually with help from higher education—certainly better than they cope with the problem represented by Dennis.

What of the social services now provided by schools—the hot lunches, counseling, medical care, and the rest? Do you jettison all this in the cause of an "intellectual" education?

Yes and no. Yes, when the services are redundant with those

233

provided at home. No, when home isn't home, when the school must substitute as parent, parent-of-last-resort. But the services thus provided must be seen as *additional* to basic educational services. Too often today they *replace* educational services, as funds are not available for both. This is sadly ironic, as the students who need social services are often the very students who require the most intensive educational service. If social services are needed, then, and can be efficiently provided through the school's systems, let this provision be added to the existing program while not undermining its essential core.

In addition, let us not confuse such social services or educational services with "social" service of publicly-paid-for parties. When the Junior Prom dominates the life of students and teachers for two weeks prior to the event, one knows that priorities are awry.

Won't students resent the narrowing of their options that is inevitable in an Essential School? Electives are seen by most as their absolute right. A school with no choices for them to make will be opposed by its students.

Initially, yes. But everyone, including the students, must go back to the beginning, to the reasons for electives in the first place. Their genesis was not so much a response to student freedom of choice as it was to accommodate student differences—different interests, aptitudes, skills. The hope was that everyone would be appropriately "placed" and successful there. (Most of us like what we're successful at.)

However, there are things in this world which are so important that we must learn them, whether we like them or not. The culture doesn't forgive us if we say we don't "like" to become literate; it merely shuts the door in our face. What is essential must be grasped, and the task of an Essential School is to adapt—to *personalize*—its program so that each student, or small group of students, can "elect" the means to that essential end, however discouraging the goal may at first appear. We're back to Charles Gross's class again: his ends there were common to all in an Essential School, but his means were tailored to his students. Pupils may "choose" among differing means and teachers may devise varying means. But the ends, albeit generally stated, remain the same.

Will the students buy this?

Eventually. They will like legitimate personalization. However, many will resist other aspects of an Essential School, particularly its emphasis on student-as-worker and on graduation on the basis of performance. The opportunity to get a diploma even when one dodges, like Melissa, or barters, as was the case in Steve Brody's class, will vanish. Some kids won't like the demise of these easy options to the work of real learning.

How does the emerging research on brain functioning and neuro-psychology, on different learning styles, affect your ideas?

The research so far clearly shows the astonishing complexity of the process of learning and the great variability among individuals. While no one yet should say with assurance precisely how to apply the findings of this research to practice, at least one general implication is demonstrably clear: schools must be personalized to the maximum feasible extent. Kids differ, one from the other, profoundly; and while we should make the best of the commonalities, we must accommodate and capitalize on those differences. Standardized practice—that panacea of so much of the contemporary reform movement—runs in precisely the opposite direction, lamentably.

But doesn't personalized instruction put a new and heavy load on teachers, an expectation for extraordinary judgment about the learning style of each youngster?

Yes, inescapably. It would be nice if there were One Best Method of schooling, but that is not to be. The variety among pupils is inconvenient, but we're stuck with it. So we'll have to trust teachers.

We can't. The profession is too weak.

We must; there isn't any alternative. The profession must be radically strengthened. Horace mustn't compromise in the ways he is forced to now. And teachers must be given the privilege of autonomy and the compliment of accountability to an unprecedented degree—if we are to take the implications of the new research seriously.

To repeat: the existing teaching force has substantial strength. We must empower and enhance the abler folk within it. Our experiment absolutely depends on able teachers. To plan otherwise is to give up.

There isn't money for all this reform.

Perhaps. We believe that we can use our existing resources better—assuming that we have the political will to change priorities. In any event, the Coalition assumes that not much more money will be available for high school education, certainly not more than 10 percent over existing per pupil expenditures, assuming inflation. Our effort, therefore, takes this financial restriction as a given.

What you want is threatening for parents. How will you get their support? Will they buy in if they think it may put their children's college chances at risk?

We insist that our Essential School program is experimental; no parent or student should have to take part. At the same time, we must persuade parents that our approach is sensible, more so than the status quo. We must also gain the understanding and endorsement of university leaders, as they are the best people to reassure parents of college-bound youngsters. Most colleges will applaud any school that awards its diploma only on the basis of the exhibition of substantial accomplishment; college admissions officers are as exasperated as anyone else with the current credit-collecting system that masks mastery.

How will you evaluate the work of the Coalition?

Slowly. First, by the staff members of each school themselves. They will quickly know what's awry, and can try to correct it. Second, by sensitive outside review, much as the better accreditation efforts are conducted. And, finally, by the performance of the students and the constructive stability of the faculties that teach them. We'll be as precise as possible, while recognizing that precision is neither possible nor wise in some areas of our business.

What is the state's or central office's role?

To support school-level work and the premise that diversity among schools is a virtue. To give principals real authority. To give the Coalition schools all possible and appropriate freedom. To give advice, and not to get upset when not all of it is taken. To give money where it is needed. To protect the experiment from those who unfairly expect quick results or whose turf is being (wisely) invaded. To have high expectations, and to be specific and honest about them. To ask probing, informed questions. To assist, sensitively, in the administration of exhibitions, as this is the place where ultimate accountability resides.

But no one cares.

Yes, too many don't care, even parents.

Few citizens really know what's going on in their schools. They settle for the familiar form and ignore the substance. The businessman who would neither copy any part of the high school's routines or structure for his own firm's training programs nor tolerate for his employees the work conditions that are standard in schools sanctimoniously takes part in pep rallies for the schools. The college professor who on principle would not stand for close state regulation of her classes of freshmen blithely endorses tight control on twelfth-grade instruction, and even assists central authorities with that standardized regulation. Hypocrisy? Not really. Just indifference. And the unwillingness to think hard and honestly about the process of education.

Perhaps the country is as docile as many of its children, wedded over twenty-two hours per week to the authority of the television set, where Johnny Carson, in contrast with Sister Michael, neither sees the yawn nor hears the scream. We seem happy to deny the complexity of learning, and are satisfied with simple remedies to the obvious ills of the schools. And perhaps Americans don't want question-askers, people who want answers. Perhaps, in sum, the unchallenging mindlessness of so much of the status quo is truly acceptable: it doesn't make waves.

But perhaps we—all of us—are better than that. That is the belief of those of us in the Coalition. Our new project, guided by that belief, tries to make an essential intellectual education joyful and accessible to all.

Acknowledgments
Notes

Acknowledgments

MY DEBTS to others are many, particularly to those who debated with and encouraged me on this project over the last five years: Nancy Sizer, Arthur Powell, Martha Landesberg, Robert Hampel, Eleanor Farrar, David K. Cohen, Philip Zaeder, and Pat West-Barker. The leaders of our two sponsoring associations, Scott Thomson of the National Association of Secondary School Principals and John Esty of the National Association of Independent Schools, were admirably helpful. The advice of the NAIS Commission on Educational Issues was always valuable: Carl Dolce (North Carolina State University), Joseph Featherstone (Commonwealth School, Boston), Chester E. Finn, Jr. (Vanderbilt University), Gerald Grant (Syracuse University), Earl Harrison (the Sidwell Friends School, Washington, D.C.), Robin Lester (Trinity School, New York City), Thomas Minter (New York City Public Schools), Cynthia Parsons (*Christian Science Monitor* and Dartmouth College), Blair Stambaugh (the Baldwin School, Bryn Mawr, Pennsylvania).

The support of six philanthropic foundations, substantive in both financial and scholarly senses, was crucial: the Charles E. Culpeper Foundation (Helen Johnson and Philip Drake), the Carnegie Corporation of New York (Alden Dunham), the Commonwealth Fund (Carleton Chapman and Margaret Mahoney), the Esther A. and Joseph Klingenstein Fund (John Klingenstein and Robert N.

Kreidler), the Gates Foundation (Charles Froelicher and Peter Grant), and the Edward John Noble Foundation (John F. Joline III). The assistance of William and Neena Dahling of Michigan is also greatly appreciated. The trustees of Phillips Academy supported my work in many ways, both while I served as the academy's headmaster and thereafter. Their commitment to the quality of secondary education beyond their own school as well as within it is exemplary and, alas, all too rare. I am especially indebted to the board's president during my tenure, Donald H. McLean, Jr. and to its current president, Melville Chapin.

I have been greatly influenced by colleagues in the schools where I have taught, from Sir Brian Hone at the Melbourne Church of England Grammar School, in Australia, where I worked in 1958, to my many Phillips Academy associates. I learned from them what was possible and from my Andover friends especially that high standards and personal caring for students need not nor cannot be separated.

Over the past decade I have visited over a hundred schools and learned from each. The specific work for this book started with a visit to some thirty Australian schools during July and August of 1981, when I was the guest of the Headmasters Association and the Association of Heads of Schools for Girls. I am especially grateful for the hospitality and counsel of S. Peter Gebhardt (Geelong College, Victoria), Father John Neil (Blackfriars Priory School, South Australia), Nigel Creese (Melbourne Grammar School, Victoria), Paul McKoewn (Canberra Grammar School, Australian Capital Territory), Mark Bishop (Cranbrook School, New South Wales), Anthony Rae (Newington College, New South Wales), Max Howell (Brisbane Grammar School, Queensland), the Reverend Dudley B. Clarke (Hutchins School, Tasmania), Philip Hughes (University of Tasmania), and Michael Pusey (University of New South Wales).

During the two years of field work, I visited over two score American secondary schools, some extensively, some briefly. Several of my visits were part of other inquiries, but I learned and benefited from all. My debt goes to many; here I can record only the schools and the principals who hosted me. During 1981: Groton-Dunstable

Regional High School, Massachusetts (David Quattrone); Greater Lawrence Regional Vocational-Technical High School, Massachusetts (Roland Cotton); Northside High School, Atlanta, Georgia (William Rudolph); Bromfield High School, Harvard, Massachusetts (Michael Horgan); Mendon High School, Pittsford, New York (Steven Stoller); Sutherland High School, Pittsford (Jerry Sollene); Edison Technical and Occupational Education Center, Rochester, New York (Eberhard (Art) Thieme); Monroe High School, Rochester (Robert Pedzich, Assistant Principal); East High School, Rochester (Theodore DeSoto); Cooley High School, Detroit, Michigan (Walter Jenkins); Northern High School, Detroit (Emeral Crosby); Spofford Juvenile Center, New York City (Luis Osorio); Hunter College High School, New York City (Bernard Miller); Martin Van Buren High School, New York City (Murray Ostrin); Canarsie High School, New York City (James Romm, Assistant Principal); Samuel Gompers Technical Vocational High School, New York City (Victor Herbert); John Bowne High School, New York City (Pearl Warner). I acknowledge special help in the Rochester area from Richard Hibschman and Robert Jordan of Pittsford and Laval Wilson and Tod and Becky Sizer of the City of Rochester. Edward Simpkins of Wayne State University welcomed me to Detroit. My days in New York City were enriched by Thomas Minter, Nathan Quinones, and especially by Kurt Paul, who accompanied me on my various visits and who described, in a strikingly perceptive way, the context in which the public schools of that great city operate. John Negley, the principal of D. C. Everest Senior High School, Schofield, Wisconsin joined me in Atlanta and shared with me his impressions of schools there.

During 1982: Chapel Hill High School, North Carolina (Robert Monson); North Carolina School of Science and Mathematics, Durham (Charles Eilber); Dominican High School, Whitefish Bay, Wisconsin (Edward Bangs, associate administrator for student affairs); Pius IX High School, Milwaukee, Wisconsin (Father Lawrence McCall); Mesa High School, Mesa, Arizona (Robert Free); Thunderbird High School, Glendale, Arizona (Timothy Waters); Nicholls High School, New Orleans, Louisiana (Russel S. Costanza, Jr.). I benefited from the counsel of Joan Lipsitz at the University of North Carolina, of Fathers John Hanley and Leslie Darnieder of Milwaukee, of George Smith in Mesa, and of Carol Allen and Theodore Cotonio in New Orleans.

Accompanied by Nancy Sizer, I visited five secondary schools in Northern California: San Francisco University High School (Dennis Collins); Tamalpais High School (Ted Mitchell); San Domenico School, San Anselmo (Sister Karen Marie); Biggs Junior-Senior High School (Walter Wilson); Shasta High School, Redding (Douglas Deason). Crayton Bedford was of special help in San Francisco. In the late spring: Lawrenceville School, New Jersey (Bruce McClellan); Wayland High School, Massachusetts (Charles Goff); Polytechnic Senior High School, Fort Worth, Texas (Marion (Jack) Jones); R. L. Paschal Senior High School, Fort Worth (Ralph Miller); Castleberry Baptist Christian School, Texas (Brother Stanley Brooke); Abilene High School, Texas (Gayle Lomax). Alexander Platt of the Wayland, Massachusetts, Public Schools has been especially helpful. Valleau Wilkie, Mollie and Garland Lasater, and Janice Hogue made my Fort Worth area visit especially useful. Martha Brooks, then of Abilene High School, helped our study in a variety of important ways.

An old friend, James Richardson of the St. Louis Public Schools, arranged for my visit to Kennard NJROTC Academy in his school system. Kennard's principal is John F. Close. Ann Campbell, Nebraska's state commissioner of education, met with me and suggested visits to two schools in her state: Broken Bow Senior High School (Wendell McConnaha) and Ansley High School (Rick Williams). Louis Stithern, the principal of Broken Bow Junior High School, was most welcoming. Jack Kennedy of the *Lincoln Journal* gave me the benefit of his wide experience as an education reporter.

Several urban schools in mid-1982: South Boston High School (Jerome Winegar); Boston Latin School (Michael G. Contompasis); Sheridan Middle School, New Haven, Connecticut (John Courtmanche); and Hillhouse High School, New Haven, (DeNorris Crosby). The latter two schools were visited as part of a study of the Yale–New Haven Teachers Institute.

My colleagues in this study carried out extensive field work in fifteen secondary schools over 1981 and 1982. I personally have visited most of these schools, and have benefited from the field notes on them all: Newton North High School, Massachusetts (Richard Mechem); Watertown High School, Massachusetts (Manson Hall); Buckingham, Browne & Nichols School, Cambridge, Massachusetts (Peter Gunness); Cambridge Rindge and Latin School, Massachusetts (Edward Sarason); Williamson High School, Mobile, Alabama (Fred Green, Jr.); Andalusia High School, Alabama (Clayton Bryant); Cleveland Central Catholic High School (Father Neil O'Connor); Findlay High School, Ohio (Robert Shamp); Colorado Academy, Englewood, Colorado (Frank Wallace); Manual High School, Denver, Colorado (Mary Gentilé); East High School, Denver (John Astuno); The Bishop's Schools, LaJolla, California (Dorothy Anne Williams); LaJolla High School (Charles Clapper); San Diego High School, California (Robert Amparan); and Vista High School, California (Alan Johnson). Sister Rosemary Hochevar of Cleveland was especially generous with her counsel and encouragement.

Martha Landesberg and I asked students at schools we could not visit to write us. In this effort we received special help from the NJROTC program, especially from Joseph C. Gilliam, chief of naval education and training, Pensacola, Florida. We are grateful to students and staff at the following schools: Concord-Carlisle High School, Massachusetts; South Brunswick High School, New Jersey; North Panola High School, Sardis, Mississippi; Jefferson County Open High School, Colorado; Dedham High School, Massachusetts; East Northport High School, Northport, New York; Dobson High School, Mesa, Arizona; Westbrook High School, Westbrook, Connecticut; Central High School, Flint, Michigan; Crystal River High School, Pensacola, Florida; South Mecklenburg High School, Pineville, North Carolina; Rancocas Valley Regional High School, Mount Holly, New Jersey; and Point Loma High School, San Diego, California.

On a variety of special questions we were helped by Diane Reinhard of the University of West Virginia; George Bereday of Teachers College, Columbia University; Kenneth Rowe, New York State Department of Education; William H. Hebert and Felix J. Zollo, Jr., of the Massachusetts Teachers Association; Rita Dunn of St. John's University; John E. Roueche of the University of Texas; Charles Bowen of the International Business Machines Corporation; David B. Tyack of Stanford University; Mark Tucker of the Carnegie

ACKNOWLEDGMENTS

Study of Technology and Education; Fred Jewett of Harvard University; William A. Garrison of Sacramento; Carl Krumpe of Phillips Academy; and the staffs of several professional associations: Charles Suhor (National Council of Teachers of English), C. Edward Siebold (American Council on the Teaching of Foreign Languages), Elizabeth Scott (National Council for the Social Studies), Bill G. Aldridge (National Science Teachers Association), and James D. Gates (National Council of Teachers of Mathematics). Bob Brown of Peterborough, New Hampshire, peppered me with useful ideas, and Myndie Nutting of Gloucester, Massachusetts, extended my reading with clippings from journals and newspapers.

I owe a special thanks to Thomas Shannon of the National School Boards Association, and to its president, Rayna Page, and the 1982–1983 executive committee, for discussing with me the virtues and perils of decentralization; and to NSBA members who sent their views to me on this subject by letter, in response to a request from Shannon in his column in *School Board News.*

The study's field staff and research assistants deepened my understanding of a variety of issues: Helen Featherstone, Lauren Young, Ruben Carriedo, Diane Franklin, Ellen Glanz, Brother Peter Holland, Barbara Neufeld, Patricia Wertheimer, Mary Jane Yurchak, Richard Berger, Richard Horn, Michael Lyden, William Ubinas, George Lowry, Joan Cawood, Lynn Sussman, and Betsy Parsons.

I am especially grateful to those who read and criticized drafts or portions of my manuscript: Gregory Anrig, Mortimer Adler, Seymour Sarason, Israel Scheffler, Thomas Hodgson, Frederic Stott, Gerald Grant, Philip Zaeder, Gilbert T. Sewall, Arthur Powell, Scott Thomson, Martha Landesberg, Robert Hampel, Eleanor Farrar, and Nancy Sizer. They gave good advice: the failings of the final work are not theirs, but mine. Fontaine Melus and Paula Foresman cheerfully and accurately typed drafts of the manuscript and of the field notes that preceded it. Cal Kolbe pulled together the last bits.

My editor at Houghton Mifflin, Austin Olney, has been a wise counselor throughout. Frances Apt edited the text with sensitivity and candor. I am grateful to them both and to their colleagues, who offered us continuing encouragement.

My final thanks are due hundreds of students and teachers in dozens of schools; to principals, superintendents, school board members, and professors whom I met at conferences and meetings and who gave counsel and sent letters and reports; and to close friends and family, who constantly gave courage. I am much in their debt.

My closest professional colleague is also my wife. Her ideas, with her wise and often wry belief in adolescents, thread through every page of this book.

Notes

Introduction

1. This teacher-student-subject triangle is a familiar metaphor in education. See, for example, David Hawkins, "I, Thou, and It," *The Informed Vision* (New York: Agathon Press, 1974) pp. 48–62.
2. See Robert S. Lynd and Helen Merrell Lynd, *Middletown: A Study in Modern American Culture* (New York: Harcourt, Brace and World, 1929, 1950), part 3, for a picture of Muncie, Indiana, schools in the mid-1920s. What is surprising is not the differences from the present, but the similarities. See also Joseph F. Kett, *Rites of Passage: Adolescence in America, 1790 to the Present* (New York: Basic Books, 1977), part 3.
3. I borrow this nice phrase from David Tyack, *The One Best System: A History of American Urban Education* (Cambridge: Harvard University Press, 1974).

Prologue

1. Portions of this section appeared under the title "In Defense of Teachers" in *The Boston Observer*, vol. 1, no. 19 (December 10, 1982), pp. 5ff.

I

1. *Boston Globe*, August 28, 1982, p. 18.
2. Robert Coles has reminded us often of this stricture from James Agee and Walker Evans' *Let Us Now Praise Famous Men*. Robert Coles, *Children of Crisis: A Study of Courage and Fear* (Boston: Little, Brown, 1964), p. 381.
3. Robert Coles has written extensively about the "narcissistic entitlement" of privileged youth. See *Children of Crisis V: Privileged Ones* (Boston: Little, Brown, 1977), part 6.

4. Edward C. Banfield has usefully analyzed "class" as an attitude toward the future. Edward C. Banfield, *The Unheavenly City: The Nature and Future of Our Urban Crisis* (Boston: Little, Brown, 1968, 1970), chapter 3.

5. Christopher Jencks et al., *Inequality: A Reassessment of the Effect of Family and Schooling in America* (New York: Basic Books), p. 27.

6. See *Chronicle of Higher Education*, October 13, 1982, pp. 1, 14.

7. See Carol Gilligan, *In a Different Voice: Psychological Theory and Women's Development* (Cambridge: Harvard University Press, 1982).

8. Paul Goodman, *Growing Up Absurd: Problems of Youth in the Organized Society* (New York: Random House, 1960), p. 72.

9. Alison Woodward, in the magazine of Melbourne Church of England Girls Grammar School (Victoria, Australia), 1982, p. 54.

10. *Psychology Today*, February 1979, p. 40.

11. James Wilde, "In Brooklyn: A Wolf in Sneakers," *Time*, October 12, 1981, pp. 10–12.

12. John Janeway Conger, *Adolescence and Youth: Psychological Development in a Changing World*, 2nd edition (New York: Harper and Row, 1973, 1977), p. 291.

13. Peter Davis, *Hometown: A Contemporary American Chronicle* (New York: Simon and Schuster, 1982), p. 42.

14. Daniel Offer, Eric Ostrov, and Kenneth I. Howard, *The Adolescent: A Psychological Self-Portrait* (New York: Basic Books, 1981), p. 123.

15. Sylvia Porter, *San Francisco Chronicle*, March 20, 1982, p. 46.

16. Davis, p. 46.

17. Conger, pp. 294, 298.

18. Ibid., pp. 283, 288; U.S. Bureau of the Census, Current Population Reports, series P-23, no. 114, *Characteristics of American Children and Youth: 1980*, pp. 7–8.

19. *Education Week*, March 3, 1982, p. 1.

20. George H. Gallup, "Gallup Poll of the Public's Attitudes toward the Public Schools," *Phi Delta Kappan*, September 1982, p. 38.

21. The *NASSP Practitioner*, vol. 8, no. 3, pp. 1–2.

22. Conger, pp. 211ff.; Offer et al., p. 71; J. G. Bachman et al., *Youth in Transition*, vol. 1: *Blueprint for a Longitudinal Study of Adolescent Boys* (Ann Arbor, 1967) quoted in Conger, p. 389; Gerald Lesser and Denise Kandel, quoted in Conger, pp. 351ff. See Samuel Bowles and Herbert Gintis, *Schooling in Capitalist America: Educational Reform and the Contradictions of Economic Life* (New York: Basic Books, 1976), pp. 144–146.

23. Franklin E. Zimring, *The Changing World of Adolescence* (New York: Free Press, 1982), pp. 91, 158–159 and chapter 7.

24. Joan S. Lipsitz's brief essay "The Hungry Student" extends this metaphor in a fruitful way. *Andover Review*, vol. 5, no. 2 (Fall 1978), pp. 55–59.

25. Neil Postman and Charles Weingartner, *Teaching As a Subversive Activity* (New York: Delacorte, 1979), p. 3.

26. Ellen S. Raphael, "Youth Employment and Its Effects on Performance in High School," unpublished M.A. policy analysis exercise, John F. Kennedy School of Government, Harvard University, p. 7.

27. Ibid., p. 28.

28. John Dewey, "The Way Out of Educational Confusion" (1931), in Reginald

D. Archambault, ed., *John Dewey on Education: Selected Writings* (New York: Random House, 1964), pp. 422–426; David Riesman, *Constraint and Variety in American Education* (Lincoln: University of Nebraska Press, 1956); Edgar Z. Friedenberg, *The Vanishing Adolescent* (Boston: Beacon Press, 1962); Paul Goodman, *Growing Up Absurd* and *Compulsory Mis-Education* (New York: Horizon Press, 1964).

29. Charles E. Silberman, *Crisis in the Classroom: The Remaking of American Education* (New York: Random House, 1970), pp. 152–153, 155.

30. Peter Holland, personal conversation.

31. Davis, p. 49.

32. David S. Seeley, *Education Through Partnership: Mediating Structures and Education* (Cambridge: Ballinger, 1981), p. 77. Robert A. Shaw of Brown University has shown how little the students are engaged in school. He asked them, "What do you do in school that makes you feel you accomplished something?" His findings are disturbing: "Even when given three chances to answer the question, fully one out of five students was unable to think of anything he or she does while in school that generates a feeling of accomplishment. In all, over half the students (52%) could think of nothing related to the school curriculum that gave them a sense of accomplishment. Rather, what sense of accomplishment they did earn in school came from sports and other extracurricular activities (20%), socializing with friends (11%), or . . . nothing at all (21%)." Unpublished paper, 1982.

33. Barbara Lerner, "American Education: How Are We Doing?" *Public Interest*, no. 69 (Fall 1982), p. 64.

34. National Assessment of Educational Progress [NAEP], "Mathematical Achievement: Knowledge, Skills, Understandings, Applications." Summary pamphlet, undated [1982].

35. NAEP, "National Assessment Results in Social Studies/Citizenship." Summary pamphlet, undated [1982].

36. NAEP, "Reading, Thinking and Writing," 1981, p. 2.

37. Ibid., p. 3.

38. Ibid., p. 5.

39. See National Research Council, *Ability Testing*, part 1 (Washington: National Academy Press, 1982), pp. 163–169, 176–180. One of the NRC's most important caveats: "No important decision about an individual's educational future should be based on a single test score considered in isolation" (p. 178). The exhibition of mastery *must* include a number of exercises; and each student should have some choice of the kind of exercise he prefers (e.g., an oral versus a written examination; a timed test versus an essay written over a period of a month).

II

1. Shasta High School, Redding, California. An eloquent and analogous statement, "The Essentials of Education," one stressing explicitly the "interdependence of skills and content" that is implicit in the Shasta High School statement, was issued in 1980 by a coalition of education associations. Organizations for the Essentials of Education (Urbana, Illinois).

250

2. Judge Arthur M. Recht, in his order resulting from *Pauley* v. *Kelly*, 1979, as reprinted in *Education Week*, May 26, 1982, p. 10. See also, in *Education Week*, January 16, 1983, pp. 21, 24, Jonathan P. Sher, "The Struggle to Fulfill at Judicial Mandate: How Not to 'Reconstruct' Education in W. Va."

3. Bureau of Education, Department of the Interior, "Cardinal Principles of Secondary Education: A Report of the Commission on the Reorganization of Secondary Education, appointed by the National Education Association," *Bulletin*, no. 35 (Washington: U.S. Government Printing Office, 1918).

4. Diane Hedin, Paula Simon, and Michael Robin, *Minnesota Youth Poll: Youth's Views on School and School Discipline*, Minnesota Report 184 (1983), Agricultural Experiment Station, University of Minnesota, p. 13.

5. I am indebted to Harold F. Sizer and Lyde E. Sizer for a survey of the diploma requirements of fifty representative secondary schools, completed for A Study of High Schools.

6. Education Research Service, Inc. *Class Size: A Summary of Research* (Arlington, Virginia, 1978); and *Class Size Research: A Critique of Recent Meta-Analyses* (Arlington, Virginia, 1980).

7. In this connection, see Patricia Albjerg Graham, "Literacy: A Goal for Secondary Schools," *Daedalus*, 210, no. 3, pp. 119–134.

8. Quoted by Fred M. Hechinger, "Who's Making School Policy?" *New York Times*, January 25, 1983.

9. There is underway useful rethinking on the proper boundaries of state generosity. See Willard Gaylin, Ira Glasser, Steven Marcus, and David Rothman, *Doing Good: The Limits of Benevolence* (New York: Pantheon, 1978), especially the essay "The State as Parent: Social Policy in the Progressive Era"; and Peter L. Berger and Richard John Neuhaus, *To Empower People: The Role of Mediating Structures in Public Policy* (Washington: American Enterprise Institute, 1977). Several secondary school reform proposals in the early 1970s recommended lowering the age of compulsory education. See B. Frank Brown, chairman, National Commission on the Reform of Secondary Education, *The Reform of Secondary Education.* (New York: McGraw-Hill, 1973).

10. Mortimer Adler, *The Paideia Proposal: An Educational Manifesto* (New York: Macmillan, 1982).

11. Frederick Rudolph, *Curriculum: A History of the American Undergraduate Course of Study Since 1636* (San Francisco: Jossey-Bass, 1977), pp. 65–75.

12. For a brief, lively essay on this independent school ritual, see Alden S. Blodget, "The Curriculum That Jack Built," *Independent School*, February 1983, pp. 9–12.

13. Jerome S. Bruner, *The Process of Education* (Cambridge: Harvard University Press, 1963), p. 66.

14. Israel Scheffler, *Reason and Teaching* (Indianapolis: Bobbs-Merrill, 1973), p. 73.

15. John Dewey, "The Nature of Subject Matter" (1916) in Reginald D. Archambault, ed., *John Dewey on Education: Selected Writings* (New York: Random House, 1964), pp. 363–364, 367.

16. Charles Dickens, *Hard Times* (1854; Signet edition, New York: New American Library, 1961), pp. 11, 12.

17. Alfred North Whitehead, *The Aims of Education* (New York: Macmillan, 1929), pp. 2, 6.

18. Bruner, p. 17.
19. Whitehead, p. 2.
20. Adler, pp. 21–31.
21. Ibid., p. 26.
22. Joshua L. Miner regaled me with this anecdote, as well as with many stimulating ideas emerging from his experience with Outward Bound and with its founder, Kurt Hahn.
23. A brief, useful analysis of these matters is found in Arnold B. Arons, "Reasoning Modes and Processes Arising in Secondary and College Level Study of Natural Science, Humanities, and the Social Sciences," *Andover Review,* vol. 5, no. 2 (Fall 1978), pp. 3–8.
24. B. F. Skinner, *The Technology of Teaching* (New York: Appleton-Century-Crofts, 1968), p. 119.
25. Bruner, pp. 58, 65.
26. They would not stay long with this teacher; children in the juvenile justice system are kept on the move. See Charles E. Silberman, *Criminal Violence, Criminal Justice* (New York: Random House, 1978), chapter 9; and Peter S. Prescott, *The Child Savers* (New York: Knopf, 1981).
27. Whitehead, p. 10.
28. Bruner, pp. 7, 25.
29. Ibid., p. 25.
30. David Hawkins, "Messing Around in Science," *Science and Children,* vol. 2, no. 2 (February 1965), p. 5.
31. Elinor M. Woods and Walt Haney, "Does Vocational Education Make a Difference?" unpublished report by the Huron Institute for the National Institute for Education, September 1981, chapter 8.
32. Edward C. Banfield, *The Unheavenly City: The Nature and Future of Our Urban Crisis* (Boston: Little, Brown, 1968, 1970), chapter 3.
33. There is a massive and argument-filled literature about the effects on student learning of class size. Martha Landesberg has reviewed it for our study. Her principal conclusion: *"Powerful* effects of class size upon student achievement, student affect, teacher affect, and classroom techniques are seen only when extremes of class size are compared . . . Within the range of class size most common in schools (roughly twenty-five to thirty-five) the addition or subtraction of a few students makes little difference." See Education Research Service, "Class Size: A Summary of Research" (Arlington, Virginia: ERS, 1978). The experience of wise teachers may be a better guide than behavioral science in this area; the numbers of variables involved are very great.
34. Under the energetic leadership of Edward A. Wynne, a group calling itself Pro-Character has organized to lessen the silence on this subject. The group's address is 1245 Westgate Terrace, Chicago, Illinois 60607.
35. This issue is usefully sorted out in *General Education in a Free Society: Report of the Harvard Committee* (Cambridge: Harvard University Press, 1945), pp. 72–78.
36. The issue of who practically decides a particular school's definition is a complicated one, obviously, and turns on that institution's form of governance. The matter is, in fact, an easier one than it may seem at first glance, because the threshold virtues of fairness, generosity, and tolerance enjoy wide, if tacit, understanding. It gets more difficult, of course, if the community from which

the students come is itself blatantly un-decent. Those kids' teachers have their jobs cut out for them.

37. I have considered the "citizenship" issue in detail in "Make Them Love America," *Andover Review,* vol. 3, no. 2 (Fall 1976), pp. 5–10.

38. Thomas Hodgson, in a letter to me, has usefully criticized the total merging of science and mathematics: "I see science as *inquiry* into the laws and explanations that bear on human sense experience. To place it together with math as a locus of certainty is to promote a misunderstanding of math (a conditional, deductive field of reasoning) and science (an intuitive, experimental field of reasoning) and a misunderstanding of the nature of the relationship between them. Math is a language of expression for science."

39. For our study, Martha Landesberg analyzed the most recent policy statements of the major professional organizations concerned with the high school curriculum. "The rhetoric of the policy statements," she writes, "is remarkably consistent and emphasizes the following key themes: *Problem-solving,* rather than rote memorization and drill, should be a central focus of the curriculum; students should be taught to *apply skills to real-life situations* (including global problems as well as more routine applications in daily life); the *curriculum must be relevant* to students' lives and connections made between what is learned and conditions in society with which students have no personal experience (for science and math 'relevance' also connotes the incorporation of new technologies into coursework); there should be *more integration of academic courses* which have traditionally remained isolated from one another in the curriculum; and, lastly, that *curriculum should be designed in stages which mirror the stages of intellectual development* evidenced by behavioral science and psychological research."

40. James Bryant Conant argued for a similar policy in 1959: "It should be the policy of the school that every student has an individualized program; there would be no classification of students according to clearly defined and labeled programs such as 'college-preparatory,' 'vocational,' 'commercial.' " *The American High School Today* (New York: McGraw-Hill, 1959), p. 46.

41. A Study of High Schools is continuing to evolve models of what we are calling "essential schools," ones that appear educationally apt and financially realistic. We hope to publish sketches of these in the near future and, if possible, to organize a network of schools interested in experimenting with them. See "Essential Schools: A First Look," NASSP *Bulletin,* October 1983, p. 33–38.

III

1. A sensible analysis of the science and art of teaching is N. L. Gage's *The Scientific Basis of the Art of Teaching* (New York: Teachers College Press, 1978), p. 20.

2. Jerome S. Bruner, *Toward a Theory of Instruction* (Cambridge: Harvard University Press, 1966), p. 118.

3. James S. Coleman, *The Adolescent Society: The Social Life of the Teenager and Its Impact on Education* (New York: Free Press, 1961), p. 315.

4. Joseph Adelson, "Rites of Passage: How Children Learn the Principles of Community," *American Educator,* Summer 1982, p. 8.

5. Jerome S. Bruner, *The Process of Education* (Cambridge: Harvard University Press, 1963), p. 33.
6. Ibid., p. 38.
7. Ibid., p. 39.
8. B. F. Skinner, *The Technology of Teaching* (New York: Appleton-Century-Crofts, 1968), pp. 95–103.
9. The new and prolific "effective school" literature stresses this point. Rutter's work has been very influential, as has the research, largely on elementary schools however, of Ronald Edmonds. See his "Making Schools Effective," *Social Policy,* September–October 1981, pp. 56–59.
10. The mobility of the poor in cities is also a problem. Families move frequently, from rented apartment to rented apartment. Adolescents will leave home, will live here or there, as transients. The less secure they are (the more hand-to-mouth, the more "lower class," as Edward Banfield would put it), the more they need stability, places that can help evoke in them the self-esteem and self-confidence that can fuel their abilities; but the less secure they are, the more they roam, paradoxically seeking a quality that their roaming often denies. Alternative settings, almost mobile schools, are needed to serve this population. See Gene I. Maeroff, *Don't Blame the Kids: The Trouble with America's Public Schools* (New York: McGraw-Hill, 1982), p. 72; and Mary Anne Raywid, "The Current Status of Schools of Choice in Public Secondary Education (pamphlet, Hofstra University, 1982). Raywid reports on 1200 schools: they "are here to stay"; "kids like alternatives"; "alternatives don't sustain segregation"; "teachers are the central ingredient"; alternatives operate at "no greater cost" than standard programs.
11. Michael Rutter et al., *Fifteen Thousand Hours: Secondary Schools and Their Effects on Children* (Cambridge: Harvard University Press, 1979), p. 178.
12. Space and scale are related. Much has been made of the differences between big schools and small schools, and whether one is more conducive to effective learning than the other. The trend in the sixties and seventies was toward larger high schools, ones that had the scale to justify a widely comprehensive program. James Bryant Conant has been given the credit for this movement, because of his recommendation in 1959 that no truly comprehensive high school should have a graduating class of fewer than 100 pupils; a four-year high school of fewer than 400 students could not provide the varied services he advocated. However, many communities have gone far beyond Conant's minimum. While the average size high school is now around 700, city schools typically run between 1200 and 4000 students. Large schools are often economically efficient, and because they usually draw from many neighborhoods, they may, at least in theory, foster class and racial integration.

The evidence about size of school is inconclusive. More important than sheer numbers is density, the traffic patterns that people use, and the organization of the school. Some big schools "feel" small, and it is the small feeling that is important. The student wants to be someone, wants a name, wants to be helped to become an individual rather than be just another unit of potential output. Likewise, teachers want to be more than cogs in a big wheel. The best of them want a group of students small enough to get to know and a corps of colleagues close enough for intense collaboration. Such hopes and expectations are proper, as schools should not be in the business of stamping out clones. One needs a feeling of intimacy in order to be the individual one wants to be.

The ERIC Clearinghouse on Educational Management recently surveyed the research in the area of school size. The finding: "If it were possible to reach conclusions on the advantages and disadvantages of different school sizes based on the traditional areas of concern, the results would be mixed." The authors imply that size is a lesser concern than "the principal's leadership, community support, and the qualities of the staff." ERIC Clearinghouse on Educational Management, "School Size: A Reassessment of the Small School," Research Action Brief no. 2, February 1982, pp. 3 and 4. See also James Bryant Conant, *The American High School Today* (New York: McGraw-Hill, 1959), pp. 77–80.

13. The most authoritative study of teachers is Dan C. Lortie, *Schoolteacher: A Sociological Study* (Chicago: University of Chicago Press, 1975). See also Michael Lipsky, *Street-Level Bureaucracy: Dilemmas of the Individual in Public Services* (New York: Russell Sage, 1980).

14. I use the word "often," because the reality is not as stark as this. Many private schools, for example, empower their teachers to a far greater extent than do their public counterparts. Many private school faculties settle issues of general curriculum, of rules and regulations, and of appointment policy by collective votes. Such teachers may not have total control of their schools (which may be a good thing), but they often have very substantial influence. Their sense of ownership is clearly manifest, and their commitment and pride with it. It gives them confidence, from which the students ultimately benefit. See Lipsky, chapters 6 and 10. Lipsky's outline of "client-processing" underscores the virtual necessity of stereotyping of students by teachers. See also David S. Seeley, *Education Through Partnership: Mediating Structures and Education* (Cambridge: Ballinger, 1981), chapter 11.

15. Data from John Esty, President, National Association of Independent Schools, from an internal research study, drawing on NEA and NAIS surveys. See also *The Condition of Education,* 1980 edition (Washington, D.C.: U.S. Government Printing Office, 1980), table 2.11.

16. San Diego Public Schools, salary pamphlet, 1982.

17. The mean earnings for this group, which includes blue- and white-collar workers, was $14,182 in 1980, the most recent year for which data are available. U.S. Bureau of the Census, Current Population Reports, series P-60, no. 132, *Money Income of Households, Families, and Persons in the United States: 1980* (Washington, D.C.: U.S. Government Printing Office, 1982), table 52, "Education and Total Money Earnings . . ." p. 179.

18. U.S. Department of Labor, Bureau of Labor Statistics, Bulletin 2145, *National Survey of Professional, Administrative, Technical, and Clerical Pay, March 1982* (Washington, D.C.: U.S. Government Printing Office, September 1982), p. 10.

19. The mean annual earnings of 55-to-64-year-old males "having five years of college or more" equaled $36,564 in 1980. U.S. Bureau of the Census, op. cit., p. 179.

20. Governor Lamar Alexander of Tennessee lobbied hard during 1983 for a "hierarchy" of categories for teachers in his state, but met fierce opposition from

organized teachers. See *Education Week,* April 20, 1983, pp. 1 and 17. Alexander's difficulties in selling his scheme highlight how difficult such a "reform" is when separated from other changes—such as school organization—which might make them politically more palatable.

21. "Chairs" have been prominently suggested by city leaders in Rochester, New York, and Dallas, Texas, as well as in other communities.

22. At last report, the assignment—which none of the affected parties wanted—had been averted.

23. Evidence on the effectiveness of decentralized schools appears in Carnegie Council on Policy Studies in Higher Education, *Giving Youth a Better Chance* (San Francisco: Jossey-Bass, 1979), pp. 170–171, and Seymour Sarason, *The Culture of the School and the Process of Change* (Boston: Allyn and Bacon, 1971), p. 222. Stewart C. Purkey and Marshall S. Smith, in a recent review of the literature on school effectiveness, wrote that "in attempting to build more effective schools we must abandon our reliance on facile solutions and the assumption that fundamental change can be brought about from the top down. Instead, a more promising notion rests on the conception of schools as functioning social systems with distinctive cultures in which the improvement effort is directed toward incremental, long-term cultural change." *Educational Leadership,* December 1982, p. 68.

24. I am indebted to members of the National School Boards Association, and particularly to its 1982–83 Executive Committee and to Thomas Shannon, NSBA's executive secretary, for providing me with substantial dialogue on these points, in person and through extensive correspondence.

25. At their best, Her Majesty's Inspectors of Schools in the United Kingdom ("HMIs") serve as an impressive model. There is no American counterpart of this respected group of professionals.

26. Data on Boston were painstakingly collected by Muriel Cohen of the *Boston Globe* and reported to us orally; data on the Wayland Public Schools were evolved by Martha Landesberg from information supplied by the superintendent's office.

27. "Regularities" is a concept used by Seymour Sarason in *The Culture of the School and the Process of Change.*

28. See Susan Moore Johnson, *Teacher Unions and the Schools,* Institute for Educational Policy Studies, Harvard University, 1982. She writes, "Labor practices . . . been adapted to fit the educational enterprise and the norms of those who work there" (p. 278). The dangers of rigidity lurk behind every collective bargaining system, but structural immovability is not inevitable.

I V

1. See Robert H. Wiebe, *The Search for Order: 1877–1920* (New York: Hill and Wang, 1967); Michael B. Katz, *Class, Bureaucracy, and Schools,* expanded edition (New York: Praeger, 1975); Raymond E. Callahan, *Education and the Cult of Efficiency* (Chicago: University of Chicago Press, 1962); and Joel H. Spring, *Education and the Rise of the Corporate State* (Boston: Beacon Press, 1972).

2. See the "Legislative Package" of California State Superintendent of Public Instruction, mimeographed, undated [1983].

3. My colleagues Arthur Powell, Eleanor Farrar, and David Cohen fully analyze what they call "anonymous individualization" in their forthcoming volume for A Study of High Schools.

4. The usual way to proceed with reform is to change the labels of courses in the curriculum. Evidence of how ineffective this approach is can be seen in the similarity of the recommended curricula in the reports of Charles W. Eliot (1893), James B. Conant (1959), and David P. Gardner (1983). All depend on labels ("English," "mathematics," and so forth) and on periods per week. Such curricular paraphernalia is necessary, but does not deal with the central issues of quality, which are, of course, far more complicated and subtler. *Report of the Committee on Secondary School Studies* (Washington: U.S. Government Printing Office, 1893). *The American High School Today* (New York: McGraw-Hill, 1959). *A Nation at Risk: The Imperative for Educational Reform* (Washington: U.S. Government Printing Office, 1983).

5. Conant, ibid., p. 40. Robert L. Hampel's review of the Conant Report for a Study of High Schools: *American High Schools Since 1940* (Boston: Houghton Mifflin, 1984).

6. Donald Erickson of UCLA, remarks at a Wingspread Conference, 1982.

7. Two such approaches were developed at Phillips Academy during the 1970s— a so-called Competence Course, in reading and expression, within the English department, and a History Qualification Test, and course patterns that flowed from its findings, by history and social studies teachers. Students are expected to take the Competence Course until they master it; it is a prerequisite to courses in literature for all students of whatever age. The HQT assists the history department in the placement of students among a variety of courses and guides the department's chairperson in the assignment of faculty. Both of these programs—and they are but two of many found at a variety of thoughtful public and private schools—are complicated and require constant adjustment. While they serve most students well, the exceptions need special arrangements. The Competence Course resulted in a textbook: *The Competence Handbook,* revised edition (Wellesley, Massachusetts: Independent School Press, 1982).

8. See Hampel, *American High Schools Since 1940.*

9. Vera Randall, "Waiting for Tim," in Thomas West Gregory, *Adolescence in Literature* (New York: Longman, 1978), p. 64.

10. From *Let Us Now Praise Famous Men,* as quoted by Robert Coles, *Children of Crisis: A Study of Courage and Fear* (Boston: Little, Brown, 1964), p. 381.

11. Personal conversation with Mr. Conant, 1972.